PMP® Q&A

Steve Caseley

Cengage Learning PTR

CENGAGE
Learning®

Professional • Technical • Reference

Australia, Brazil, Japan, Korea, Mexico, Singapore, Spain, United Kingdom, United States

CENGAGE
Learning

Professional • Technical • Reference

PMP® Q&A
Steve Caseley

Publisher and General Manager,
Cengage Learning PTR:
Stacy L. Hiquet

Associate Director of Marketing:
Sarah Panella

Manager of Editorial Services:
Heather Talbot

Senior Product Manager:
Mitzi Koontz

Project Editor/Copy Editor:
Cathleen D. Small

Technical Reviewer:
Chris Ward

Interior Layout Tech:
Bill Hartman

Cover Designer:
Mike Tanamachi

Indexer:
Larry Sweazy

Proofreader:
Sue Boshers

© 2015 Cengage Learning PTR.

WCN: 01-100

> For product information and technology assistance, contact us at
> **Cengage Learning Customer & Sales Support, 1-800-354-9706**
> For permission to use material from this text or product, submit all requests online at **cengage.com/permissions**
> Further permissions questions can be emailed to
> **permissionrequest@cengage.com**

Library of Congress Control Number: 2014949652

ISBN-13: 978-1-305-49197-7

ISBN-10: 1-305-49197-1

Cengage Learning PTR
20 Channel Center Street
Boston, MA 02210
USA

Cengage Learning is a leading provider of customized learning solutions with office locations around the globe, including Singapore, the United Kingdom, Australia, Mexico, Brazil, and Japan. Locate your local office at: **international.cengage.com/region**

Cengage Learning products are represented in Canada by Nelson Education, Ltd.

For your lifelong learning solutions, visit **cengageptr.com**

Visit our corporate website at **cengage.com**

Printed in the United States of America
1 2 3 4 5 6 7 16 15 14

Computers

Some respond

Others still

Just tell you what they want you to do

If you know how

Even a simple man

Can talk to his toy

Unpublished work by Gordon C. Adams (1975)

This book is dedicated to all those who wish to learn to talk to their toys—in this case, learn to become better project managers and demonstrate their knowledge by becoming certified project managers.

ACKNOWLEDGMENTS

My involvement with project management goes way back in my career, when my boss at the time convinced me to lay down my coding pencil and begin to manage projects. More importantly, she knew that it wasn't a natural transition from coding to management, and she provided me with hours of coaching, mentoring, and support. My eternal thanks go to Yolande McDonald Delmar for starting me down this exciting project management career path. Without her encouragement, I might still be writing COBOL programs and wondering why the world was leaving me behind.

Over the years, I was lucky enough to work for a number of organizations that recognized the importance of project management, and I received the ongoing education and on-the-job experience to allow me to fine-tune my project management skills and "toolbox."

About 15 years ago, I got the opportunity to teach an introductory project management course for the Dalhousie University Continuing Education Department. This whetted my appetite for training and helping others to become better project managers. This also furthered my desire to get engaged and give back to the project management community. In the 15 years since I started my professional teaching career, I have taught project management at the graduate and undergraduate levels, delivered PMP and CAPM preparation courses, and recently distance-delivered CBT courses. With every course delivered, my appreciation and understanding of project management has increased as a result of interacting with my students and helping them resolve their project challenges.

I would also be remiss if I didn't thank the wonderful folks at Cengage Learning, specifically Cathleen Small and Mitzi Koontz, for their care, support, and attention in helping move this book from a series of thoughts to a publishable book.

ABOUT THE AUTHOR

Steve Caseley has worked in the project management field for more than 30 years and has a wealth of practical experience in successful project delivery. He has more than 10 years of development of Online CBT training modules for PM and IT management, including Microsoft Project and PMI PMP certification preparation series. He has also delivered IT and project management courses for a number of universities, with classes delivered in the adult continuing education, bachelor's, and master's programs at these universities.

As a result, he has many battle scars, but none has been fatal. Over the years, Steve has helped a wide range of companies implement PPM systems and best practices and has practical, hands-on PM experience in a wide range of industries, project types, and sizes. Steve's passion is working with organizations to improve overall project delivery efficiency through the implementation and adaption of industry best practices in project and portfolio management and implementation of effective PPM tools supporting these best practices.

Steve has presented at international PM conferences and Microsoft Project User Groups over the years.

CONTENTS

INTRODUCTION

Congratulations! If you have purchased this book, you are most likely well along the path to securing a very important certification of your competency as a project manager, the Project Manager Professional (PMP) certification from the Project Management Institute (PMI). If you have not already downloaded and reviewed both the Project Management Professional (PMP) Handbook and the Project Management Professional Examination Content Outline, both of which are available free from the PMI website (www.pmi.org), I would strongly encourage you to do so, as both documents provide valuable information about the qualifications for the PMP certification and the format and delivery of the actual certification exam.

The PMP certification is an internationally recognized certification of project management expertise and is definitely not an entry-level certification. If you are new to the project management profession, I strongly encourage you to explore the PMI CAPM certification as opposed to the PMP as an entry-level project manager. First, you will be challenged to satisfy the eligibility requirements, and second, you most likely will have difficulty with some of the experiential questions in the exam itself, because there are many exam questions designed to measure project management in action, as opposed to validating an understanding of project management theory.

While I have *no* intention of repeating the details contained in the PMI documents, I feel compelled to provide a very high-level overview of both the prerequisites for the certification and the exam format.

PMP ELIGIBILITY REQUIREMENTS

To be considered eligible for the PMP exam, all candidates must demonstrate either 60 months of professional project management experience with at least 7,500 hours of hands-on application directly leading or managing a project management for candidates who do not have a four-year degree, or 36 months and 4,500 hours of direct experience for candidates who have a four-year degree.

You will need to put considerable effort into collecting and documenting these professional experience requirements, as you must provide full specifics, including the project name, role, project management processes, and most importantly verifiable references for each project. While not all PMP applications are validated by PMI, random applications are selected and verified by contacting the supplied references to ensure that the level of experience reported is accurate and appropriate. PMI takes the eligibility requirements very seriously to ensure that only fully qualified candidates are granted permission to take the certification exam.

In addition, you must demonstrate attending a minimum of 35 hours of formal project management education that has been completed prior to the submission of the application. These 35 hours must be formal classroom-style education and must be focused specifically on project management; general management education is not eligible. PMI is also very explicit that this formal education must be verifiable and that self-education, such as reading reference books, browsing project management websites, and even participating in non-controlled computer-based training sites, does not qualify for this requirement.

Assuming you satisfy these requirements, the next step is to go to www.pmi.org, complete the application form, and submit it, along with full payment for the certification (currently $555 U.S. for non-PMI members and $405 U.S. for PMI members, but subject to change so please verify the costs at the time of your application). Please remember that you will need to provide the full details for your professional experience at the time of the application, so it is important to have names, dates, and reference contact details on hand before you start the application. But the good news is, if you are missing some details, you can save a partially completed application and complete it any time within 90 days.

PMI will respond within five business days of final submission with one of the following:

- Your eligibility letter to take the exam
- A notification that your application is being audited (randomly—so don't get too worried if you get this response; it doesn't mean your application is at risk)
- A denial of your application

If you do get an audit notification, you have 90 days to provide the additional details requested.

Once you receive your eligibility letter, you have up to one year from the date of the eligibility letter to take and pass the certification exam. If you do not happen to pass the exam, you can retake the exam up to two more times within the one-year eligibility period. There is an additional fee each time you complete the examination.

PMP Exam Format

The PMP exam consists of 200 multiple-choice questions. While PMI does not publish a formal passing grade (the pass/fail is based on a psychometric analysis), it is commonly felt that the passing grade is in the 60 percent range. You have a maximum of four hours to complete the exam, and experience has shown that you should plan to use the entire four hours because many of the questions will require considerable thought and contemplation to select the most appropriate, experience-based best answer.

And speaking of the "most appropriate" answer, you can expect to find many questions on the exam that have more than one right answer, but you will be required to provide only a single answer. In these instances, the most appropriate or best answer incorporates the other right answers or is substantially a better or more appropriate answer.

Another thing to keep in mind when selecting the "most appropriate" answer is to select the answer that most closely aligns with the Project Management Body of Knowledge (PMBOK).

The questions in the exam will follow several formats:

- A question and you select the answer
- A sentence with a missing word or phrase and you select the missing word/phrase
- A negative question where you select a word or phrase that does not meet the question criteria
- A problem or equation and you select the answer

Each question in the exam will have four possible answers, and in some instances All of the Above or None of the Above will be one of the four possible answers. Please note that while the exam will only have four possible answers, in this book I have deliberately provided five (and in a few instances more than five) answers to make these sample questions a little more challenging than the actual exam to help you be prepared to take and pass your actual exam in a single try.

The questions in the exam will be drawn from all areas of the PMBOK and presented in a totally random fashion; you are equally likely to have your first question on closing a project as you are to have it on initiating a project. Having said that the questions are presented randomly, PMI does provide an expected distribution of questions based on the five Project Management Process Groups.

- Initiating: 13%
- Planning: 24%
- Executing: 30%
- Monitoring and Controlling: 25%
- Closing: 8%

A last piece of information you need to be aware of is that although the exam has 200 questions, only 175 will be scored to determine your passing grade for your certification. The other 25 questions are new/pretest questions that are being evaluated as potential future exam questions. You will have no way of knowing whether a question is scored or under evaluation, so my recommendation is to ignore the fact that there are evaluation questions and focus on getting the right answer for all 200 questions. The only reason I even bring this up is so that you are aware that these evaluation questions exist. Should you get a question that you find exceptionally difficult to understand or have trouble selecting the most appropriate answer, it is likely an evaluation question that may need to be further improved. Therefore, if you do get a question that just doesn't feel right, simply tell yourself that it's an evaluation question, don't let it shake your confidence in your abilities, select the best answer, and move on.

WHAT TO EXPECT ON THE EXAM

The exam questions have been professionally prepared and are designed to test both your understanding of project management best practices and the application of these best practices in real-world applications. One of the best pieces of advice I can give you regarding the exam questions is to ignore all the "free advice" you may get from friends and peers— statements like "The longest answer is always correct," "The correct answer always begins with a positive description," and "The right answer is never A" have no value for the PMP exam. As I just stated, the questions are professionally prepared and even pretested by other exam takers, so there are no secrets for getting the right answer. Read each question slowly and carefully to ensure you understand it thoroughly, and then read each potential answer slowly and carefully so you can select the most appropriate answer.

A significant change with this version of the PMP exam is that there will be no questions explicitly discussing the Project Manager Code of Ethics and Professional Responsibility. These are now integrated into the questions related to the Project Management Process Groups. This doesn't mean that the Code of Ethics and Professional Responsibility is no longer important. In fact, I believe it makes it *more* important, because you will be answering questions about how to behave as a PMI member in an experiential project delivery situation, as opposed to directed theoretical questions about professionalism and social responsibility.

When preparing for the PMP exam, be alert for "PMIisms" (specific terms and processes defined by PMI in the PMBOK). In other words, when you are selecting the right answer for a question, if you put each right answer into the context of PMI and the PMBOK, it should help you select the most appropriate answer.

Finally, you need to be prepared for direct PMBOK-based questions explicitly validating your understanding of the Knowledge Areas, Processes, Inputs, Techniques, and Outputs. The best (and only?) way to get these answers right is to memorize that section of the PMBOK; specifically, Annex A1, "The Standard for Project Management of a Project," does a wonderful job of consolidating these key relationships. I personally find Table A1-1, "Project Management Process Groups and Knowledge Area Mapping," to be key to understanding and remembering the PMBOK.

HOW THIS BOOK CAN HELP YOU PREPARE FOR THE EXAM

The best way this book can help you prepare for the exam is for you to complete each and every one of the sample questions, compare your answers to the correct answers, and then review the justification for each correct answer. I have put a lot of thought into each correct answer justification to ensure that each one is more than simply repeating the question and right answer and that there is also a detailed explanation or justification of the theory as to why each answer is correct. Each answer is designed to be a mini-learning exercise.

While each of you has your own learning style, I recommend you complete the series of questions for each chapter, record your answers, and then once the entire chapter is completed, compare your answers to the correct answer and review the justifications as needed.

In my experience preparing for my own PMP, as well as other certification exams, a better learning experience is possible from a focused session of answering questions, followed by a review and evaluation period, as opposed to reviewing single questions/answers/justifications.

There is a 50 question pre-test designed to be completed in approximately one hour (50 questions rather than 200 questions in one hour rather than four). The questions in the pre-test are randomized as they will be in the exam, but I've provided a scoring grid, which will allow you to determine how well you did on each Knowledge Area as well as on the quiz as a whole. The results of this pre-test should allow you to determine which Knowledge Areas you may need to focus on.

Next, I present 11 chapters with questions focused on each Knowledge Area. I have deliberately presented the questions in each chapter in a non-random fashion and follow the initiating/planning/executing/monitoring and controlling/closing sequence of the PMBOK because I feel this is a more natural way to review each Knowledge Area and should make it easier for you to go back to the PMBOK or any other reference books you have used and improve your knowledge in any area that the questions indicate you may be weak in.

Finally, I present another 50-question post-test, again designed to be completed in approximately one hour, to allow you to validate improvements in areas you may have been weak in and/or to identify areas where you may still need to do additional review.

One note of special caution on your pre/post results: Because the sample size is small (50 questions), the question distribution for some of the Knowledge Areas will be relatively small with only three questions; therefore, a passing grade will be two out of three correct, while a failing grade will be only one less question right at one out of three. Don't get too concerned about pass/fail at individual Knowledge Areas as opposed to the overall pre- and post-test results. My intention is to evaluate at the Knowledge Area level simply to help you understand where you should focus any additional study, as opposed to truly evaluating your chances of success at the full PMP certification exam.

What Else Do I Need to Do to Pass the PMP Exam?

If you haven't already purchased a copy of the PMBOK Fifth Edition, do so immediately. It has to be the current edition because the exam will be explicitly testing your understanding of this edition. You should be prepared to read this book several times. Unless you have a photographic memory, I don't believe you will absorb everything in this book on a single pass. I would suggest at least three readings are necessary. And as mentioned earlier, focus on Annex 1, because it provides a terrific summary of the core principles of the PMBOK. I suggest you memorize this Annex or at least have a solid appreciation of the five Project Management Process Groups, 10 Knowledge Areas, and 47 project management processes.

In addition to the PMBOK guide, I strongly recommend purchasing at least two other project management reference books that are based on the PMBOK. There are many excellent reference books on the market, including *PMP In Depth: Project Management Professional Study Guide for the PMP Exam* (Cengage, 2009). The reason I recommend at least two other reference books is that they will provide additional insight into the practical application of the PMBOK necessary to correctly answer the questions related to the application of the best practices in real-world scenarios.

And finally, be prepared for questions related to Earned Value Management and Network Analysis. It's my experience that these are the two subject areas most people taking the PMP certification exams are least prepared for. There *will* be questions on your exam requiring you to do both Earned Value and Network calculations and analysis. Ensure that you understand both the theory and practical application of both Earned Value Analysis and Network Analysis.

COMPANION WEBSITE DOWNLOADS

You may download the companion website files from www.cengageptr.com/downloads.

CHAPTER

1

PRE-TEST

1. The _____ estimating method involves developing an optimistic, a pessimistic, and a most likely estimate.
   a. Parametric
   b. Three-point
   c. Analogous
   d. Peer
   e. Work effort

2. A controlling PMO:
   a. Measures compliance to project management processes.
   b. Directly manages projects.
   c. Augments the project management team.
   d. Supplies templates, best practices, and training.
   e. Consolidates project reports into organizational reports.

3. Plan Risk Responses is:
   a. A reactive process that takes place once the risk has materialized on the project.
   b. A proactive process that takes place approximately one month before the risk is expected to materialize.
   c. A proactive process that takes place once Qualitative and Quantitative Risk Analysis are complete.
   d. A one-time process that takes place during project planning.
   e. An ongoing process that takes place during weekly status meetings.

4. Which of the following is *not* a classification of stakeholder engagement?
   a. Unaware
   b. Resistant
   c. Neutral
   d. Unimpressed
   e. Leading

5. A project manager can create a positive team environment by:
   a. Providing individual team members with challenges and opportunities.
   b. Ensuring timely performance feedback.
   c. Implementing reward and recognition programs.
   d. Organizing team-building activities.
   e. Handling conflicts in an efficient manner.
   f. All of the above.

6. A project will have:
   a. A single contract covering all procurement requirements of the project.
   b. A single contract covering each phase of the project lifecycle.
   c. One contract for each item the project must procure.
   d. Multiple contracts for each item the project must procure.
   e. Contracts for only the items requiring a formal definition of the procurement process.

7. Cause-and-effect diagrams are used to:
   a. Allocate responsibilities to team members to ensure that issues can be directed to the appropriate person.
   b. Trace problems back to an actionable root.
   c. Identify continuous process improvements.
   d. Map requirements to the appropriate business resource.
   e. Assign responsibilities for resolving quality issues.

8. In a _____ dependency relationship, a successor cannot start until a predecessor has started.
   a. Finish-to-start
   b. Finish-to-finish
   c. Start-to-start
   d. In-progress-to-start
   e. Start-to-finish

9. WBS decompositions do *not* contain which of the following elements?
   a. Identifying and analyzing deliverable and related work
   b. Structuring and organizing the WBS
   c. Breaking high-level elements into more details
   d. Ensuring project management activities are included in the WBS
   e. Developing and assigning WBS codes to each element

10. Stakeholder analysis is focused on:
    a. Documenting the hierarchical relationships of stakeholders to identify the most senior stakeholders.
    b. Identifying stakeholders, analyzing the impact the stakeholder has on the project, and assessing how the stakeholder will react to various project situations.
    c. Classifying stakeholders as supporter, neutral, or adversary.
    d. Classifying stakeholders as influencer, decision maker, or impacted by.
    e. Documenting stakeholder names, role/title, phone number, and email address

11. The objective of Project Risk Management is to:
    a. Prevent risks from impacting the project.
    b. Increase the likelihood of positive events and decrease the likelihood of negative events.
    c. Ensure that the project is isolated from risks and other negative events.
    d. Develop contingencies to cover all project impacts from risks and other negative events.
    e. Eliminate risk events before they can impact the project.

12. Product scope and project scope can be considered to be equivalent terms.
    a. True
    b. False

13. The Project Charter:
    a. Kicks off the project.
    b. Documents the project scope and delivery approach.
    c. Formally authorizes the project and commits resources to the project.
    d. Defines how the project will be delivered.
    e. Assigns the project manager to the project.

14. EVM stands for:
    a. Extra Value Management.
    b. Extremely Valuable Management.
    c. Every Value Measured.
    d. Extreme Valuables Measured.
    e. Earned Value Management.

15. There are six members on a project team who must communicate with each other. How many communications channels does this represent?
    a. 5
    b. 6
    c. 10
    d. 12
    e. 15

16. A RACI chart refers to:
    a. Responsible, Acting, Clarifying, and Informational.
    b. Ready, Available, Capable, and Informed.
    c. Responsible, Available, Consulted, and Informed.
    d. Responsible, Accountable, Consulted, and Informed.
    e. Ready, Accountable, Consulted, and Informed.

17. Scope, time, and cost are often described as the project triple constraints. If the scope of a project increases, what is likely to happen to time and cost?
    a. Both will increase.
    b. At least one, and possibly both, will increase.
    c. Cost will increase, but time will decrease.
    d. Time will increase, but cost will decrease.
    e. Neither time nor cost will change.

18. Which of the following is *not* a focus for identifying policies and procedures in Plan Cost Management?
    a. Identifying the project budget.
    b. Spending the project budget.
    c. Managing the project budget.
    d. Controlling the project budget.
    e. Approving the project budget.

19. Which of the following is *not* addressed in the PMI Code of Ethics and Professional Conduct?
    a. Responsibility
    b. Respect
    c. Fairness
    d. Legality
    e. Honesty

20. In a weak matrix organization, staff report:
    a. Exclusively to the functional manager.
    b. Primarily to the functional manager and secondarily to the project manager.
    c. Primarily to the project manager and secondarily to the project manager.
    d. Exclusively to the project manager.
    e. Equally to the functional and project managers.

21. Which of the following documents should be considered when producing the Scope Management Plan?
    a. Project Charter
    b. Existing Project Management Plans
    c. Organizational Process Assets
    d. Enterprise Environmental Factors
    e. None of the above
    f. All of the above

22. Known risks that cannot be managed proactively should:
    a. Be ignored, since there are no direct actions that can be taken to minimize them.
    b. Be assigned a contingency reserve.
    c. Be documented to management so that the project is absolved of responsibility.
    d. Be assigned a management reserve.
    e. Be added as a WBS element so that resources can be assigned to it.

23. Which of the following statements about activities and work packages is true?
    a. Activities and work packages are the same. They are different terms used to differentiate between Scope Management and Time Management processes.
    b. Activities are composed of work packages.
    c. Work packages are composed of activities.
    d. Work packages are referenced in written documentation, and activities are used in the project scheduling tool.
    e. Work package is an old term that is being phased out by the PMI and is being replaced by activities.

24. The Project Management Plan integrates content from which of the following Knowledge Areas?
    a. Project Integration Management
    b. Project Scope Management
    c. Project Scope Management and Project Time Management
    d. All Knowledge Areas except Procurement Management
    e. All Knowledge Areas except Integration Management

25. Having an external firm provide a needed project interface for a negotiated price is an example of what type of contract?
    a. Unit price
    b. Fixed price
    c. Cost plus
    d. Time and materials
    e. Risk sharing

26. Training requirements are:
    a. Not to be considered when staffing the project.
    b. Clearly defined in the human resource plan to ensure that project-specific training requirements are known and planned for.
    c. Defined once the team is assigned, to backfill any missing skills.
    d. Identified once the project is underway, to address any shortcoming once the team has been evaluated based on performance.
    e. Not required, as the project should be staffed with qualified resources.

27. According to the PMI Code of Ethics and Professional Conduct, respect is:
    a. Understanding cultural differences.
    b. Understanding that different team members work in different ways.
    c. Understanding the chain of authority within the project and the organization.
    d. Showing a high regard for ourselves, others, and the resources entrusted to us.
    e. Giving all team members a second and third chance to perform to expected levels.

28. Project Communications Management is focused on:
    a. Formal project communications.
    b. Informal project communications.
    c. Project status reports.
    d. Written communications.
    e. All of the above.

29. Contingencies' financial reserves should (select two):
    a. Be combined into a single account.
    b. Be allocated to specific contingencies.
    c. Be included in the overall cost estimates.
    d. Include a project-level contingency.
    e. Be defined by senior management.

30. Risk and uncertainty are typically highest at:
    a. Project startup.
    b. End of planning.
    c. End of project design.
    d. Beginning of project acceptance.
    e. End of the project.

1

31. A message that is *not* understood because the receiver was unable to understand what the message meant suffers from an issue in what step in the communications model?
    a. Encode
    b. Transmit
    c. Decode
    d. Acknowledge
    e. Feedback

32. When identifying risks, it is important to:
    a. Validate the reasonableness of the risk before documenting it.
    b. Identify the top 10 risks only.
    c. Identify any and all risks that could impact the project.
    d. Confirm with the project sponsor before documenting any risks.
    e. Obtain consensus of the team before documenting any risks.

33. Perform Integrated Change Control is performed:
    a. During project planning.
    b. During project delivery.
    c. As part of acceptance when defects are discovered.
    d. Only when the business requests a significant change.
    e. At any time during the project.

34. Project Quality Management is focused on:
    a. Ensuring that the project is completed with zero defects.
    b. Defining the testing processes to be applied.
    c. Defining the quality assurance to be applied.
    d. Defining the quality control to be applied.
    e. Ensuring that the project satisfies the needs for which it was undertaken.

35. During which project management process are lessons learned documented?
    a. Initiating
    b. Planning
    c. Executing
    d. Monitoring and controlling
    e. Closing

36. In a _____ organization, the project manager has little to no authority.
    a. Functional
    b. Weak matrix
    c. Balanced matrix
    d. Strong matrix
    e. Projectized

37. A Requirements Traceability Matrix:
    a. Requires a dedicated, specialized tool.
    b. Can be easily supported using a spreadsheet.
    c. Can be provided using manual/paper methods.
    d. Is part of the Requirement Documents.
    e. Is optional.

38. Develop Schedule is a(n):
    a. Ongoing process throughout the project.
    b. One-time process during project planning.
    c. Iterative process during project planning.
    d. Iterative process throughout the project.
    e. Continuous process occurring daily.

39. The Project Work Breakdown Structure (WBS) should initially be based on:
    a. The team's determination of what work is required to complete the project.
    b. An industry-standard template for the type of project.
    c. A detailed list of every task the team will complete.
    d. The deliverables defined in the Project Scope Statement.
    e. The PMI PMBOK Guide processes.

40. Project stakeholders are:
    a. Individuals assigned to provide project oversight.
    b. Individuals or groups who have an interest in the project; they could impact or be impacted by the project.
    c. Senior management of the delivery team and receiving organizational units involved in the project.
    d. Senior members of the project team.
    e. The group that reviews and approves all Project Change Requests.

41. Project Human Resource Management is:
    a. A standalone Knowledge Area focused on ensuring that the team performs effectively.
    b. A one-time process needed at the beginning of the project to staff the team.
    c. A process repeated at each phase of the project to ensure that the team complement supports the requirements for each phase.
    d. Often done outside the project by the human resources department.
    e. An integrated project process to ensure that all changes to the project team are evaluated across all other Knowledge Areas.

1

42. Project Procurement Management defines:
   a. What the project must acquire from a third party.
   b. The contracts or purchase orders to acquire items from a third party.
   c. Managing the contracts in place for the project.
   d. Closing the contracts in place for the project.
   e. All of the above.

43. The requirements form the basis for the development of which of the following?
   a. WBS
   b. Budget
   c. Schedule
   d. Quality
   e. Procurement
   f. All of the above

44. Leadership is focused on:
   a. Defining work and monitoring results.
   b. Mentoring and coaching.
   c. Directing and controlling.
   d. Focusing efforts toward a common goal.
   e. Encouraging and training.

45. Qualitative Risk Analysis is:
   a. A one-time event completed during planning.
   b. An ongoing process repeated for each new risk identified.
   c. Always performed at the same time as Quantitative Risk Analysis.
   d. Typically not completed because it is very time-consuming for all but the most complicated risks.
   e. Performed weekly in the project team meetings.

46. Deliverables are:
   a. Any pieces of work completed by the project team.
   b. Produced at the end of the project only.
   c. Always printed documents.
   d. Specific to the project's defined requirements.
   e. Rarely used on projects because they limit adaptability.

47. The Plan Schedule Management process does *not* focus on:
   a. Defining the processes to be followed to identify the schedule inputs.
   b. Defining the processes for entering the schedule inputs into an automated tool.
   c. Defining the processes for managing the project schedule.
   d. Defining the process for controlling the project schedule.
   e. Defining the process for executing the project schedule.

48. Resource leveling is a technique:
    a. That is rarely used because the project scheduling software does this automatically.
    b. That adjusts activity dates to balance resource demands.
    c. That often extends the project dates.
    d. That is commonly used to accommodate activities that share resources.
    e. All of the above.
    f. All except A.

49. Quality control:
    a. Tests the product.
    b. Ensures that quality processes are followed.
    c. Validates that the results satisfy the requirements.
    d. Audits the project and reports violations.
    e. Is typically not required on projects.

50. Which of the following documents are *not* updated as part of stakeholder management?
    a. Issue Log
    b. Change requests
    c. Project budget
    d. Communications Management Plan
    e. Stakeholder register

2

PROJECT MANAGEMENT PROCESSES, ORGANIZATIONAL STRUCTURES, AND PROFESSIONALISM

1. The PMI Code of Ethics and Professional Conduct:
    a. Defines specific rules and regulations that project managers must follow.
    b. Guides project management practitioners and describes the expectations that they should hold for themselves and others.
    c. Is a legal statement that defines how project managers must act.
    d. Is a set of guidelines to be followed when contracting out project management work.
    e. Is a set of recommendations on how project managers should behave in North America.

2. A project is:
    a. A defined engagement to create a result.
    b. An organized team working together to satisfy stated requirements.
    c. An endeavor focused on achieving results.
    d. A temporary arrangement to complete a piece of work to achieve a desired result.
    e. A temporary endeavor to create a unique product, service, or result.

3. A project is different from operations because:
    a. A project has a project manager assigned, and operations has an operations manager.
    b. A project produces a unique result, and operations produce a repetitive output.
    c. A project is ongoing, and operations have a defined start and end date.
    d. A project requires funding, and operations do not.
    e. A project requires management oversight, and operations do not.

4. What is the relationship between portfolios, programs, and projects?
    a. A portfolio contains programs, which contain projects.
    b. A program contains projects, which support portfolios.
    c. A program contains portfolios, which contain projects.
    d. A project defines programs and portfolios.
    e. There are no relationships between these three items.

5. Which of the following is *not* a Project Management Process Group?
    a. Initiating
    b. Planning
    c. Costing
    d. Executing
    e. Closing

6. Which of the following is *not* a project constraint?
    a. Budget
    b. Scope
    c. Acceptance
    d. Resources
    e. Schedule

7. It is important for the project manager and project acceptor to review and understand the relationships between scope, time, and cost because:
    a. All three will need to be managed for the project to be a success.
    b. The project acceptor needs to understand that it is not possible to change any of them.
    c. The project acceptor needs to understand that these are the project triple constraints, and all three will be changing throughout the project.
    d. The project acceptor needs to identify which of the three is least important to allow the project manager to manage changes most effectively.
    e. The project manager will present the impact to each as part of each change request.

8. Progressive elaboration is:
    a. Developing the Project Management Plan as an iterative activity.
    b. Defining the project requirements only as needed for immediate planned activities.
    c. Developing the solution as a series of iterations, each building on the next.
    d. Adding more team members as needed to maintain the schedule.
    e. Defining the acceptance criteria before the requirements are finalized.

9. With respect to change, a program:
   a. Defines processes while managing and controlling changes.
   b. Expects change and is prepared to manage it.
   c. Monitors change in the broader internal and external environment.
   d. Manages change through an iterative development process.
   e. Does not support change.

10. A project measures success as:
    a. On time and on budget.
    b. Acceptance of results.
    c. The quality of product, timeliness, budget compliance, and customer satisfaction.
    d. The degree by which results satisfy the stated needs and benefits for which the project was undertaken.
    e. The aggregate performance and benefit realization.

11. A program measures success as:
    a. On time and on budget.
    b. Acceptance of results.
    c. Quality of product, timeliness, budget compliance, and customer satisfaction.
    d. Degree by which results satisfy the stated needs and benefits for which the program was undertaken.
    e. Aggregate performance and benefit realization.

12. A portfolio measures success as:
    a. On time and on budget.
    b. Acceptance of results.
    c. Quality of product, timeliness, budget compliance, and customer satisfaction.
    d. Degree by which results satisfy the stated needs and benefits for which the portfolio was undertaken.
    e. Aggregate performance and benefit realization.

13. Which of the following is *not* a type of Project Management Office (PMO)?
    a. Supportive
    b. Controlling
    c. Budgeting
    d. Directive
    e. All are types of PMOs

14. A supportive PMO:
    a. Measures compliance to project management processes.
    b. Directly manages projects.
    c. Augments the project management team.
    d. Supplies templates, best practices, and training.
    e. Consolidates project reports into organizational reports.

15. A directive PMO:
    a. Measures compliance to project management processes.
    b. Directly manages projects.
    c. Augments the project management team.
    d. Supplies templates, best practices, and training.
    e. Consolidates project reports into organizational reports.

16. Operations management is responsible for:
    a. Identifying projects.
    b. Overseeing projects.
    c. Interfacing with projects.
    d. Overseeing, directing, and controlling business operations.
    e. Delivering the processes and training requirements for projects.

17. Projects and operations typically overlap:
    a. At phase closeout.
    b. At project closeout.
    c. When a project is developing a product, service, or results for operations.
    d. All of the above.
    e. None of the above.

18. What role should operations management play in a project?
    a. It should be included only when the project is explicitly being delivered for the operations department.
    b. It should be included as part of the project stakeholders and involved based on the stakeholder analysis.
    c. It should be engaged at the conclusion of phases and the project to transfer ownership of completed deliverables.
    d. It should be engaged during the testing phase to ensure that operational requirements are fully tested.
    e. Operations should not be involved in project activities to ensure a clear delineation of responsibilities.

2

19. A project-based organization (PBO) is:
    a. An organization with many projects ongoing at any time.
    b. An organization that focuses on delivering projects under contract to a third party—for example, a consulting firm.
    c. An organization that conducts the majority of its work as projects.
    d. An organization where projects are given a higher priority for resources than operations.
    e. Typically a subset of an organization, often called a Project Management Office.

20. The relationship between organizational strategy and a project is:
    a. Critical to project success, because the project should be aligned with organizational strategy.
    b. Not important, because the project is defined by the Scope Management Plan.
    c. That project strategy should always be a subset of the organizational strategy.
    d. Important only when the project has senior management as the project acceptor.
    e. Important only when the project is designated as a mission-critical project.

21. What are the three key competencies for a project manager?
    a. Knowledge, leadership, and courage
    b. Leadership, performance, and courage
    c. Knowledge, leadership, and soft skills
    d. Leadership, personality, and scheduling
    e. Leadership, performance, and soft skills

22. Which of the following is *not* a required interpersonal skill for a project manager?
    a. Leadership
    b. Negotiating
    c. Conflict management
    d. Requirements analysis
    e. Communications

23. The relationship between organizational culture and a project is:
    a. Independent, because the project must develop its own culture.
    b. That the project's culture should be adapted to model that of the organization.
    c. That the project manager should be aware of the organizational culture and adopt the project approaches as needed to work harmoniously.
    d. Important only when the project has to be delivered globally.
    e. Important only when the project is designated as a mission-critical project.

24. Which of the following is *not* an organizational structure?
    a. Functional
    b. Hierarchical
    c. Strong matrix
    d. Weak matrix
    e. Projectized

25. In a _____ organization, the project manager has moderate to high authority.
    a. Functional
    b. Weak matrix
    c. Balanced matrix
    d. Strong matrix
    e. Projectized

26. In a _____ organization, the project manager has low to moderate control over resource availability.
    a. Functional
    b. Weak matrix
    c. Balanced matrix
    d. Strong matrix
    e. Projectized

27. In a strong matrix organization, the _____ manages the budget.
    a. Chief financial officer
    b. Project sponsor
    c. Project acceptor
    d. Project manager
    e. PMO

28. In a functional organization, each member of a functional unit:
    a. Reports to both the functional manager and the project manager.
    b. Reports primarily to the functional manager.
    c. Reports primarily to the project manager.
    d. Changes reporting relationships on a regular basis.
    e. Is never assigned to work outside the functional area.

29. Functional organizations are typically structured:
    a. By job classification.
    b. By seniority level on the organization.
    c. By specialty.
    d. By physical location.
    e. By role.

30. In a balanced matrix organization, staff report:
    a. Exclusively to the functional manager.
    b. Primarily to the functional manager and secondarily to the project manager.
    c. Primarily to the project manager and secondarily to the functional manager.
    d. Exclusively to the project manager.
    e. Equally to the functional and project managers.

31. In a strong matrix organization, staff report:
    a. Exclusively to the functional manager.
    b. Primarily to the functional manager and secondarily to the project manager.
    c. Primarily to the project manager and secondarily to the functional manager.
    d. Exclusively to the project manager.
    e. Equally to the functional and project managers.

32. In a weak matrix organization, the project manager:
    a. Does not exist or has limited power and acts in a coordination role only.
    b. Has escalation power to senior management.
    c. Has total power to resolve project issues.
    d. Reports within the functional area for which the project is being completed.
    e. Reports to the PMO.

33. In a balanced matrix organization, the project manager:
    a. Does not exist or has limited power and acts in a coordination role only.
    b. Has escalation power to senior management.
    c. Has total power to resolve project issues.
    d. Reports within the functional area for which the project is being completed.
    e. Reports to the PMO.

34. In a strong matrix organization, the project manager:
    a. Does not exist or has limited power and acts in a coordination role only.
    b. Has escalation power to senior management.
    c. Has total power to resolve project issues.
    d. Reports within the functional area for which the project is being completed.
    e. Reports to the PMO.

35. In a projectized organization:
    a. The project manager reports directly to senior management.
    b. The project manager is permanently assigned staff.
    c. The project manager and project team are assigned for the duration of the project.
    d. The project manager reports to the functional manager for which the project is being delivered, but the project team reports directly to the project manager.
    e. The project manager and team all report to the PMO.

36. A project sponsor:
    a. Is a senior manager who has final approval authority for a project.
    b. Supports the project acceptor when the project acceptor cannot or will not make a project decision.
    c. Backs up the project acceptor when the project acceptor does not have time for the project.
    d. Is the person who provides resources ($) and support for the project and is accountable for enabling success.
    e. An honorary position with little to no power on the project.

37. Project governance:
    a. Defines how project acceptance is to be completed.
    b. Defines the structure, processes, decision-making models, and tools for managing the project.
    c. Defines reporting relationships.
    d. Defines authority levels.
    e. All of the above.

38. A project lifecycle is:
    a. Initiating, Planning, Executing, Monitoring and Controlling, and Closing.
    b. Analysis, Design, Construction, and Implementation.
    c. Project Charter, Project Plan, Project Status, and Acceptance.
    d. Project Management, Project Development, and Acceptance.
    e. A series of phases that a project passes through from initiation to closing.

39. Which of the following is *not* a type of project lifecycle?
    a. Predictive
    b. Variable
    c. Plan-driven
    d. Adaptive
    e. Change-driven

40. A project lifecycle is the same as the Project Management Process Groups.
    a. True
    b. False

41. Cost of changes is typically highest at:
    a. Project startup.
    b. End of planning.
    c. End of project design.
    d. Beginning of project acceptance.
    e. End of the project.

42. Which of the following is *not* a characteristic of a project phase?
    a. The work completed has a distinct focus.
    b. The work will be completed over a short timeframe.
    c. Results are based on controls or processes specific to the phase.
    d. Results are transferred for use outside the phase.
    e. All of the above.

43. A predictive lifecycle:
    a. Has a defined path with the scope, time, and cost defined early in the lifecycle.
    b. Is based on significant input from the business and is responsive to business needs.
    c. Has repeating cycles where the same phases provide incremental functionality to the project.
    d. Uses a rolling-wave planning process.
    e. Has very short (two- to four-week) fixed time and cost iterations.

44. An iterative lifecycle:
    a. Has a defined path with the scope, time, and cost defined early in the lifecycle.
    b. Is based on significant input from the business and is responsive to business needs.
    c. Has repeating cycles where the same phases provide incremental functionality to the project.
    d. Uses a rolling-wave planning process.
    e. Has very short (two- to four-week) fixed time and cost iterations.

45. An adaptive lifecycle:
    a. Has a defined path with the scope, time, and cost defined early in the lifecycle.
    b. Is based on significant input from the business and is responsive to business needs.
    c. Has repeating cycles where the same phases provide incremental functionality to the project.
    d. Uses a rolling-wave planning process.
    e. Has very short (two- to four-week) fixed time and cost iterations.

46. An adaptive lifecycle is used when:
    a. There is no scope defined.
    b. The business cannot define the acceptance criteria.
    c. There will be very high levels of change.
    d. The business wishes to be able to fund the project from an operational rather than a capital budget.
    e. A project acceptor is not available.

47. Which of the following is *not* a Project Management Process Group?
    a. Initiating
    b. Planning
    c. Delivering
    d. Monitoring and controlling
    e. Closing

48. The five Project Management Process Groups are:
    a. Executed serially.
    b. Executed in parallel.
    c. Executed with initiating first, followed by planning, then monitoring and controlling and executing in parallel, with closing as the final process.
    d. Executed with initiating first, with planning and executing as a repeat loop, with closing as a final process, and with monitoring and controlling active for the duration of the project.
    e. Executed with initiating first, followed by planning, then monitoring and controlling and executing in a repeating loop, and then closing as a final process.

49. During which project management process is the Project Charter created?
    a. Initiating
    b. Planning
    c. Executing
    d. Monitoring and controlling
    e. Closing

50. During which project management process are risks managed and closed?
    a. Initiating
    b. Planning
    c. Executing
    d. Monitoring and controlling
    e. Closing

51. During which project management process are project deliverables created?
    a. Initiating
    b. Planning
    c. Executing
    d. Monitoring and controlling
    e. Closing

52. During which project management process is the Communications Management Plan created?
    a. Initiating
    b. Planning
    c. Executing
    d. Monitoring and controlling
    e. Closing

53. Which of the following is *not* part of the Closing process group?
    a. Gain final acceptance
    b. Harvest reusable artifacts
    c. Finalize project deliverables
    d. Conduct lessons learned workshops
    e. Complete employee evaluations

54. A project deliverable has been presented to the project acceptor for final acceptance. What Project Management Process Group are you in?
    a. Initiating
    b. Planning
    c. Executing
    d. Monitoring and controlling
    e. Closing

55. Work performance data consist of:
    a. Raw observations and measurements taken during project delivery.
    b. Information provided by the project management scheduling software.
    c. Performance data collected, analyzed, and integrated across areas.
    d. A physical representation of project information compiled for presentation.
    e. Timesheets provided by team members.

56. Work performance information consists of:
    a. Raw observations and measurements taken during project delivery.
    b. Information provided by the project management scheduling software.
    c. Performance data collected, analyzed, and integrated across areas.
    d. A physical representation of project information compiled for presentation.
    e. Timesheets provided by team members.

57. Work performance reports consist of:
    a. Raw observations and measurements taken during project delivery.
    b. Information provided by the project management scheduling software.
    c. Performance data collected, analyzed, and integrated across areas.
    d. A physical representation of project information compiled for presentation.
    e. Timesheets provided by team members.

58. The relationship between the Project Management Process Groups is best described as follows:
    a. The Project Management Process Groups are all the processes the project management team should follow.
    b. The outputs from one process group typically become the input to the next process group.
    c. The process groups are related through the 10 Knowledge Areas.
    d. The process groups are injected into the project lifecycle to provide an integrated delivery environment.
    e. The process groups are independent and have no relationship to each other.

59. Team building is focused on:
    a. Conducting team building sessions.
    b. Encouraging and training.
    c. Resolving conflicts.
    d. Developing a team motto and name.
    e. Helping a group of individuals work together toward a common goal.

60. Which of the following is *not* a team-building activity?
    a. Encouraging team-member commitment
    b. Defining project objectives
    c. Creating a team identity
    d. Managing conflicts
    e. Promoting trust

61. Which of the following would *not* result in team-member motivation?
    a. Job satisfaction
    b. Sense of accomplishment
    c. Challenging work
    d. Career growth
    e. Comfortable chairs

62. Which of the following has been identified as the single biggest reason for project success?
    a. Communication
    b. Proper tools
    c. Adequate project contingency
    d. Well-trained team
    e. Clear scope definition

63. What are the four styles of decision making?
    a. Command, delegation, consensus, and random
    b. Command, consultation, delegation, and consensus
    c. Command, consultation, consensus, and random
    d. Delegation, consensus, consultation, and random
    e. Delegation, consensus, individual, and random

64. Which of the following is *not* a step in the decision-making model?
    a. Problem definition
    b. Problem solution generation
    c. Ideas to action
    d. Solution evaluation planning
    e. Implementation

65. The PMI Code of Ethics and Professional Conduct is based on which of the following values?
    a. Responsibility, accountability, respect, and honesty
    b. Accountability, respect, fairness, and honesty
    c. Responsibility, accountability, respect, and honesty
    d. Responsibility, respect, fairness, and honesty
    e. Respect, predictability, fairness, and honesty

66. According to the PMI Code of Ethics and Professional Conduct, responsibility is:
    a. Ensuring that the PMBOK Knowledge Areas are adhered to.
    b. Owning the project schedule and budget and committing to successful project delivery.
    c. Taking ownership for the actions and decisions we make or fail to make and the consequences that result.
    d. Accepting responsibility for all project results.
    e. Committing to deliver the scope of the project.

67. As a PMI member, you have been requested to make a payment to secure a permit to allow your company to bid on a very important piece of business in a foreign country. When you question the legality of the payment, you are informed that this is the normal process in the country and that everyone does it. What should you do?
    a. Include the cost for the permit in the project budget.
    b. Inform management that a payment to secure a permit is required and facilitate the delivery.
    c. Investigate the legal system of the country and validate the legality of the request.
    d. Inform management that a payment to secure a permit is required, but inform them that as a PMI member, you cannot participate in the delivery.
    e. Refuse to participate in the acquisition of the permit.

68. You have been offered an opportunity to manage a dream project. However, this dream project is more than a stretch and is most likely beyond your current abilities. What should you do?

    a. Accept the position with the intention of putting in as many extra hours as needed.

    b. Inform management that you are honored by the offer, but that you must decline because you don't believe you have the skills to be successful.

    c. Inform management that you would like to take the position provided they would agree to fund extra training to help you develop the needed skills.

    d. Accept the position and quickly appoint a "second in command" with skills to backfill some of your weak areas.

    e. Accept the position. If management offered it, they must have confidence that you can do it.

69. According to the PMI Code of Ethics and Professional Conduct, fairness is:

    a. Treating all team members equally.

    b. Treating all stakeholders equally.

    c. Treating all vendors equally.

    d. Making decisions and acting impartially and objectively.

    e. Ensuring that personal feelings never influence professional decisions.

70. As a PMI member and as a project manager for a consulting firm managing a contract for a customer, you discover a situation on your project that cannot be resolved without either your employer or the customer suffering a loss. What should you do?

    a. Protect the customer's interest, because an unhappy customer will never be a repeat customer.

    b. Protect your employer's interest to ensure ongoing employment.

    c. Continue to look for a solution that will be a win-win.

    d. Declare a conflict of interest and inform both parties of the facts.

    e. Continue to monitor the situation in the hopes that it will resolve itself.

71. According to the PMI Code of Ethics and Professional Conduct, honesty is:

    a. Never withholding information.

    b. Reporting all information as required.

    c. Understanding the truth and acting in a truthful manner in communication and conduct.

    d. Seeking all possible information.

    e. Relaying all information in the same form as it was received.

72. Who has the most power in a projectized organization?
    a. Team members
    b. Project manager
    c. Functional manager
    d. PMO
    e. All share power equally

73. Who has the most power in a functional organization?
    a. Team members
    b. Project manager
    c. Functional manager
    d. PMO
    e. All share power equally

74. The project schedule cannot be created until which of the following is complete?
    a. Risk Register
    b. Project budget
    c. Staffing plan
    d. Work Breakdown Structure
    e. Quality manual

75. Once the Project Charter is approved, what is the next step in the project?
    a. Define the team staffing plan.
    b. Document the project scope.
    c. Initiate integrated change control.
    d. Begin work on satisfying the requirements of the Project Charter.
    e. Define the quality assurance processes.

76. The optimal time to assign a project manager to a project is during:
    a. Initiating.
    b. Planning.
    c. Executing.
    d. Monitoring and controlling.
    e. Closing.

77. Which project management process typically requires the most time and resources?
    a. Initiating
    b. Planning
    c. Executing
    d. Monitoring and controlling
    e. Closing

78. A work authorization system is used to:
    a. Allocate team members to a project.
    b. Ensure that WBS activities are completed by the right resource in the right order.
    c. Ensure that all team members have a full workload.
    d. Match the project schedule to task lists.
    e. Record time worked on WBS activities.

79. The difference between the cost budget and the Cost Baseline is:
    a. The cost budget has a time-based component.
    b. The Cost Baseline does not reflect any contingencies.
    c. The cost budget reflects the amount the business unit is willing to spend, while the Cost Baseline reflects the actual cost of the project.
    d. The Cost Baseline does not reflect the management reserve.
    e. The Cost Baseline does not reflect any sunk costs.

80. Which of the following officially starts a project?
    a. Project Charter
    b. Project Management Plan
    c. Project schedule and budget
    d. Formal acceptance of the Project Charter
    e. Project kickoff meeting

81. Which of the following would be considered a project constraint?
    a. A business deadline defining the last possible date on which the project can be completed before the project benefits are no longer valid
    b. A concern that there will be a labor dispute at one of the project's vendors
    c. A milestone on the project schedule
    d. The assignment of a key project resource at 50 percent availability
    e. All of the above

82. You have been informed that your project has been cancelled. What should you do next?
    a. Review your resume and begin looking for a new job.
    b. Immediately schedule a meeting with the project sponsor to try to have the project restarted.
    c. Execute the closing process to properly close the cancelled project.
    d. Meet with human resources to determine your next assignment.
    e. Meet with the team to develop a plan to accelerate all project deliverables in an attempt to have the project restarted.

83. The Requirements Traceability Matrix cannot be used in which of the following instances?
    a. Tracing requirements to the project scope
    b. Tracing test cases to the requirements
    c. Tracing requirements to risk plans
    d. Tracing defects to requirements
    e. Tracing requirements to system components

84. You are managing a project that will be making a major project procurement. A close member of your family works for one of the companies that will be bidding on this procurement. What should you do?
    a. Do nothing; the procurement process has been defined to be fair and defendable.
    b. Advise your relative that his or her organization cannot bid on the work.
    c. Ask to be removed from the project.
    d. Fully disclose the potential conflict of interest and request to be removed from the vendor-selection committee.
    e. Inform senior management of the situation and ensure that they understand that you will not let the relationship interfere with your project responsibilities.

85. Which of the following defines the total scope of the project?
    a. Project Work Breakdown Structure
    b. Project schedule
    c. Project budget
    d. Project Management Plan
    e. All of the above

86. Your project is currently actively seeking approval of a project deliverable. What process is the project performing?
    a. Perform Quality Assurance
    b. Control Quality
    c. Validate Scope
    d. Control Scope
    e. Monitor and Control Project Work

87. Your project is processing a number of highly urgent and critical changes to the scope. What is the first step?
    a. Notify the project acceptor that work will begin on these changes immediately to ensure minimal impact to the schedule.
    b. Instruct the team to begin working on the changes immediately.
    c. Initiate the Perform Integrated Change Control process.
    d. Notify the project acceptor that urgent changes will only delay the project and recommend that the changes not be made.
    e. Request additional resources to allow for the changes to be made without impacting the schedule.

88. During an internal project meeting, a team member tells a story that could be considered offensive. No one present at the meeting seems to be offended by the story, and most laugh and encourage the teller to proceed. What should you as a PMI project manager do?
    a. Immediately request that the story be stopped and remind the teller that we must show respect at all times.
    b. Carefully monitor the team to see whether anyone is offended and discuss this with the storyteller.
    c. Meet with the storyteller privately after the meeting and advise him or her that the story was not respectful and that in the future this will not be tolerated.
    d. Notify human resources and request that they meet with the storyteller.
    e. Do nothing, as no one was offended.

CHAPTER

3

PROJECT INTEGRATION MANAGEMENT

1. There are _____ processes in Project Integration Management.
   a. 4
   b. 5
   c. 6
   d. 7
   e. 8

2. Manage and Control Project Team is one of the Project Integration Management processes.
   a. True
   b. False

3. The focus of the Project Integration Management process is to:
   a. Ensure that the project processes are followed throughout the project.
   b. Ensure that individual processes interact to integrate related activities.
   c. Summarize the other nine Knowledge Areas into a single Knowledge Area.
   d. It currently has no value; it was the original Knowledge Area and has been preserved for continuity.
   e. Integrate change management into all other Knowledge Areas.

4. Which of the following is *not* an input to the Project Charter?
   a. Business Case
   b. Benefits statement
   c. Organizational Process Assets
   d. Project Statement of Work
   e. Enterprise Environmental Factors

5. The preferred time for a project manager to be assigned is:
   a. Before the Project Charter can be started.
   b. Once the Project Charter has been approved.
   c. As soon as feasible, ideally while the Project Charter is being created.
   d. At the start of planning.
   e. When planning is complete.

6. Who is responsible for the Project Charter?
   a. The project manager
   b. The project team
   c. Executive management
   d. Business management
   e. The sponsoring entity

7. The Project Statement of Work (SOW) contains which of the following?
   a. Project scope, budget, and timeline
   b. Business need, budget, and timeline
   c. Business need, project scope, and strategic plan
   d. Budget, timeline, and strategic plan
   e. Legal contract and payment terms

8. The Business Case is produced in the Develop Project Charter process.
   a. True
   b. False

9. Which of the following would *not* typically be part of a Project Charter?
   a. Project purpose
   b. High-level risks
   c. Detailed project schedule
   d. Stakeholder list
   e. Assigned project manager

10. The Project Management Plan focuses on the execution and monitoring and controlling phases of the project.
    a. True
    b. False

11. The Project Management Plan is updated during which phases of the project?
    a. All phases
    b. All phases except closing
    c. Initiating and planning only
    d. Planning and executing
    e. Planning, execution, monitoring and controlling

12. Which elements must be included in the main Project Management Plan and can-not be provided through a subsidiary plan?
    a. Scope Management Plan
    b. Scope and Time Management Plans
    c. Stakeholder Management Plan
    d. Cost Management Plan
    e. None of the above

13. When can the Project Management Plan be changed without requiring the Perform Integrated Change Control process?
    a. During initial creation
    b. During initiation and planning
    c. During the replanning process for each subsequent project phase
    d. At any time during the project
    e. Never

14. Direct and Manage Project Work focuses on:
    a. Team management
    b. Time and budget management
    c. Quality management
    d. Work authorization system
    e. All of the above

15. One of the primary outputs of Direct and Manage Project Work is:
    a. Project status.
    b. Team training.
    c. Project deliverables.
    d. Planning for the next phase.
    e. Lessons learned and post-mortem analysis.

16. Which of the following is *not* a meeting type defined by PMI?
    a. Information exchange
    b. Status updates
    c. Brainstorming
    d. Decision making
    e. None of the above

17. Meetings are most effective when:
    a. As many topics are covered as possible to use all available time.
    b. They are dynamic and can be set up whenever required.
    c. They follow a defined agenda.
    d. They follow a defined agenda with enough free time to cover other topics.
    e. Extra participants are added as needed to discuss the current topic.

18. Work performance data are:
    a. Only produced on large projects over one million dollars or more than one year in duration.
    b. Raw data measurements of the project work activities.
    c. Produced by schedule- and budget-tracking tools.
    d. Of interest to only the project managers.
    e. No longer required because most projects use project portals.

19. Change requests are needed when:
    a. The project budget increases.
    b. The project timeline increases.
    c. A change occurs on an accepted project component.
    d. Any change occurs on the project.
    e. Either A or B.

20. Monitor and Control Project Work is a process in:
    a. The Monitoring and Controlling process group.
    b. Project Scope Management.
    c. Routine daily project management activities.
    d. Project Integration Management.
    e. None of the above.

21. The Monitor and Control Project Work process does *not* include which of the following?
    a. Comparing performance to plan.
    b. Identifying corrective actions needed.
    c. Conducting status meetings.
    d. Producing status reports.
    e. All of the above are part of Monitor and Control Project Work.

22. Who can initiate a Project Change Request?
    a. Only the project manager
    b. Only the project acceptor
    c. Only the project sponsor
    d. Anyone
    e. Any of A, B, or C

23. Who can approve a Project Change Request?
    a. The project manager
    b. The project sponsor
    c. The individual most impacted by the change
    d. Individual(s) identified in the Scope Management Plan
    e. Executive management

24. Approved change requests require:
    a. No additional changes, as the change request documents the approved changes.
    b. Changes to the Project Management Plan to reflect the changes.
    c. Changes to all project documents impacted by the change.
    d. Changes to the project schedule and budget.
    e. Changes to documents currently in development only.

25. At what level should change requests be formalized as written documents as opposed to verbal discussions and/or meeting minutes?
    a. When the schedule impact is greater than one day
    b. When the budget impact is greater than $1,000
    c. When the schedule impact is greater than one week
    d. When the budget impact is greater than $10,000
    e. For any change, independent of schedule or budget impacts
    f. A or B
    g. C or D

26. A Change Control Board (CCB) is required on a project when:
    a. The project is part of a larger portfolio of projects.
    b. The project is defined as strategic for the organization.
    c. The project has been selected as a "watch project."
    d. It is defined in the Scope or Change Management Plan.
    e. A CCB is required only for large or complex change requests.

27. A Project Change Log:
    a. Tracks all approved changes.
    b. Tracks all rejected changes.
    c. Tracks only changes that have a time or budget impact.
    d. Tracks all changes.
    e. Is used only for small projects not using an automated Project Management Information System.

28. Close Project or Phase occurs:
    a. Once at the end of a project.
    b. As required by the project manager or project acceptor.
    c. Only when formal deliverables are implemented and put into service.
    d. Only when the project is being cancelled.
    e. At the end of every phase.

29. Which of the following is *not* part of a Change Management Plan?
    a. Change policies
    b. Review meetings
    c. Change request templates
    d. Lessons learned
    e. Approval levels

30. A minor change request has been submitted by the team. The change is minor and can easily be accommodated. What is the first step to processing this change?
    a. Get the team to do the work so you can demonstrate the results.
    b. Review the change and determine the full project impacts.
    c. Contact the project acceptor and validate that the change is needed.
    d. Submit a change request to the Change Control Board.
    e. Tell the team member that all changes must come from the project acceptor.

31. You are assigned to an in-flight project. The outgoing project manager provides access to the project information system and demonstrates that the project is performing within both Cost and Schedule baselines. However, the outgoing project manager also informs you that the project acceptor is *not* happy with the project. What should you do?
    a. Review all information in the project information system to validate that the project is in fact within baseline.
    b. Meet with the team to validate their confidence in the project information system.
    c. Replan the project to ensure that you support the remaining estimates.
    d. Meet with the project acceptor to understand why he or she is unhappy.
    e. Allow things to continue as is for one month to get a feel for how things are operating.

32. The project acceptor has submitted a request to change the scope of the project. The project has completed the Control Scope processes. What is the next step?
    a. Begin work on the changes.
    b. Complete Integrated Change Management.
    c. Inform the project acceptor that the change is ready for acceptance.
    d. Meet with the project acceptor to understand why the change was submitted and determine whether others are likely to be submitted.
    e. Inform the project acceptor that the change will be difficult and that you recommend it not proceed.

33. A Change Control Board is:
    a. Made up of the project management team, project acceptor, and project sponsor.
    b. Made up of the senior members of the project team, who are responsible for analyzing project changes.
    c. An external group, typically composed of senior management, who approve all changes for a project.
    d. An external group, typically composed of senior management, who approve all changes for all projects.
    e. A group of senior managers from the business area who approve all changes for a project.

34. Close Project or Phase is *not* appropriate when:
    a. A project is moving from one phase to another.
    b. A project is completing.
    c. A project is cancelled early.
    d. A project is reinitiated.
    e. A phase is completing.

3

4

PROJECT SCOPE MANAGEMENT

1. Managing the project scope is primarily concerned with:
   a. Creating the Project Scope Document.
   b. Meeting with the business to define and then manage project scope.
   c. Defining and controlling what is and is not included in the project.
   d. Creating the project scope box.
   e. Processing change requests to ensure that the project scope is accurate.

2. The Project Scope Baseline:
   a. Is a one-time document produced during project planning to initially define the project scope.
   b. Changes daily for the life of the project as the team adjusts it based on new information gathered.
   c. Is updated at the end of each phase to reflect the new Scope Baseline for the next phase.
   d. Is a formal document and is updated only with formal change request approval.
   e. Is optional and often not produced by a project.

3. The Project Scope Baseline is used to:
   a. Evaluate change requests against.
   b. Be the basis on which scope is validated and controlled.
   c. Report project progress on a weekly basis.
   d. Deny all project changes.
   e. Justify any project delays or budget exceptions.

4. Once the Scope Management Plan is created, the Project Management Plan is no longer needed.
   a. True
   b. False

5. The Scope Management Plan:
   a. Is required only on large or complex projects.
   b. Is required on all projects.
   c. Must always be produced as a separate standalone document.
   d. Can be a "chapter" in the Project Management Plan.
   e. None of the above.
   f. All of the above.
   g. A and C.
   h. A and D.
   i. B and C.
   j. B and D.

6. The goal of the Scope Management Plan:
   a. Is to eliminate scope creep.
   b. Is to support scope creep.
   c. Is to control scope creep.
   d. Is to encourage scope creep.
   e. Has nothing to do with scope creep.

7. Which of the following is *not* considered to be a component of the Scope Management Plan?
   a. The process for preparing the Project Scope Statement.
   b. The process for creating the WBS.
   c. The process for project acceptance of work products.
   d. The process for implementing project scope items.
   e. The process for changing the project scope.

8. The Requirements Management Plan contains:
   a. Requirements reporting processes.
   b. Configuration management processes.
   c. Prioritization processes.
   d. Requirements metrics processes.
   e. Requirements traceability processes.
   f. All except B.
   g. All except B and C.
   h. All except D.
   i. All of the above.

9. Collect Requirements is completed:
   a. During project planning.
   b. After project planning but before project startup.
   c. During project delivery.
   d. Throughout the project.
   e. During analysis only.

10. Requirements definition during planning:
    a. Is high-level only, and therefore it is acceptable to miss requirements at this stage.
    b. Focuses on the solution and therefore should reject any requirements that will be difficult to implement.
    c. Forms the foundation for the project and therefore must identify all business requirements.
    d. Must address both business and technical requirements.
    e. Is optional if the Project Charter is considered to be accurate and complete.

11. Target dates and budget constraints should be considered requirements collection.
    a. True
    b. False

12. Which of the following is *not* considered an appropriate technique for collecting requirements?
    a. Interviews
    b. Focus groups
    c. Web searches
    d. Prototypes
    e. Document analysis

13. Using interviewing as a technique can be advantageous because it:
    a. Allows for spontaneous questions.
    b. Is formal and follows a predefined interview script.
    c. Allows for confidential information to be gathered.
    d. A and B.
    e. B and C.
    f. A and C.
    g. All of the above.

4

14. Advantages of using focus groups as a technique include which of the following?
    a. It allows for multiple participants.
    b. Interactive discussions may yield additional details.
    c. It requires no special skills.
    d. A and B.
    e. B and C.
    f. A and C.
    g. All of the above.

15. One key advantage of facilitated workshops is that they:
    a. Require no special skills or support.
    b. Can be scheduled and executed with no advanced planning.
    c. Reconcile differing requirements between stakeholders.
    d. Are effective for obtaining final project acceptance.
    e. Allow the facilitator to direct the conclusion to the desired result.

16. Which of the following is *not* a group creative technique?
    a. Brainstorming
    b. Requirements review
    c. Nominal group technique
    d. Idea/mind mapping
    e. Affinity diagram
    f. All are group creative techniques

17. Which of the following is *not* a group decision-making technique?
    a. Unanimity
    b. Majority
    c. Plurality
    d. Dictatorship
    e. All are group decision-making techniques

18. Advantages of questionnaires and surveys include the following:
    a. They ensure a quick turnaround.
    b. They ensure answers to predetermined questions.
    c. They support geographically dispersed respondents.
    d. They support numerical analysis.
    e. All of the above.

19. Which of the following is *not* an advantage of the observations technique?
    a. It is done on the job and therefore doesn't take the individual away from regular activities.
    b. It is natural, and observations directly reflect work activities.
    c. It supports information gathering where requirements are hard to articulate.
    d. It may identify hidden requirements not previously identified.
    e. All except B.
    f. All of the above.

20. Advantages of prototyping include the following:
    a. It involves a tangible model to allow for better and early feedback.
    b. Prototypes can be reused so no extra effort is required.
    c. It is a one-time event, so it can be accommodated with no schedule impact.
    d. It can be done by the business users, so no additional effort is required from the project.
    e. All of the above.

21. Advantages of the benchmarking technique include the following:
    a. It requires limited advance knowledge of the requirements.
    b. It compares project requirements to best practices and/or industry norms.
    c. It provides a basis for evaluating requirements for "reasonableness."
    d. Benchmarks can be internal or external.
    e. B and C.
    f. A and D.
    g. B, C, and D.
    h. A, B, and C.
    i. A, B, C, and D.

22. The document analysis technique:
    a. Allows for determining requirements without requiring business unit participation.
    b. May not identify all requirements.
    c. Allows for additional techniques to gather additional details.
    d. Is often the first source for requirements gathering.
    e. All of the above.

23. Which of the following must be satisfied before the Requirements Document can be baselined?
    a. Requirements must be unambiguous.
    b. Requirements must be traceable.
    c. Requirements must be fully defined.
    d. Requirements must be accepted by the key stakeholders.
    e. All of the above.
    f. All except A.
    g. All except B.
    h. All except C.
    i. All except D.

24. A Requirements Traceability Matrix is:
    a. Created during project delivery.
    b. Created during initial requirements identification.
    c. Required only on projects with more than 1,000 requirements.
    d. Required only on projects with more than 10,000 requirements.
    e. Required only in IT projects, as requirements are typically intangible.

25. The Define Scope process produces:
    a. A business document, which is produced by the key stakeholders.
    b. A project document, which is used exclusively by the project team.
    c. A project document, which is produced by the project team and accepted by key stakeholders.
    d. An informal document, which is updated regularly and does not require formal acceptance.
    e. A one-time document approved by key stakeholders and then not updated.

26. The key input to the Define Scope process is the:
    a. Scope Management Plan.
    b. Project Charter.
    c. Requirements Documentation.
    d. Organizational Process Assets.
    e. All are equally important.

27. Some requirements in the Requirements Document may *not* be included in the project scope.
    a. True
    b. False

28. The Define Scope process should consider:
    a. The Requirements Document only.
    b. Requirements, risks, assumptions, and constraints.
    c. Requirements, risks, assumption, constraints and all previous project documentation.
    d. Starting fresh to ensure that the scope is not contaminated with previous work.
    e. The Project Charter, as it clearly defines the business objectives and Business Case.

29. The Define Scope process is:
    a. Done once during project planning.
    b. Done during project planning and as part of each phase replan.
    c. Done initially during project planning and continuously as needed as part of Project Change Management.
    d. A daily process done continuously during the project to allow for timely resolution of all delivery challenges.
    e. A monthly process to ensure that the project scope remains relevant.

30. Expert judgment, a technique commonly used in the PMBOK, can make use of:
    a. Other organizational units.
    b. Consultants.
    c. Stakeholders.
    d. Professional associations.
    e. Industry groups.
    f. Subject-matter experts.
    g. All of the above.
    h. None of the above: Expert Judgment must be provided by the project team.

31. The Project Scope Statement contains the following components:
    a. Project scope.
    b. Project deliverables.
    c. Acceptance criteria.
    d. Project schedule.
    e. Project exclusions.
    f. All of the above.
    g. All except A.
    h. All except B.
    i. All except C.
    j. All except D.
    k. All except E.

32. The Project Scope Statement contains only the project's scope. The product scope is documented only in the Project Charter.
    a. True
    b. False

33. The Project Scope Statement should identify:
    a. Major deliverables only.
    b. All deliverables.
    c. Only deliverables that will be presented for acceptance.
    d. A single deliverable that represents project completion.
    e. The Project Scope Plan.

34. It is important to document exclusions in the Project Scope Statement because:
    a. Doing so identifies the work that the team doesn't feel is important.
    b. Explicitly stating what is *not* to be delivered helps define what *will* be delivered.
    c. Doing so identifies the work that the project manager expects from the business team.
    d. Doing so ensures that the team won't do extra work.
    e. Exclusions should *not* be included in the Project Scope Statement, because negative statements will undermine the relationship with the key stakeholders.

35. Assumptions and constraints are important in a Project Scope Statement because:
    a. They provide a collection of all the items that the team didn't have time to consider.
    b. They support negotiations for future change requests.
    c. They ensure that the project can't be held responsible for the Project Scope Statement.
    d. They clearly document limiting factors and conditions on which the Project Scope Statement is based.
    e. They document the areas on which the project team and the business team could not agree.

36. During scope planning, the WBS should identify activities.
    a. True
    b. False

37. The WBS created in Project Scope Management identifies the work to:
    a. Accomplish the project objectives.
    b. Assign activities to team members.
    c. Create the required deliverables.
    d. Define the total scope of the project.
    e. All of the above.
    f. All except A.
    g. All except B.
    h. All except C.
    i. All except D.

4

38. When creating the WBS, the project team may consider using which of the following?
    a. Organizational Process Assets
    b. Industry-specific WBS standards
    c. WBS from vendors and other involved parties
    d. All of the above
    e. None of the above: The WBS must be developed from the project's deliverables list.

39. The WBS should be decomposed into how many levels?
    a. 3
    b. 4
    c. 5
    d. Depends on the project manager's management method
    e. Depends on the size and complexity of the deliverable

40. WBS decomposition should be based on:
    a. Project phases.
    b. Project deliverables.
    c. Project components/subcomponents.
    d. Existing templates.
    e. All of the above.
    f. Any of the above.
    g. None of the above.

41. Based on the diagram, which WBS decomposition method is being used?

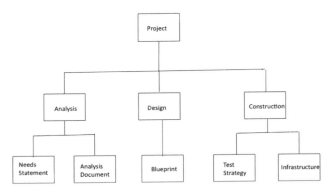

a. Deliverable
b. Phase
c. Components
d. PMBOK
e. Industry standard

42. Based on the diagram, which WBS decomposition method is being used?

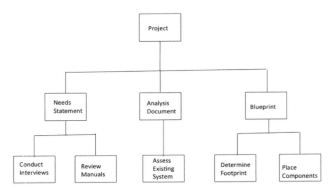

a. Deliverable
b. Phase
c. Components
d. PMBOK
e. Industry standard

43. Based on the diagram, which WBS decomposition method is being used?

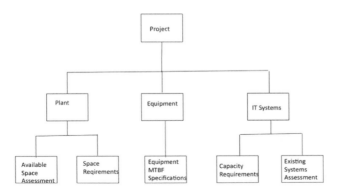

a. Deliverable
b. Phase
c. Components
d. PMBOK
e. Industry standard

44. A WBS can be verified as complete when:
    a. All deliverables are defined.
    b. The sum of the decomposed elements identify all work to produce the deliverable.
    c. No work packages exist that don't directly contribute to a deliverable.
    d. All decomposition paths are at the same depth.
    e. All of the above.
    f. All except A.
    g. All except B.
    h. All except C.
    i. All except D.

45. Rolling-wave planning is:
    a. Not recommended.
    b. Acceptable only for large projects.
    c. Acceptable when required details are not available.
    d. Recommended, as it reduces unknowns.
    e. Suitable only for IT projects.

46. The Scope Baseline includes:
    a. The Scope Statement.
    b. The WBS.
    c. The WBS Dictionary.
    d. Stakeholder approval of the scope.
    e. All of the above.

47. A control account is assigned:
    a. To every element of the WBS.
    b. At a predefined level of the WBS—for example, all Level 3 elements.
    c. To the lowest-level elements of each WBS branch.
    d. To elements of the WBS that represent management control points.
    e. To WBS elements, which identify the project deliverables.
    f. To WBS elements, which will require formal project acceptance.

48. A WBS Dictionary:
    a. Further describes each WBS element.
    b. Is required for WBS structures to be distributed outside the core project group.
    c. Provides business definitions to project terms.
    d. Matches WBS elements to resources assigned to complete it.
    e. Is not required.

49. Validate Scope is focused on:
    a. Confirming work is within the project scope definition.
    b. Processing Project Change Requests.
    c. Validating the project schedule, including all scope elements.
    d. Managing the team to ensure that they don't complete any unplanned work.
    e. Managing the formal acceptance of the completed project deliverables.

50. Control Quality produces verified deliverables, whereas Validate Scope produces accepted deliverables by the stakeholders.
    a. True
    b. False

51. The Validate Scope process can result in:
    a. Project Change Requests.
    b. Defect reports.
    c. Project acceptance documents.
    d. Work performance information.
    e. All of the above.

52. Validate Scope is typically performed before Control Quality for each deliverable.
    a. True
    b. False

53. Control Scope is focused on:
    a. Reviewing Project Change Requests.
    b. Processing Project Change Requests.
    c. Managing the team to ensure that no unauthorized work is completed.
    d. Monitoring and managing changes to the Scope Baseline.
    e. It is not needed if Perform Integrated Change Control is included in the project.

54. Control Scope's main focus is:
    a. To avoid all scope changes.
    b. To manage scope changes.
    c. To make scope changes so expensive that they will not be accepted.
    d. Needed only during the early phases of the project.
    e. To identify deviations from the Scope Baseline.

55. The Control Scope process must integrate with:
    a. The project management team.
    b. The Perform Integrated Change Control process.
    c. The Control Time and Control Costs process.
    d. The Perform Integrate Change Control, Control Time, and Control Costs processes.
    e. All control processes defined in the respective Knowledge Areas.

56. Which of the following project documents would *not* be used in the Control Scope process?
    a. Scope Baseline
    b. Scope Management Plan
    c. Requirements Traceability Matrix
    d. Quality Management Plan
    e. Requirements Document

57. What tools and techniques would be used by the Control Scope process?
    a. Questionnaires
    b. Interviews
    c. Variance analysis
    d. Stakeholder analysis
    e. Status reporting

58. What is the first step in creating the project scope?
    a. Writing the Scope Statement
    b. Defining the WBS
    c. Identifying the requirements
    d. Identifying the deliverables

59. The lowest level of the WBS is typically referred to as the:
    a. Deliverables.
    b. Work packages.
    c. Task assignments.
    d. Milestones.
    e. Phases.

60. The Project Scope Baseline is composed of which of the following?
    a. The WBS
    b. The Scope Statement
    c. The WBS and the Scope Statement
    d. The WBS, the WBS Dictionary, and the Scope Statement
    e. The WBS, the deliverables list, and the Scope Statement

61. Which of the following is *not* produced by the Control Scope process?
    a. Work performance information
    b. Project acceptance documents
    c. Project Change Requests
    d. Project Management Plan updates
    e. Project document updates

62. The main purpose of the WBS is to:
    a. Develop the project schedule.
    b. Identify what components of the project must be purchased externally.
    c. Organize and define the project's scope.
    d. Assign work to the team.
    e. None of the above.

5

PROJECT TIME MANAGEMENT

1. There are _____ processes in Project Time Management.
   a. 4
   b. 5
   c. 6
   d. 7
   e. 8

2. On small projects, it is okay to complete Define Activities, Sequence Activities, Estimate Activity Resources, Estimate Activity Durations, and Develop Schedule as a single process.
   a. True
   b. False

3. A schedule model is referred to as:
   a. The starting point from which a schedule is developed.
   b. A "perfect" specimen of a project schedule on which to model each project.
   c. The combination of the schedule data and the schedule calculations on a scheduling tool.
   d. The result of the Project Time Management processes—the schedule model that the project is delivered against.
   e. The Project Management project lifecycle.

4. The Schedule Management Plan is:
   a. A standalone document always produced for every project.
   b. A standalone document or integrated into the Project Management Plan depending on size, complexity, and project's specific requirements.
   c. Only needed if the schedule is to be developed manually, as project scheduling tools automate the schedule management processes.
   d. Required only on large and complex projects.
   e. Optional.

5. Project scheduling tools (for example, Microsoft Project) must be used for effective Project Time Management.
   a. True
   b. False

6. Project Schedule Management should *not* consider which of the following?
   a. Organizational culture
   b. Resource skills
   c. Prior project results
   d. Usability of the project scheduling tools
   e. Prior experience of the team with the business area

7. A key consideration of the Schedule Management Plan is:
   a. Schedule management, including time tracking and activity updates.
   b. Historical information, which impacts how the current schedule should be created.
   c. Use and functionality of schedule management software.
   d. Schedule change techniques, such as fast tracking and crashing.
   e. Estimating techniques.
   f. All of the above.
   g. All except A.
   h. All except B.
   i. All except C.
   j. All except D.
   k. All except E.

8. The Schedule Management Plan does *not* contain:
   a. Scheduling methodology.
   b. Level of accuracy.
   c. Schedule maintenance approach.
   d. Resource assignments.
   e. Control thresholds.

9. The Define Activities process:
   a. Is the same as the Create WBS process, as they both focus on the WBS.
   b. Replaces Create WBS because it comes later in the planning process.
   c. Augments the Create WBS and further decomposes the WBS.
   d. Creates a second WBS that replaces the original WBS created in Project Scope Management.
   e. Identifies the steps for entering the WBS into the schedule management tool.

10. The output of the Define Activities process is:
    a. A fully scheduled list of project activities.
    b. A complete list of project activities that must be completed to produce the project deliverables.
    c. A detailed list of activities that should be assigned to team members.
    d. Detailed team member timesheets identifying the activities they are to work on.
    e. A medium-level decomposition of the WBS, more detailed than work packages but not yet detailed enough for project scheduling.

11. The project management scheduling software to be used should be considered when creating WBS activities because:
    a. If the activity list is in the right format, it will make using the tool easier.
    b. Some project scheduling tools require a specific noun/verb construction for activity names.
    c. The activity decomposition will need to be limited to conform to a maximum number of WBS levels defined by the tool.
    d. Most project scheduling tools won't support spaces in activity names; therefore, attention must be paid to how names can be entered into the tool.
    e. All of the above.
    f. None of the above.

12. Activity decomposition should stop when:
    a. There are six levels in the WBS.
    b. All WBS branches have the same number of levels.
    c. The time allocated in the plan for activity decomposition is complete.
    d. The activity is estimable and assignable.
    e. Based on expert judgment, it feels like the right level of decomposition.

13. Activity decomposition should:
    a. Ignore the WBS Dictionary.
    b. Maintain the WBS Dictionary if activity decomposition made any changes at the WBS levels.
    c. Maintain the WBS Dictionary for all new activities added to the WBS.
    d. Ensure that the team member assigned to the activity updates the WBS Dictionary as soon as work is started on the activity.
    e. Cut and paste the WBS Dictionary details from the WBS levels into the children activity elements.

5

14. Decomposing work packages into activities is best completed by:
    a. The business team, because they fully understand the requirements.
    b. The PMO, because they will ensure that organizational decomposition best practices are applied.
    c. The project management team, because they will ensure that overall project estimates are preserved during the decomposition process.
    d. Using external guidelines and templates.
    e. The project team members who will be completing the work identified by the activities.

15. A WBS typically:
    a. Is two levels deep: deliverable and activity.
    b. Is three levels deep: project, deliverable, and activity.
    c. Is four levels deep: project, deliverable, subdeliverable, and activity
    d. Varies by project complexity, but all branches should be the same.
    e. Varies by deliverable complexity.

16. The activity list and activity attributes are the equivalent of the WBS and WBS Dictionary.
    a. True
    b. False

17. Activity names should:
    a. Be as short as possible to make it easier for the team to reference them.
    b. Be self-sufficient so that they can be referenced outside the project schedule and still describe the activity's place in the schedule.
    c. Contain the complete path of the WBS: project/deliverable/subdeliverable/activity group/etc.
    d. Be unique within each deliverable path.
    e. Be unique within each activity group.

18. What is the difference between a milestone and an activity?
    a. Milestones have no duration.
    b. Milestones are always entered in ALL CAPITALS.
    c. Milestones have the word milestone at the end of the name.
    d. Milestones are no different than activities.
    e. Milestones do not have attributes.

19. The Sequence Activities activity:
    a. Is optional and typically not completed.
    b. Identifies the relationships between project activities.
    c. Defines the logical sequence of the schedule.
    d. All of the above.
    e. All except A.
    f. All except B.
    g. All except C.

20. In a well-defined project schedule:
    a. Dependencies exist for the key deliverables to ensure that they are completed in the correct order.
    b. All activities except the project start and project end should have at least one predecessor and one successor.
    c. Most dependencies in a project should be start-to-start to ensure that activities start as soon as possible.
    d. Most dependencies in a project should be end-to-end to ensure that the activities complete on time.
    e. A complete dependency network defines both activity and resource dependencies.

21. Requirements for dependencies come from:
    a. The order in which the activities are entered into the schedule.
    b. The availability of resources to work on the activities.
    c. The activity attributes (or WBS Dictionary).
    d. The project manager, who defines the order in which the project is to be completed.
    e. Subject-matter experts.

22. Milestones should *not* be included in the Sequence Activities activity.
    a. True
    b. False

23. Which of the following is *not* a valid dependency type?
    a. Start-to-start
    b. Finish-to-start
    c. Start-to-finish
    d. In-progress-to-start
    e. Finish-to-finish

5

24. In a _____ dependency relationship, a successor cannot start until a predecessor has finished.
    a. Finish-to-start
    b. Finish-to-finish
    c. Start-to-start
    d. In-progress-to-start
    e. Start-to-finish.

25. In a _____ dependency relationship, a successor cannot finish until a predecessor has finished.
    a. Finish-to-start
    b. Finish-to-finish
    c. Start-to-start
    d. In-progress-to-start
    e. Start-to-finish

26. In a _____ dependency relationship, a successor cannot finish until a predecessor has started.
    a. Finish-to-start
    b. Finish-to-finish
    c. Start-to-start
    d. In-progress-to-start
    e. Start-to-finish

27. _____ is the most commonly used dependency type.
    a. Finish-to-start
    b. Finish-to-finish
    c. Start-to-start
    d. In-progress-to-start
    e. Start-to-finish

28. _____ is the least commonly used dependency type.
    a. Finish-to-start
    b. Finish-to-finish
    c. Start-to-start
    d. In-progress-to-start
    e. Start-to-finish

29. The diagram below depicts what type of dependency?

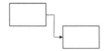

   a. Finish–to–start
   b. Finish–to–finish
   c. Start–to–start
   d. In–progress–to–start
   e. Start–to–finish

30. The diagram below depicts what type of dependency?

   a. Finish–to–start
   b. Finish–to–finish
   c. Start–to–start
   d. In–progress–to–start
   e. Start–to–finish

31. The diagram below depicts what type of dependency?

   a. Finish–to–start
   b. Finish–to–finish
   c. Start–to–start
   d. In–progress–to–start
   e. Start–to–finish

5

32. The diagram below depicts what type of dependency?

    a. Finish–to–start
    b. Finish–to–finish
    c. Start–to–start
    d. In–progress–to–start
    e. Start–to–finish

33. The Precedence Diagramming Method (PDM):
    a. Is rarely used in developing project schedules.
    b. Is used by most project management software packages.
    c. Represents the schedule with activities on nodes and relationships between the nodes.
    d. Represents the schedule with activities on arrows and nodes as connectors.
    e. Both A and C.
    f. Both A and D.
    g. Both B and C.
    h. Both B and D.

34. Which of the following is *not* a valid dependency type?
    a. Mandatory
    b. Project
    c. Discretionary
    d. External
    e. Internal

35. Which dependency type should be defined most often on a project?
    a. Mandatory
    b. Project
    c. Discretionary
    d. External
    e. Internal

36. Which dependency type should be defined least often on a project?
    a. Mandatory
    b. Project
    c. Discretionary
    d. External
    e. Internal

37. Which dependency type identifies dependencies outside the project scope?
    a. Mandatory
    b. Project
    c. Discretionary
    d. External
    e. Internal

5

38. Activity dependencies can be modified by:
    a. Combining dependency types to give multiple ways activities can be linked.
    b. Adding leads and lags to the dependencies.
    c. Making dependencies optional.
    d. Removing the dependency and manually adjusting the schedule.
    e. Dependencies cannot be modified once they are set.

39. A lead of two days on a start-to-finish dependency results in:
    a. Nothing—there is no such thing as a lead.
    b. A delay of the start of the first activity by two days.
    c. An advance of the start of the first activity by two days.
    d. A delay of the start of the second activity by two days.
    e. An advance of the start of the second activity by two days.

40. A lag of two days on a finish-to-finish dependency results in:
    a. Nothing—there is no such thing as a lag.
    b. A delay of the start of the first activity by two days.
    c. An advance of the start of the first activity by two days.
    d. A delay of the start of the second activity by two days.
    e. An advance of the start of the second activity by two days.

41. The project schedule network diagram represents:
    a. The technical environment that supports the project.
    b. The activities and their dependency relationships.
    c. The communications network between the project and the business unit.
    d. The order in which the activities were entered into the project schedule.
    e. The order in which the project manager will assign the tasks to the team members.

42. A project schedule network diagram is typically:
    a. Not produced.
    b. Produced by the project manager using an advanced drawing tool.
    c. Produced by the scheduling software.
    d. Hand-drawn by the project manager.
    e. Not used.

43. Which of the following requirements is *not* identified by the Estimate Activity Resources process?
    a. Materials
    b. Human resources (team)
    c. Equipment
    d. Supplies
    e. Budget

44. When estimating activity resources, which of the following are required?
    a. Resource rate/costs
    b. Resource calendars
    c. Material availability
    d. Equipment availability
    e. All of the above
    f. A and D
    g. B, C, and D
    h. All except B

45. Costs for resources should *not* be considered when estimating activity resources.
    a. True
    b. False

46. Which of the following techniques should be considered when estimating activity resources?
    a. Expert judgment
    b. Alternatives analysis
    c. Published estimating data
    d. Bottom-up estimating
    e. All of the above
    f. All except A
    g. All except B
    h. All except C
    i. All except D

47. When estimating activity resources, if it is difficult to accurately determine the resource requirements, it is best to:
    a. Estimate as well as possible and continue to the next activity.
    b. Further decompose the activity until it can be resourced.
    c. Assign a senior resource to the activity to ensure that it can be completed appropriately.
    d. Estimate as well as possible and add extra resources as a contingency.
    e. Estimate and continue, as estimations are never accurate.

48. The outputs from the Estimate Activity Resource process are:
    a. The complete project schedule.
    b. The resource requirements list.
    c. The activity resource requirements.
    d. The Resource Breakdown Structure.
    e. All of the above.
    f. A and B.
    g. A and C.
    h. A and D.
    i. B and C.
    j. B and D.
    k. C and D.

49. The Estimate Activity Durations process can be done:
    a. In isolation of all other Project Time Management activities.
    b. After the project schedule has been completed.
    c. Once the activity resources are identified.
    d. After the activity dependencies are identified.
    e. After the activities are identified.

50. Which of the following is required to estimate activity durations?
    a. Required resource types
    b. Resource calendars
    c. Activity scope of work
    d. Estimated resource quantities
    e. All of the above

51. Which of the following estimating methods is appropriate for determining activity duration estimates?
    a. Parametric
    b. Three-point
    c. Analogous
    d. Peer
    e. Work effort
    f. All of the above
    g. A, B, and C
    h. A, C, and E
    i. All except C
    j. All except E

52. The _____ estimating method involves using a standardized measure of effort to complete a unit of work.
    a. Parametric
    b. Three-point
    c. Analogous
    d. Peer
    e. Work effort

53. The _____ estimating method involves basing the task estimate on a similar activity from the past, with adjustments for project-specific conditions.
    a. Parametric
    b. Three-point
    c. Analogous
    d. Peer
    e. Work effort

54. The formula for the beta distribution three-point estimate is:
    a. (Optimistic + Most Likely + Pessimistic) / 3
    b. Optimistic – Confidence Factor
    c. Most Likely + Contingency Factor
    d. Pessimistic + Confidence Factor
    e. (Optimistic + 4 ★ Most Likely + Pessimistic) / 6

55. The formula for the triangular distribution three-point estimate is:
    a. (Optimistic + Most Likely + Pessimistic) / 3
    b. Optimistic – Confidence Factor
    c. Most Likely + Contingency Factor
    d. Pessimistic + Confidence Factor
    e. (Optimistic + 4 ★ Most Likely + Pessimistic) / 6

56. PERT (or Program Evaluation and Review Technique) has been replaced by triangular and beta distribution.
    a. True
    b. False

57. An activity estimate is determined based on estimating the detailed task lists for all the individual work items. What type of estimate method was used?
    a. Bottom-up
    b. Top-down
    c. Analogous
    d. Parametric
    e. Expert

58. Duration estimates should:
    a. Be accurate and complete.
    b. Consider unknowns, risks, and other factors by including contingency reserves.
    c. Define both estimate and contingency reserves separately.
    d. Identify contingency reserves for allocation at the project level.
    e. Not consider contingency reserves, as risks are covered in a separate Knowledge Area.

59. If the optimistic estimate is 10, the most likely is 12, and the pessimistic is 20, what is the beta distribution estimate?
    a. 10
    b. 12
    c. 13
    d. 14
    e. 20

60. If the optimistic estimate is 10, the most likely is 12, and the pessimistic is 20, what is the triangular distribution estimate?
    a. 10
    b. 12
    c. 13
    d. 14
    e. 20

61. What is the duration of a milestone?
    a. A milestone has no duration.
    b. The total of all the activity durations.
    c. The duration of the longest activity that is part of the milestone.
    d. The total of all the activity work estimates.
    e. The largest of the activity work estimates that make up the milestone.

62. Contingency reserves should be:
    a. Included in the duration estimate so that it cannot be questioned or reduced by management.
    b. Calculated at the activity level but added to the project at the deliverable or project level.
    c. Included as a separate component of the activity duration estimate so it can be managed independently.
    d. Calculated as a single number at the deliverable or project level.
    e. Not required, as Project Risk Management has specific processes for dealing with risk.

63. Contingency reserves may also be referred to as (select two):
    a. Management overhead.
    b. Time reserves.
    c. Risk mitigation plans.
    d. Buffers.
    e. Rainy-day funds.

64. Risk reserves at the activity level are associated with:
    a. Risk events.
    b. Known–unknowns.
    c. Unknown–knowns.
    d. Unknown–unknowns.
    e. Risk mitigation plans.

65. Risk reserves at the deliverable or project level are also referred to as:
    a. Risk events.
    b. Known–unknowns.
    c. Unknown–knowns.
    d. Unknown–unknowns.
    e. Risk mitigation plans.

66. Unknown–unknown contingency reserves are also referred to as management reserves.
    a. True
    b. False

67. Activity duration estimates should:
    a. Be presented as a single number indicating the activity estimate.
    b. Include any leads and lags associated with predecessors.
    c. Include any estimating ranges determined as part of the estimate.
    d. Include contingency reserves.
    e. Always be presented as a range to cover any efforts in estimation.

68. The Develop Schedule process does *not* require input from which of the following processes?
    a. Define Activities
    b. Estimate Costs
    c. Sequence Activities
    d. Estimate Activity Resources
    e. Estimate Activity Durations

69. The Project Schedule Baseline is used to:
    a. Define the starting state for the project.
    b. Motivate the team to achieve the baseline.
    c. Measure project progress against and identify corrective actions.
    d. Obtain project startup approval.
    e. Project Schedule Baselines are not used—only Project Budget Baselines.

70. Development of the project schedule is (select two):
    a. A labor-intensive process that should only be undertaken after all other schedule details are finalized.
    b. An interactive process that requires updates to the resource assignments and activity dependencies to fine-tune the schedule.
    c. Typically completed by project scheduling software with little involvement from the project management team.
    d. An iterative process using project scheduling software.
    e. Often not required, as end dates are provided by the project sponsor and the team simply works to achieve the required date.

71. The project schedule is typically developed using schedule network analysis. This consists of:
    a. The critical path method.
    b. The critical chain method.
    c. What-if analysis.
    d. Resource optimization.
    e. All of the above.
    f. None of the above—project scheduling software should be used.

72. The critical path method:
    a. Is used for manual scheduling only.
    b. Is used by scheduling software only.
    c. Is used for both manual and software scheduling.
    d. Is theoretical only and doesn't apply to actual project scheduling.
    e. Is an old method that is being retired.

73. The critical path method calculates:
    a. Early start.
    b. Early finish.
    c. Late start.
    d. Late finish.
    e. All of the above.
    f. None of the above—it calculates the project schedule.

74. A project with multiple critical paths:
    a. Is easy to manage.
    b. Is hard to manage.
    c. Is best avoided because it is distracting to the team.
    d. Must be changed by adding contingency, making the most complex path the critical path.
    e. Must be discussed with the project sponsor to find ways to remove some dependencies.

75. The critical path method calculates:
    a. Minimum project duration.
    b. Scheduling flexibility.
    c. Maximum project duration.
    d. All of the above.
    e. None of the above—it calculates the project schedule.

76. The project's critical path is:
    a. The sequence of activities that determine the project finish date.
    b. The activities that are the most critical tasks for completing the project because they provide the maximum business value.
    c. The activities that have the largest risk to successful completion.
    d. The activities in which the key stakeholders are most interested.
    e. The activities the project manager has identified as most important to project success.

77. Based on the following diagram, what is the project end date?

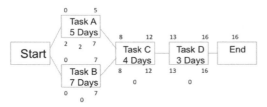

a. Day 13
b. Day 16
c. Day 17
d. Cannot be calculated using the information provided
e. None of the above

78. Based on the following diagram, what is the critical path?

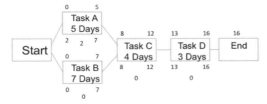

a. A–C–D
b. B–C–D
c. A–B–C–D
d. Cannot be calculated using the information provided
e. None of the above

79. Based on the following diagram, what is the project slack?

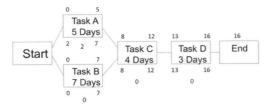

a. 0
b. 1
c. 2
d. Cannot be calculated using the information provided
e. None of the above

80. The critical path method:

    a. Requires resources to be leveled in advance.

    b. Does not consider resource availability.

    c. Determines resource requirements.

    d. Optimizes resource loads.

    e. Tolerates resource loads within a +/− range of 50 percent.

81. Based on the following diagram, how much can the start/finish or duration of Task C change without impacting the finish date?

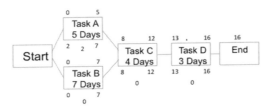

    a. 0 days

    b. 1 day

    c. 2 days

    d. 3 days

    e. None of the above

82. Based on the following diagram, how much can the start/finish or duration of Task A change without impacting the finish date?

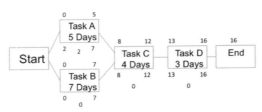

    a. 0 days

    b. 1 day

    c. 2 days

    d. 3 days

    e. None of the above

83. Negative slack is:
    a. What happens when a task on the critical path is delayed.
    b. What results when a constraint is placed on the project that violates the dates calculated by the critical path.
    c. What happens when a task not on the critical path begins to slip and therefore consumes some of the available slack.
    d. What happens when a team member completes a task that isn't scheduled at this time.
    e. This is not a term used in project management.

84. A project typically has:
    a. No critical path.
    b. A single critical path.
    c. Multiple critical paths.
    d. A critical path and several almost-critical paths.
    e. All of the above.
    f. All except A.

85. The critical chain method is (select two):
    a. Another name for the critical path method.
    b. A method for adding buffers to a project schedule.
    c. A method for accounting for limited resources or other project uncertainties.
    d. Used only for manual project scheduling.
    e. Used only for automated project scheduling.

86. Buffers are added to the project schedule based on the critical chain method as:
    a. Additional dependencies to delay selected project tasks.
    b. Additional activities to introduce additional time into the schedule.
    c. They are not added; the project end date is simply extended to include the buffer.
    d. Additional activities to identify and staff needed resources to complete the project.
    e. Additional dependencies to identify and staff needed resources to complete the project.

87. When using project scheduling software, the critical chain method:
    a. Is particularly relevant, because the software needs to be told about resource constraints.
    b. Applies for both manual and automated scheduling.
    c. Is not required for automated scheduling, because the software has complex resource-leveling algorithms that perform the same functionality as the critical chain method.
    d. Is useful for explaining the approach but cannot be implemented using either manual or automated scheduling.
    e. Is obsolete and is being retired from the PMBOK.

88. Resource smoothing (select two):
    a. Is the same as resource leveling.
    b. Is the adjustment of activity dates within available slack.
    c. May still result in resource over-allocation.
    d. Is dealing with conflicts between team members.
    e. Is validating the willingness of resources to work on the project.
    f. All except B.
    g. All except C.

89. Crashing is:
    a. What happens when resources are over-allocated and burn out from overwork.
    b. What happens when the project has no slack and the project dates cannot be met.
    c. A technique to shorten the project schedule by adding resources.
    d. A technique to shorten the project schedule by completing work in parallel.
    e. What happens when you've been completing too many PMP Prep Exams.

90. Fast tracking is:
    a. What happens when you deliver your project on time and on budget.
    b. What happens when you reduce the estimates on activities to get the project done sooner.
    c. A technique to shorten the project schedule by adding resources.
    d. A technique to shorten the project schedule by completing work in parallel.
    e. A technique to recalculate the critical path to allow the project to be done sooner.

91. Which of the following is an example of crashing?
    a. Doubling the number of resources on an activity.
    b. Adding tools to reduce the effort to complete an activity.
    c. Changing the delivery approach for completing an activity.
    d. All of the above.
    e. None of the above.

92. A project activity has an early start of 5, an early finish of 12, a late start of 7, and a late start of 14. What can be determined about this task?
    a. It is on the critical path.
    b. It is not on the critical path.
    c. A lag of two days has been defined for the activity.
    d. A lead of two days has been defined for the activity.
    e. Not enough information is provided to make any determination.

93. Midway through a project, it is becomes apparent that the project is forecasted to be two weeks late. What should you do?
    a. Inform the project sponsor that the project will be two weeks late.
    b. Submit a Project Change Request to extend the project's end date by two weeks.
    c. Explore alternatives to recover the schedule and discuss options with the project sponsor.
    d. Inform the team that overtime is needed to get back on schedule.
    e. Continue to monitor and hope the schedule delay is resolved over time.

94. Which of the follow is an example of fast tracking?
    a. Removing a dependency between two activities
    b. Adding a lead to a dependency
    c. Moving a dependency from a predecessor activity to a later (non–critical path) activity in the plan
    d. All of the above
    e. None of the above

95. The Schedule Baseline is:
    a. A formal project deliverable subject to approval and change management processes.
    b. A living document that changes weekly and in which project progress is tracked.
    c. Updated monthly as part of management status reporting.
    d. An internal document used by the project management team and therefore not approved.
    e. Optional.

5

96. The project schedule is typically presented as:
    a. Bar charts.
    b. Milestone charts.
    c. Schedule network diagrams.
    d. All of the above.
    e. None of the above.

97. A bar chart is the same as a Gantt chart.
    a. True
    b. False

98. The Control Schedule process is focused on:
    a. Ensuring that all activities are completed as defined in the baseline schedule.
    b. Changing the project schedule so that it always reflects the current status.
    c. Updating project progress and managing changes to the schedule.
    d. Reporting status to senior management.
    e. Rescheduling the project to ensure that resources are always fully loaded.

99. The Control Schedule process identifies the current status of the project from:
    a. The project management software tool's ability to update the plan to record that work has been completed as planned.
    b. Work performance data, which include detailed timesheets and updated project estimates.
    c. Information gathered as part of team status meetings.
    d. Individual one-on-one meetings with each team member.
    e. Exception reporting only.

100. The Control Schedule process is:
    a. Identical to the Monitor and Control Project Work process.
    b. Identical to the Perform Integrated Change Control process.
    c. Closely integrated with the Monitor and Control Project Work and Perform Integrated Change Control processes.
    d. Only required if the Monitor and Control Project Work process is not used.
    e. Only required if the Perform Integrated Change Control process is not used.

101. The Control Schedule process is concerned with:
    a. Determining the current project schedule status.
    b. Analyzing variances to the project schedule.
    c. Understanding why changes have happened.
    d. Managing changes to the project schedule.
    e. All of the above.

102. Which of the following techniques is *not* appropriate for the Control Schedule process?
    a. Trend analysis
    b. Critical path analysis
    c. Timesheets
    d. Critical chain analysis
    e. Earned Value Management

103. Trend analysis is a technique that:
    a. Interviews team members to get their opinion on why the project schedule is changing.
    b. Examines schedule variances over time to determine whether the situation is improving or deteriorating.
    c. Tracks and reports on variances for each activity between baseline and current status.
    d. Provides extensive written narratives on the root cause of variations.
    e. Is usable only on projects with more than 100,000 data points.

104. Critical path analysis is a schedule control technique that:
    a. Identifies the critical path for the project.
    b. Identifies any changes to the critical path for the project.
    c. Allows for the identification of near–critical path tasks that are becoming more critical.
    d. Focuses attention on the tasks that impact the project schedule.
    e. All of the above.

105. Critical chain method is a schedule control technique that:
    a. Tracks the project contingency.
    b. Determines changes in the critical path.
    c. Identifies changes to project buffers.
    d. Focuses the team on the activity chain that leads to a schedule delivery.
    e. Is a schedule development technique only.

106. Earned Value Management is a schedule control technique that:
    a. Only applies to cost management.
    b. Tracks project schedule performance to baseline.
    c. Predicts future schedule performance.
    d. B and C.
    e. All of the above.

5

107. The results of the Control Schedule process are (select two):
    a. Updated schedule forecasts reflecting current project status.
    b. Project Change Requests.
    c. Remediation actions.
    d. Senior management updates.
    e. Project cancelation requests.

108. You determine that the estimate for an activity is 60 hours because it will involve conducting 12 interviews of 5 hours each. This is based on what estimating approach?
    a. Bottom–up
    b. Top-down
    c. Parametric
    d. Analogous
    e. Expert judgment

109. A dependency where the walls cannot be built before the floor is finished is a(n):
    a. Mandatory dependency.
    b. Discretionary dependency.
    c. External dependency.
    d. Recommended dependency.
    e. Optional dependency.

6

PROJECT COST MANAGEMENT

1. There are _____ processes in Project Cost Management.
   a. 4
   b. 5
   c. 6
   d. 7
   e. 8

2. Project Cost Management is the most important of the Knowledge Areas because it is focused on the financial control of the project.
   a. True
   b. False

3. On small projects, it is acceptable to consider cost estimating and cost budgeting at the same time.
   a. True
   b. False

4. Project Cost Management is typically:
   a. Integrated with the corporate finance department.
   b. Deliberately separated from corporate finance to maintain project independence.
   c. Managed using PMBOK financial-management approaches.
   d. Focused on cost only; financial-management principles do not apply.
   e. Done exclusively by corporate finance without any project involvement.

5. Project Cost Management is concerned with:
   a. Project cash flow.
   b. Project accounting.
   c. Accounts receivables and payables.
   d. Discount rates and other financial calculations.
   e. All of the above.

6. The Cost Management Plan is typically:
   a. Delivered as a separate plan, because it must integrate with finance.
   b. Delivered as part of the Project Management Plan.
   c. Delivered separately or as part of the Project Management Plan, depending on project requirements.
   d. Not needed, because the project will always follow corporate financial policies.
   e. Not needed, because corporate finance does all cost management for the project.

7. The Cost Management Plan would *not* contain which of the following?
   a. Level of precision requirements
   b. Control thresholds
   c. Financial methods
   d. Funding sources
   e. Project cost accounting methods

8. Estimate Costs should (select two):
   a. Be done independently of the WBS to ensure that all costs are calculated.
   b. Be based on the costs to complete each activity in the WBS.
   c. Be based on the anticipated budget, which is then divided across the WBS.
   d. Ensure that risks and contingencies are included in the project costs.
   e. Be prepared by corporate, because they are the financial experts.

9. Cost estimates for WBS activities should include:
   a. Resource costs.
   b. Material costs.
   c. Costs for supplies.
   d. Costs for equipment.
   e. All costs required to complete the activity.

10. Cost estimates are always based on money/currency.
    a. True
    b. False

11. Cost estimates should be _____ at the completion of cost planning.
    a. 100 percent accurate
    b. 90 percent accurate
    c. 75 percent accurate
    d. ROM (rough order of magnitude)
    e. As accurate as possible

12. The cost for the human resources assigned to a project comes from:
    a. Corporate finance.
    b. Each team member.
    c. Human resources.
    d. The Human Resources Management Plan.
    e. The Project Management Office.

13. Project costs should include:
    a. Direct costs only.
    b. Direct and indirect costs.
    c. Direct salary costs plus fringe.
    d. Corporate overhead allocation.
    e. All of the above.
    f. None of the above.
    g. It depends!

6

14. When determining human resource costs, you should use the total hours per resource multiplied by the appropriate rate.
    a. True
    b. False

15. Which of the following is considered an appropriate method for cost estimating?
    a. Analogous estimating
    b. Parametric estimating
    c. Bottom-up estimating
    d. Three-point estimating
    e. All of the above
    f. None of the above—corporate finance is responsible for cost estimating

16. How should cost estimates be calculated?
    a. Using project scheduling software
    b. By corporate finance
    c. Using spreadsheets and other mathematical tools (including simulation tools)
    d. Manually
    e. Using actual costs as purchases are made

17. The project budget differs from the cost estimate because it:
    a. Combines the estimates into a budget and a baseline.
    b. Documents the cash-flow requirements for the project.
    c. Allocates costs to business units.
    d. Documents the approved costs.
    e. All of the above.

18. Which of the following are *not* needed when determining the project budget?
    a. Activity cost estimates
    b. Project schedule
    c. Human resource plan
    d. Risk plans
    e. Purchase agreements

19. The Determine Budget process consists of which of the following steps?
    a. Aggregate costs by work package.
    b. Aggregate work packages to higher-level WBS elements.
    c. Allocate costs to a time-phased budget.
    d. Determine reserve budget.
    e. Apply financial-management principles.
    f. All of the above.

20. Contingency reserves and management reserves do *not* mean the same thing.
    a. True
    b. False

21. Management reserves are always included in the Cost Baseline.
    a. True
    b. False

22. Management reserves are always included in the project budget.
    a. True
    b. False

23. Project actual costs are obtained from:
    a. Corporate accounting systems.
    b. Vendor invoices.
    c. Team-member timesheets.
    d. Interoffice charges.
    e. All of the above.

24. When uncontrollable project cost overruns are detected, the project manager should:
    a. Update the project baseline, because cost overruns often cannot be controlled.
    b. Accept the overrun and report the project as over budget.
    c. Process a Project Change Request to document the overrun and increase the project budget.
    d. Use project contingency to absorb the cost overrun.
    e. All of the above.

25. Project costs should be managed in isolation to ensure that an accurate project status can be produced.
    a. True
    b. False

26. Controlling project costs involves:
    a. Ensuring that the total project baseline is not exceeded.
    b. Ensuring that the project costs do not exceed the time-phased baseline.
    c. Ensuring that the project costs do not exceed the WBS-level baseline.
    d. Ensuring that the project costs do not exceed planned activity costs.
    e. All of the above.

27. Which of the following is *not* an Earned Value Management term?
    a. PV
    b. AC
    c. DC
    d. CPI
    e. BAC

28. Earned Value Management should be used for what type of projects?
    a. Fixed cost delivery
    b. Large projects over $1,000,000
    c. Projects involving external partners
    d. Critical projects
    e. All projects

29. Earned Value Management requires:
    a. The Scope Baseline.
    b. The Cost Baseline.
    c. The Schedule Baseline.
    d. Actual results.
    e. All of the above.

30. _____ is the authorized budget assigned to scheduled work.
    a. Planned value
    b. Earned value
    c. Actual cost
    d. Budget at completion
    e. Estimate at completion

6

31. _____ is the measure of work performed.
    a. Planned value
    b. Earned value
    c. Actual cost
    d. Budget at completion
    e. Estimate at completion

32. _____ is the realized cost for the work performed.
    a. Planned value
    b. Earned value
    c. Actual cost
    d. Budget at completion
    e. Estimate at completion

33. Planned value:
    a. Is the total cost of the project.
    b. Is the planned cost for each component of the project.
    c. Is the accumulated planned cost for a specified time in the project.
    d. Is the accumulated planned cost for planned components.
    e. Includes management reserve.

34. Earned value is:
    a. A calculated value that has meaning only for EVM calculations.
    b. The actual level of work completed for a specified time.
    c. Actual costs times percent complete.
    d. Planned costs times percent complete.
    e. Actual costs divided by planned costs.

35. Actual cost is:
    a. Costs actually consumed by the project.
    b. Financial allocations of overhead for the project.
    c. Actual invoices paid by the project.
    d. Charges approved by the project manager.
    e. Team-member costs based on timesheets.

36. EV − PV is the formula for:
    a. SV
    b. SPI
    c. CV
    d. CPI
    e. EAC

37. EV − AC is the formula for:
   a. SV
   b. SPI
   c. CV
   d. CPI
   e. EAC

38. EV / PV is the formula for:
   a. SV
   b. SPI
   c. CV
   d. CPI
   e. EAC

39. EV / AC is the formula for:
   a. SV
   b. SPI
   c. CV
   d. CPI
   e. EAC

40. Schedule variance measures:
   a. How late the project is.
   b. The amount the project is ahead of or behind schedule.
   c. The percentage complete of the project.
   d. The percentage the project is ahead of or behind schedule.
   e. The project manager's assessment of the schedule.

41. Cost variance measures:
   a. How over-budget the project is.
   b. The amount the project is over or under budget.
   c. The percentage of the budget spent.
   d. The percentage the project is over or under budget.
   e. The project manager's assessment of the budget.

6

Use these values for the next set of questions: PV = 1000, AC = 1250, EV = 980

42. What is SV?
    a. 20
    b. −20
    c. 0
    d. 270
    e. −270

43. What is CV?
    a. 20
    b. −20
    c. 0
    d. 270
    e. −270

44. What is CPI?
    a. .98
    b. 1.02
    c. 1
    d. .78
    e. 1.28

45. What is SPI?
    a. .98
    b. 1.02
    c. 1
    d. .78
    e. 1.28

46. Based on these calculations, what can be determined about the project's health?
    a. The project is experiencing cost issues but is fine on schedule.
    b. The project is experiencing scheduling issues but is fine on budget.
    c. The project is experiencing both cost and budgeting issues.
    d. The project is fine on both budget and schedule.
    e. Not enough information is available to make a statement.

47. A project has a CV of 125 and an SPI of .87. What can be determined about the project's health?
    a. The project is experiencing cost issues but is fine on schedule.
    b. The project is experiencing scheduling issues but is fine on budget.
    c. The project is experiencing both cost and budgeting issues.
    d. The project is fine on both budget and schedule.
    e. Not enough information is available to make a statement.

48. A project has an SV of 125 and a CPI of 1.32. What can be determined about the project's health?
    a. The project is experiencing cost issues but is fine on schedule.
    b. The project is experiencing scheduling issues but is fine on budget.
    c. The project is experiencing both cost and budgeting issues.
    d. The project is fine on both budget and schedule.
    e. Not enough information is available to make a statement.

49. EAC is:
    a. Early Action Correction.
    b. Estimate Actual Costs.
    c. Easy at Cost.
    d. Estimate at Completion.
    e. Early Actual Completion.

50. EAC is calculated as:
    a. AC + Bottom-Up ETC
    b. AC + (BAC: EV)
    c. BAC / CPI
    d. AC + [(BAC: EV) / (CPI ★ SPI)]
    e. All of the above.

51. Given a planned project total cost of 50,000 and a CPI of .98, what is a reasonable estimate for the current total project cost?
    a. 48,000
    b. 50,000
    c. 51,020
    d. 52,500
    e. Unable to determine

6

52. Given a planned project total cost of 50,000 and a CPI of 1.04, what is a reasonable estimate for the current total project cost?
    a. 48,000
    b. 50,000
    c. 51,020
    d. 52,500
    e. Unable to determine

53. The To Complete Performance Index (TCPI):
    a. Measures the cost performance required to achieve the stated goals.
    b. Is used to forecast when the project will complete.
    c. Measures future project performance.
    d. Predicts the CPI at completion.
    e. Isn't an EVM term.

54. The TCPI formula is:
    a. CPI / SPI
    b. (BAC: EV) / (BAC: AC)
    c. BAC ★ EAC / (BAC: EAC)
    d. EV ★ SPI
    e. SPI / (EAC: BAC)

55. Which are the three variance calculations in Earned Value Management?
    a. Schedule variance
    b. Earned variance
    c. Cost variance
    d. Calculated variance
    e. Completion variance

56. If a risk event passes and the contingency reserve has *not* been used, what should be done?
    a. The contingency reserve should be maintained for other identified risk events.
    b. The contingency reserve can be used to cover any other project budget overruns.
    c. The contingency reserve should be used to reward the team for ensuring that the risk didn't happen.
    d. The contingency reserve should be added to the management reserve.
    e. All of the above.
    f. None of the above.

7

PROJECT QUALITY MANAGEMENT

1. There are _____ processes in Project Quality Management.
   a. 3
   b. 4
   c. 5
   d. 6
   e. 7

2. Plan Quality Management is:
   a. Not required, as the project will follow corporate quality practices.
   b. Often combined with Project Test Management.
   c. Condensed to address Control Quality only.
   d. Required on all projects to ensure that quality matches the business expectations.
   e. Deferred to the delivery phase of the project because quality is better expressed at that time.

3. Project Quality Management should:
   a. Be unique to each project.
   b. Be consistent with corporate policies even if it doesn't meet business expectations.
   c. Meet business expectations, with deviations from corporate policy documented and approved.
   d. Meet corporate policy, with deviations from business expectations documented and approved.
   e. Balance corporate policy and business expectations.

7

4. Process improvement is:
   a. Integrated with the project quality statement.
   b. Considered as part of project closing.
   c. Documented for future projects but should not be considered during a project, as the Project Management Plan has been signed off.
   d. Submitted as modifications to the corporate quality statement.
   e. Deferred until the next project phase.

5. Which of the following statements is correct?
   a. Quality assurance is more important than quality control because it ensures that the project follows the proper processes.
   b. Quality control is more important than quality assurance because it ensures that the results satisfy the requirements.
   c. With adequate quality control in place, quality assurance is not required.
   d. Quality assurance and quality control are both required for a successful project.
   e. The project acceptor will identify whether quality assurance or quality control is more important at each milestone in the project.

6. For a project to be accepted:
   a. Quality must be high.
   b. Grade must be high.
   c. Both quality and grade must be high.
   d. Quality must be high and grade must be average.
   e. Quality and grade must satisfy quality expectations.

7. From a quality perspective, grade is defined as:
   a. Usability.
   b. Evaluation completed by an external inspector.
   c. A numerical score based on the project's time and cost performance.
   d. Only applicable for projects delivering physical results that can be evaluated using laboratory tests.
   e. An obsolete term being retired from the PMBOK because is was deemed to be too inflexible.

8. From a quality perspective, quality is referred to as:
   a. Number of defects.
   b. Amount of testing completed.
   c. Conformance to requirements.
   d. Usability of the solution.
   e. Time to resolve defects.

9. A project with low grade could be accepted.
   a. True
   b. False

10. A project with low quality could be accepted.
    a. True
    b. False

11. Modern Quality Management, consistent with ISO, consists of:
    a. Customer satisfaction.
    b. Prevention over inspection.
    c. Continuous improvement.
    d. Management responsibility.
    e. Cost of Quality.
    f. All of the above.

12. Quality Management should be focused on:
    a. Following defined policies.
    b. Planning and designing effective quality processes.
    c. Inspecting the product to catch (and fix) defects.
    d. Effective defect-remediation processes.
    e. Effective change control to change the scope to match quality delivered.

13. Plan-Do-Act-Check is an example of continuous improvement.
    a. True
    b. False

14. Which of the following is an acceptable continuous improvement process?
    a. Plan-Do-Act-Check
    b. Total Quality Management
    c. Six Sigma
    d. Lean Six Sigma
    e. All of the above

15. Cost of Quality is:
    a. The total cost for the project.
    b. The cost of the testing on the project.
    c. The sum of the cost of conformance work and nonconformance work.
    d. The cost of rework.
    e. The cost of defect resolution post project completion.

7

16. The Plan Quality Management process:
    a. Should always be completed on every project.
    b. Is only required for organizations without quality policies.
    c. Is typically required only on very large projects.
    d. Is required only on software projects due to the amount of testing required.
    e. Is typically applied only on mission-critical or high-priority projects.

17. Quality planning is best performed:
    a. As the first planning step, because it is needed before any other plans can be produced.
    b. As the last planning step, because it is based on all other project plans.
    c. Once the scope is defined, because it is focused on validating the scope.
    d. Once the scope, schedule, and budget are complete, because these three plans provide the parameters under which quality planning can be performed.
    e. In parallel with all planning activities.

18. Which of the following is *not* required when developing the Project Quality Plan?
    a. Scope Baseline
    b. Human resource plan
    c. Schedule Baseline
    d. Cost Baseline
    e. All are needed.

19. The Quality Management Plan should consider:
    a. Project scope.
    b. Project schedule.
    c. Project budget.
    d. Governmental regulations.
    e. Industry standards.
    f. All of the above.

20. The Quality Management Plan should consider which of the following?
    a. Organizational quality policies
    b. Historical results
    c. Prior project lessons learned
    d. All of the above
    e. None of the above—the Quality Management Plan should be unique for each project

21. Which of the following is *not* a recommended technique for the Plan Quality Management process?
    a. Cost-benefit analysis
    b. Cost of Quality
    c. Benchmarking
    d. Bottom-up estimating
    e. Statistical sampling

22. Which of the following is *not* a Cost of Quality cost category?
    a. Prevention costs
    b. Internal failure costs
    c. Contract negotiation costs
    d. External failure costs
    e. Appraisal costs

23. Which of the following can be considered a cost of conformance cost?
    a. External failure costs
    b. Prevention costs
    c. Labor costs
    d. Rework
    e. Warranty work

24. Which of the following can be considered to be a cost of nonconformance cost?
    a. Training
    b. Appraisal costs
    c. Deliverable preparation
    d. Rework
    e. Prevention costs

25. 7QC tools refers to:
    a. 7 Quick Configuration tools.
    b. 7 Quick Check tools.
    c. 7 Quality Control tools.
    d. 7 Quality Configuration tools.
    e. 7 Quantifiable Control tools.

7

26. Graphical tools, such as histograms, control charts, and scatter diagrams, are useful quality control tools because:
    a. They are easy to create in spreadsheet tools.
    b. They create pictures that can be shared with senior management.
    c. They combine the cost and schedule into a single view.
    d. They present the earned value data on a graph.
    e. They allow for viewing of large amounts of quality data in a meaningful way.

27. Checksheets are useful because:
    a. They define the required steps and allow for checking them off as completed.
    b. They are useful for gathering data in an effective way.
    c. They ensure that team members have a list of planned daily activities.
    d. They document the daily checks for the project.
    e. They identify which team members are working onsite on a daily basis.

28. Pareto diagrams are used to:
    a. Create bar charts.
    b. Categorize problems with the goal of identifying the main problem sources.
    c. Report analysis results of problem areas.
    d. Represent cause-and-effect relationships on a bar chart.
    e. Identify all problem causes.

29. A Pareto diagram is:
    a. A line graph with time on the Y-axis and number of defects on the X-axis.
    b. A horizontal bar chart with time on the Y-axis and number of defects on the X-axis.
    c. A vertical bar chart with number of defects on the Y-axis and defect categories on the X-axis.
    d. A line graph with number of defects on the Y-axis and duration of defects on the X-axis.
    e. A pie chart showing the defects by category.

30. A control chart is used to:
    a. Identify control points in the project, typically associated with project milestones.
    b. Designate upper and lower control limits on a specific project result/ measurement.
    c. Summarize team-member timesheets, showing hours spent versus hours planned.
    d. Show management control points for submitting results to senior management.
    e. Identify action items, risks, and issues.

31. Benchmarking allows for:
    a. Comparing actual practices to comparable projects.
    b. Generating ideas for improvements.
    c. Measuring performance.
    d. All of the above.
    e. None of the above.

32. A statistical method for identifying factors that influence a process or result is:
    a. Statistical sampling.
    b. Benchmarking.
    c. 7QC tools.
    d. Design of experiments.
    e. Brainstorming.

33. A quality checklist:
    a. Identifies the required steps to be performed for a specific quality process.
    b. Defines the end-of-day/end-of-week and end-of-month quality report that must be produced.
    c. Documents the variations between corporate and project quality policies.
    d. Is used as a precursor to project acceptance.
    e. Is used to validate data required to produce quality reports.

34. Quality assurance is focused on:
    a. Validating deliverables.
    b. Testing products.
    c. Reviewing deliverables for grammar and spelling.
    d. Validating that quality processes are used.
    e. Satisfying the audit department.

35. A key benefit of quality assurance is that:
    a. It guarantees deliverables will be accepted.
    b. It ensures that the deliverables meet standards.
    c. It identifies team members that are not following processes.
    d. It provides evidence for audits.
    e. It is used for governmental compliance reports.

36. Quality assurance is likely to detect:
    a. Deliverables that do not meet requirements.
    b. Deliverables that are missing sections.
    c. Deliverables that are late.
    d. Deliverables that are inaccurate.
    e. None of the above.

7

37. Quality assurance is often provided by:
    a. The project manager.
    b. The acceptor.
    c. The team.
    d. The quality assurance department.
    e. The audit department.

38. Quality assurance is reported on as which Cost of Quality category?
    a. Prevention
    b. Appraisal
    c. Rework
    d. Warranty
    e. Training

39. As quality assurance is being performed on a project, which of the following could occur?
    a. A deliverable is rejected because it does not meet standard.
    b. A standard is recommended for change because nonvaluable results are detected.
    c. Processes are changed to streamline and improve them.
    d. All of the above.
    e. None of the above.

40. The 7QC tools are used to complete quality assurance activities on a project.
    a. True
    b. False

41. An affinity diagram is used to:
    a. Help the team move from the storming to the norming stage.
    b. Help the team move from the forming to the storming stage.
    c. Generate ideas to link patterns to resolve problems.
    d. Create cluster diagrams.
    e. Combine requirements into deliverables.

42. A PDPC is a:
    a. Policy Document Project Control.
    b. Process Description Pending Correction.
    c. Process Decision Program Chart.
    d. Policy Decision Program Chart.
    e. Pending Decision Project Change.

43. An interrelationship digraph is typically used:
    a. Only for simple problems.
    b. For problems when no other problem-solving method has been successful.
    c. For moderately complex problems with up to 50 items.
    d. As an alternative to a fishbone diagram.
    e. When external factors must be accommodated.

44. Tree diagrams are useful diagrams:
    a. To define nested or parent/child relationships.
    b. To present the project schedule in a diagram.
    c. To solve complex problems.
    d. To present the project budget in a graph.
    e. To assign activities to team members.

45. Tree diagrams are useful for:
    a. Work Breakdown Structures.
    b. Risk Breakdown Structures.
    c. Organizational Breakdown Structures.
    d. Decision trees.
    e. All of the above.
    f. None of the above.

46. Prioritization matrices are useful because:
    a. Spreadsheets can easily create them.
    b. Important items can be identified and acted on.
    c. Prioritization criteria can be identified.
    d. Priorities can be weighted.
    e. Items can be sorted as required for specific management decisions.

47. Prioritization matrices capture:
    a. Priorities and issues.
    b. Issues, evaluation criteria, and weights.
    c. Issues and evaluation criteria.
    d. Priorities, evaluation criteria, and weights.
    e. Issues and assigned weights.

48. Matrix diagrams are used to:
    a. Perform complex mathematical models.
    b. Store large amounts of numbers.
    c. Match relationships between two variables.
    d. Show the strength of relationships between factors, causes, or objectives.
    e. Combine project data based on time and costs.

7

49. Quality audits are performed on projects to:
    a. Determine whether the project complies with corporate and project policies.
    b. Identify individuals not following policies.
    c. Punish projects not following policies.
    d. Punish individuals not following policies.
    e. Ensure project acceptance.

50. Quality audits are best conducted:
    a. As surprises by an non-project resource.
    b. Routinely to ensure project compliance with quality plans.
    c. By the project team, as they are familiar with the processes.
    d. By a non-project resource.
    e. By the audit department.

51. The objectives of a quality audit may include:
    a. Identifying practices being used.
    b. Identifying deviations from the quality plan.
    c. Identifying good practices to share outside the project.
    d. Identifying process-improvement opportunities.
    e. Improving corporate quality processes.
    f. All of the above.

52. Which of the following is a typical output from the Perform Quality Assurance process?
    a. Change requests
    b. Project Management Plan updates
    c. Project document updates
    d. Organizational Process Assets updates
    e. All of the above
    f. None of the above

53. The Perform Quality Control process:
    a. Tests the deliverables for completeness.
    b. Tests the deliverables for accuracy.
    c. Demonstrates that the deliverables meet the acceptance criteria.
    d. Produces performance metrics to satisfy compliance reports.
    e. Is only required if the project acceptor doesn't have time to test the results.

54. During quality control, inspections are used to:
    a. Review the processes to validate that they were followed.
    b. Inspect the team timesheets to ensure that time was coded to quality activities.
    c. Inspect the defect list to ensure timely resolution.
    d. Review the action list to ensure that all actions associated with a deliverable are closed.
    e. Examine the work products to ensure that they conform to expectations.

55. Quality control would use:
    a. Peer review.
    b. Inspections.
    c. Walkthroughs.
    d. Testing.
    e. All of the above.
    f. None of the above.

56. Which of the following is *not* a result of quality control?
    a. Defect reports
    b. Verified deliverables
    c. Review of rework
    d. Acceptance documents
    e. Change request

57. The project team decides to implement some new functionality because they believe that it will greatly increase the system's usability. This in an example of:
    a. Ensuring customer satisfaction.
    b. Gold plating.
    c. Using contingency for the benefit of the project.
    d. Team building.
    e. Discretionary change control.

7

8

PROJECT HUMAN RESOURCE MANAGEMENT

1. Project Human Resource Management is focused on:
   a. The full-time team members who will be working on the project for its entire duration.
   b. The part-time team members, to ensure that they are utilized most effectively.
   c. All project team members, full-time and part-time, temporary or permanent.
   d. The project management team.
   e. The relationships between the team and the business.

2. The project team is typically:
   a. Assigned at the beginning of the project and remains intact for the life of the project.
   b. Assigned at the beginning of each phase and remains intact for the duration of the phase.
   c. Focused on full-time team members, because they have the largest contribution to the project.
   d. Dynamic and can change as project needs and organizational resource requirements evolve.
   e. Always assigned 100 percent by the project manager.

3. When resources are replaced on a project, the project manager should:
   a. Ensure "as good or better" resources to ensure no project impact.
   b. Refuse to allow resources to be replaced.
   c. Evaluate each resource change and process a change request to document the project impacts.
   d. Accept that resources will be replaced and use project contingency to mitigate impacts.
   e. Accept new resources and use them as the excuse for any delivery issues.

4. Which of the following activities is *not* part of Plan Human Resource Management?
   a. Identify and document project roles
   b. Plan team kickoff party
   c. Identify skills required
   d. Create staffing management plan
   e. Document reporting relationships

5. The staffing plan identifies:
   a. Named individuals, starting dates, and project rates.
   b. Skills required, starting dates, ending dates, and allocation percentage.
   c. Named individuals, starting dates, and allocation percentage.
   d. Skills required and allocation percentage.
   e. Assignment of team to project activities.

6. The human resource plan should:
   a. Define the reporting relationship for the project.
   b. Avoid defining the reporting relationship because this cannot be determined until the skills of the team are known.
   c. Avoid defining the reporting relationship because this cannot be determined until the personalities of the team are known.
   d. Define the top-level reporting relationship for the project.
   e. Focus on defining the skills needed; once the right resources are on the project, the reporting relationships will naturally evolve.

7. Which of the following should *not* be included in the human resource plan?
   a. Reward and recognition program
   b. Career plans
   c. Team-building strategies
   d. Safety issues
   e. Training needs

8. The Human Resources Management Plan should:
   a. Be a standalone document so it can be sent to the human resources department.
   b. Always be integrated into the Project Management Plan, as it is a minor plan and should never receive the attention a standalone document would receive.
   c. Be produced as a standalone document or integrated with the Project Management Plan, depending on specific project needs.
   d. Only be required if the project will be staffed with external resources.
   e. Rarely be produced because staffing a project is a dynamic negotiation with the human resources department.

9. Which of the following project documents is *not* required to develop the Human Resources Management Plan?
   a. Project Management Plan
   b. Project schedule
   c. WBS
   d. Project budget
   e. Risk plan

10. The Project Management Plan is a key input to the Human Resources Management Plan because:
    a. It defines the scope of the project.
    b. It defines the acceptance criteria the team must deliver against.
    c. It defines the project lifecycle and the processes that will be used on the project.
    d. It defines how the project will be staffed.
    e. None of the above.

11. The WBS is needed to develop the human resource plan because:
    a. It identifies the work to be done.
    b. It defines the schedule for the project.
    c. It allows for resources to be assigned to activities.
    d. It determines the human resource needs for the project.
    e. It allows the project team to be decomposed based on the deliverable breakdown.

12. Project organization charts and position descriptions are important to:
    a. Define roles and responsibilities.
    b. Define reporting relationships.
    c. Define escalation points.
    d. Assign work packages to an unambiguous owner.
    e. All of the above.
    f. Both A and C.
    g. All except D.
    h. All except A.

13. Project organization charts and position descriptions typically are:
    a. Presented as tree-based organization charts.
    b. Presented as written role descriptions.
    c. Presented as responsibility matrices.
    d. Presented as a combination of tree-based charts and written role descriptions/responsibility matrices.
    e. Defined at the project management team level only to provide flexibility to activity assignments.

8

14. The Organizational Breakdown Structure (OBS):
    a. Is another name for the WBS.
    b. Is directly connected to the WBS, assigning resources to each element of the WBS.
    c. Defines how the organization is structured.
    d. Maps the team members back to the organization.
    e. Has no value in a project environment.

15. The Resource Breakdown Structure (RBS) is:
    a. Another name for the WBS.
    b. Directly connected to the WBS, assigning resources to each element of the WBS.
    c. A definition of the organizational structure of the project.
    d. Used to map the team members back to the organization.
    e. Useful only when external resources are used on a project.

16. A RACI chart can be developed:
    a. At the activity level only.
    b. At the deliverable level only.
    c. At the major activity level only.
    d. At any level of the WBS.
    e. None of the above—the RACI is too detailed for the WBS.

17. In a RACI chart, it is normal to:
    a. Have a single resource in the Responsible column.
    b. Not have anyone assigned the Responsible role.
    c. Have multiple resources responsible.
    d. Have the project manager responsible for all lines.
    e. Have the acceptor responsible for all lines.

18. In a RACI chart, it is normal to:
    a. Have multiple resources assigned in the Consulted column.
    b. Have multiple resources assigned in the Informed column.
    c. Have a single resource assigned in the Accountable column.
    d. All of the above.
    e. All except A.
    f. All except B.
    g. All except C.

19. The staffing plan should:
    a. Identify when resources are required to join the project.
    b. Identify when resources will be released from the project.
    c. Identify the number of resources required.
    d. Show staff rotation plans.
    e. All of the above.
    f. All except C.
    g. All except D.

20. What should be done when the human resources department cannot provide the resources with the required skills and/or in the required timeframe?
    a. Halt the project until appropriate resources can be assigned to it.
    b. Understand the alternative staffing offered and replan the project accordingly.
    c. Escalate the senior management to ensure that human resources comply with the project's requirements.
    d. Review options with human resources and develop alternate staffing and delivery plans, documenting any changes in a Project Change Request.
    e. Accept the resources and attempt to deliver the project based on the original plan.

21. The Acquire Project Team process typically:
    a. Involves negotiation to ensure the best possible team.
    b. Should never deviate from the human resource plan.
    c. Is delegated to the human resources department.
    d. Rarely follows the human resource plan and often results in many unfilled team positions.
    e. Is only required when external subcontractors will be on the team.

22. Pre-assignment is a staffing technique typically applied when:
    a. The project manager has staffing preferences based on prior project experiences.
    b. Human resources have staff with high availability who must be assigned to projects ASAP.
    c. Team members request assignment to a specific project.
    d. Senior management define who will work on a project.
    e. Competitive proposals require identification of key staff as part of the proposal.

23. Which of the following is a potential source for obtaining project staff?
    a. Functional managers
    b. Other project managers
    c. External organizations
    d. All of the above
    e. None of the above

24. Virtual teams:
    a. Should never be considered for project work because the project team needs to co-locate to facilitate ease of communication.
    b. Provide an ideal way to acquire the needed project staff because they leverage the entire organization.
    c. Should be considered only when all other resource options are exhausted.
    d. Can be used, but only when all project estimates are doubled.
    e. Provide the best option for project resourcing.

25. Which of the following is *not* an appropriate selection criterion for acquiring the project team?
    a. Availability
    b. Experience
    c. Prior experience with the individual
    d. Knowledge
    e. Attitude

26. A multi-criteria decision matrix is a valid tool for selecting the project team.
    a. Definitely not—it reduces the human factors to a series of mathematical models.
    b. Absolutely—it ensures optimal candidates based on the decision criteria that are selected.
    c. It should be used only when personal interviews cannot be conducted.
    d. It should be used only to select virtual team members.
    e. It should be one of the tools used for selecting the project team.

27. The Develop Project Team process is:
    a. Critical to ensure that each team member is performing to his or her full potential.
    b. Required only if the Acquire Team process has to accept less than optimal resources.
    c. Required only if the human resource plan identified project-specific training requirements.
    d. Used when team members join an in-flight project.
    e. The responsibility of the human resources department.

28. Project managers are:
    a. Not involved in ensuring effective team performance—the human resources department looks after this.
    b. Partners with human resources to ensure effective team performance.
    c. Interested in, but not involved with, effective team performance, because the team must do this on their own.
    d. Directly responsible for ensuring effective team performance.
    e. None of the above—effective team performance occurs naturally and cannot be influenced.

29. Projects delivered in a multicultural environment should:
    a. Ensure that each culture is managed individually based on cultural norms.
    b. Integrate all cultures into a common team culture that recognizes the cultural differences.
    c. Integrate all cultures into a common team culture that focuses on the project's success.
    d. Operate based on the culture of the largest team.
    e. Operate based on the culture of the project manager.

30. Which of the following is *not* a Develop Project Team technique?
    a. Interpersonal skills
    b. Training
    c. Team building
    d. Resource Breakdown Structure
    e. Recognition and rewards

31. Interpersonal skills are vital project management skills because they:
    a. Equip the project manager to deal with junior resources.
    b. Round out the project manager's skills necessary for promotion to the next management level.
    c. Ensure that the project manager has balanced hard and soft skills.
    d. Are vital skills for developing the project team.
    e. Are highly overrated. Project managers should focus on time, budget, and quality management.

32. Project team training should be:
    a. Delivered as documented in the human resource plan.
    b. Used only when necessary because training time reduces time available for project delivery.
    c. Done outside the project time because it should be considered a corporate employee development activity.
    d. Delivered as documented in the human resource plan and augmented for any skills shortfalls identified during the Acquire Project Team process or during project delivery.
    e. Used as a staff motivation technique.

33. Which of the following is *not* one of the Tuckman Team building stages?
    a. Performing
    b. Admiring
    c. Storming
    d. Norming
    e. Adjourning

8

34. If the majority of team members have worked together in the past, it's acceptable to assume that the early stages of the Tuckman model can be ignored and that the performing stage will be in place.
    a. True
    b. False

35. When moving from phase to phase, with minor 10 to 15 percent changes in the team, which stage of the Tuckman model should be applied?
    a. Forming
    b. Storming
    c. Norming
    d. Performing
    e. Adjourning

36. When ending a phase of a project with very few team members leaving the project, which stage of the Tuckman model should be applied?
    a. Forming
    b. Storming
    c. Norming
    d. Performing
    e. Adjourning

37. Ground rules are effective:
    a. For teams with new hires or external consultants, because they need to understand how the organization works.
    b. For teams with junior team members, because they may never have been on a project before.
    c. For all projects, because it's important for all team members to operate from the same basic set of operating principles.
    d. Only for virtual teams.
    e. Only for teams where business resources are working with project resources.

38. Who is responsible for developing project ground rules?
    a. Project management team
    b. Human resources
    c. Communications
    d. The team
    e. No one—ground rules should be based on corporate guidelines

39. Who is responsible for enforcing project ground rules?
    a. Project management team
    b. Human resources
    c. Communications
    d. The team
    e. No one—ground rules should be based on corporate guidelines

40. Project-based rewards and recognition:
    a. Should be used as motivational techniques at the project, team, and individual levels.
    b. Should be used as motivational techniques at the project and team levels.
    c. Should be used as motivational techniques at the project and individual levels.
    d. Should be used as motivational techniques at the team and individual levels.
    e. Should be used as motivational techniques at the individual level only.
    f. Should not be used as project technique because this should be done corporately, as part of existing reward and recognition programs.

41. The most effective reward and recognition systems are:
    a. Monetary.
    b. Non-monetary, such as free lunches and other team perks.
    c. Career-based, such as training and learning opportunities.
    d. Endorsements for the annual employee review process.
    e. All of the above.

42. Input into a team member's annual assessment should be:
    a. Used as a threat to ensure high performance levels.
    b. Used as a reward to ensure high performance levels.
    c. Built into the project and defined in advance in the Human Resources Management Plan.
    d. Isolated from the project because the project manager should be focused exclusively on delivering the project.
    e. Completed only at project completion.

43. Team member assessments should be:
    a. Used to identity strengths that can be leveraged on the project and weaknesses that can be improved with appropriate project support.
    b. Used to focus on weaknesses because they must be documented in case human resources need to be engaged.
    c. Focused on strengths to motivate the individual.
    d. Left until the project completes, because they can distract the team.
    e. Discussed informally with the team members immediately.

44. The Manage Project Team process is focused on:
    a. Ensuring that timesheets are submitted on time.
    b. Motivating the team to complete work on time.
    c. Finding ways to accelerate project delivery.
    d. Tracking team performance and managing team-member issues.
    e. Interfacing with human resources to ensure that the team is happy.

45. Managing the project team is primarily:
    a. The responsibility of the human resources department.
    b. Soft skills, such as communications, conflict management, and leadership.
    c. Hard skills, such as time tracking and task assignment.
    d. Best left to the team to self-manage.
    e. Typically not part of the project manager's responsibility.

46. When conflicts are detected in the team, the project manager is best advised to:
    a. Replace one of the team members because conflicts can quickly destroy project morale.
    b. Carefully monitor the conflict and intervene as soon as it appears to be becoming unresolvable.
    c. Encourage the conflict because conflict resolution often results in innovative project approaches.
    d. Intervene immediately and arbitrate a solution to the conflict.
    e. Instruct the team members that the conflict must be resolved within the next business day.

47. Managing the project team is best accomplished by:
    a. Carefully tracking project status to allow for early recognition of deviations from the plan.
    b. One-on-one meetings with all team members.
    c. Regular project status meetings.
    d. Observation and communications.
    e. Using project management software.

48. Team-member performance appraisals should be:
    a. Integrated into the overall team management approach.
    b. Completed as required by corporate policies.
    c. Separated from project management to avoid potential conflicts between project and career goals.
    d. Not done until the project is complete to avoid any demotivation that may result from a poor performance review.
    e. Done as soon as an appraisal-worthy activity is noticed, positive or negative.

49. Project conflict is:
    a. Best avoided.
    b. Strongly encouraged.
    c. Inevitable.
    d. Beneficial in limited amounts.
    e. Best eliminated as soon as detected.

50. Project conflict can be caused by:
    a. Lack of resources.
    b. Scheduling priorities.
    c. Personality types.
    d. Work styles.
    e. All of the above.

51. Project conflicts can be minimized by:
    a. Ground rules.
    b. Group norms.
    c. Good project management.
    d. A reasonable schedule and budget.
    e. All of the above.

52. Conflict can be beneficial to a project.
    a. True
    b. False

53. Which of the following defined conflict-resolution approaches will typically produce a lasting result?
    a. Withdrawal
    b. Smoothing
    c. Compromise
    d. Force
    e. Collaborate

54. Which conflict-resolution approach is being used when the member says, "Go ahead; I don't have time to discuss right now"?
    a. Withdrawal
    b. Physical
    c. Smoothing
    d. Compromise
    e. Collaborate

55. A new project acceptor is assigned to a project and requests to see what team members are responsible for. What is the best tool to show him or her?
    a. Project schedule
    b. Project organization chart
    c. Dependency diagram
    d. RACI chart
    e. Resource histogram

56. A project manager responsible for managing a weak matrix team needs to motivate the team. What power base would be most effective?
    a. Reward
    b. Penalty
    c. Expert
    d. Formal
    e. Referent

57. Which of the following is *not* a defined conflict-resolution approach?
    a. Withdrawal
    b. Physical
    c. Smoothing
    d. Compromise
    e. Collaborate

58. Which of the following is the preferred conflict-resolution approach?
    a. Withdrawal
    b. Smoothing
    c. Compromise
    d. Force
    e. Collaborate
    f. All of the above
    g. None of the above

59. The project management team should intervene in a conflict:
    a. Immediately.
    b. Only when requested.
    c. When the conflict worsens.
    d. When the level of conflict escalates.
    e. When a resolution appears to be impossible.

60. Which of the following is *not* a project management interpersonal skill?
    a. Leadership.
    b. Time tracking.
    c. Influencing.
    d. Decision making.
    e. Conflict management.

61. Which of the following tools can be used to determine resource load levels?
    a. Project schedule
    b. Resource assignment matrix
    c. Resource histogram
    d. Resource Breakdown Structure
    e. RACI matrix

62. The resource management plan should identify release dates as well as starting dates because (select two answers):
    a. Human resources needs to know when resources will be available for other assignments.
    b. Team members need to understand how long they will be assigned to a project.
    c. The project schedule is based on the release dates.
    d. Costs can be reduced by removing team members from the project as quickly as possible.
    e. Conflicts can be minimized because team members can "wait it out" until they are off the project.

63. An effective recognition and reward system would *not* contain which of the following?
    a. Measurable criteria
    b. Achievable results
    c. Stretch goals
    d. External factors
    e. Meaningful rewards

64. Team building is:
    a. An upfront activity performed during project kickoff.
    b. Always done offsite to remove project distractions.
    c. Moderated by trained consultants to ensure optimal results.
    d. Any activity, formal or informal, that can help the team work better together.
    e. Optional if most of the team already knows each other.

8

65. Which of the following is *not* a form of power that a project manager typically has?
    a. Reward
    b. Referent
    c. Expert
    d. Formal
    e. Penalty

66. When team-management issues impact the overall project status and team-member changes must be made, the project manager should:
    a. Find a way to replace a team member without having to notify the stakeholders.
    b. Absorb any cost or schedule impacts from the project contingency.
    c. Create a change request documenting the change and the impacts.
    d. Stick it out, as a new team member will have ramp-up impacts and would worsen the situation.
    e. Demand extra resources at no cost to the project to bring the project back on track.

9

PROJECT COMMUNICATIONS MANAGEMENT

1. Project Communications Management is focused on:
   a. Improving communications styles.
   b. Effective and timely distribution of project information.
   c. Obtaining project status from the team members.
   d. Improving the relationship between the project manager and the project acceptor.
   e. Producing more meaningful project status reports.

2. The Plan Communications Management process is:
   a. A critical process to ensure that an effective communications process is defined for the project.
   b. Required on projects when there are multiple members on the project management team, to ensure that each project management team member clearly understands the communications protocols.
   c. Only required on virtual projects because it is critical that communications flow effectively to all virtual team members.
   d. Only required when the project manager and project acceptor are in different locations.
   e. Typically not needed because communications is a natural process for project managers.

3. The Plan Communications Management process is focused on:
   a. Outbound communications to project stakeholders.
   b. Outbound communications to senior management.
   c. Internal communications within the project team.
   d. Communications between the project team and the business area.
   e. All communications needed to collect and distribute appropriate project information.

4. Which of the following is a required input to communications planning?
   a. Project budget
   b. Project schedule
   c. Stakeholder register
   d. Risk Register
   e. All of the above
   f. None of the above

5. What is the formula for determining the number of communications channels?
   a. $n(n - 1) / n$
   b. $(n + 1)(n - 1) / n$
   c. $n(n - 1) / 2$
   d. $n^2 / 2$
   e. $N / 2$

6. On a project with 21 team members, the maximum number of communications channels is 210. Recognizing that this is an unmanageable number, how can the number of channels be reduced?
   a. Forbid the team members to communicate with more than five individuals.
   b. Create teams with specific focuses that can operate independently.
   c. Publish a project newsletter that communicates all key information.
   d. Create a project portal with a chat site where questions can be posed (and answered).
   e. Have all communications go through the project management team.

7. Which of the following would *not* be a factor in the choice of a project's communication approach?
   a. Urgency of communications
   b. Availability of technology
   c. Sensitivity of information
   d. Language to be used
   e. Usability of technology

8. A message that is *not* understood because it was *not* properly prepared suffers from an issue in what step in the communications model?
   a. Encode
   b. Transmit
   c. Decode
   d. Acknowledge
   e. Feedback

9. What step in the communications model is required for the sender of a message to ensure that the message was understood?
   a. Encode
   b. Transmit
   c. Decode
   d. Acknowledge
   e. Feedback

10. A message that is *not* understood because there was too much noise in the room suffers from an issue in what step in the communications model?
    a. Encode
    b. Transmit
    c. Decode
    d. Acknowledge
    e. Feedback

11. Failure of a stakeholder to confirm receipt of a weekly status report shows a failure in what step in the communications model?
    a. Encode
    b. Transmit
    c. Decode
    d. Acknowledge
    e. Feedback

12. As part of the communications model, the sender is responsible for (select two):
    a. Encode.
    b. Transmit.
    c. Decode.
    d. Acknowledge.
    e. Feedback.

13. A deliverable that contains a lot of technical buzzwords and industry-specific terms could result in a reader from another department experiencing issues with what step in the communications model?
    a. Encode
    b. Transmit
    c. Decode
    d. Acknowledge
    e. Feedback

9

14. Which of the following is *not* a communications distribution tool?
    a. Written reports
    b. Emails
    c. Databases of project data
    d. Project portals
    e. Presentations

15. A project status report is an example of what type of communication?
    a. Informal/verbal communication
    b. Informal/written communication
    c. Formal/verbal communication
    d. Formal/written communication
    e. Presentation

16. What is the appropriate communications method to be used when the project manager needs to review a number of options before a change request is submitted?
    a. Interactive communication
    b. Push communication
    c. Pull communication
    d. All of the above
    e. None of the above

17. What is the appropriate communications method to be used when the project manager needs to distribute the monthly status report to the identified stakeholders?
    a. Interactive communication
    b. Push communication
    c. Pull communication
    d. All of the above
    e. None of the above

18. What is the appropriate communications method to be used when the project manager needs to provide access to the project status archives to allow any stakeholders to review old status reports as needed?
    a. Interactive communication
    b. Push communication
    c. Pull communication
    d. All of the above
    e. None of the above

19. What is the appropriate communications method to be used when the project manager needs to obtain project updates from the team?
    a. Interactive communication
    b. Push communication
    c. Pull communication
    d. All of the above
    e. None of the above

20. Meetings:
    a. Are the single largest waste of time on projects.
    b. Should be used only when no other communication methods can be used.
    c. Should be carefully managed to ensure effective use of participants' time.
    d. Should always be held in the morning, so afternoons can be used to complete project work.
    e. Should never take more than one hour.

21. During the startup of a meeting, an uninvited individual shows up and asks to attend. What is the appropriate response?
    a. Invite the person in because he or she might add value to the meeting.
    b. Forbid the person to attend as he or she wasn't invited.
    c. Validate why the person wishes to attend and determine whether he or she would add value to the meeting.
    d. Call the project sponsor to validate whether the person should be allowed to attend.
    e. Adjourn the meeting to assess who should be invited.

22. During a meeting, an attendee introduces a new item that was *not* on the agenda. What is the appropriate response?
    a. Apologize for missing the item and begin to discuss it.
    b. Confirm whether there is time to discuss the additional item, and include it only if the meeting still can be completed on time.
    c. Confirm with the other attendees whether they would like to add the additional item.
    d. Inform the person that this item was not on the agenda and refuse to discuss it.
    e. Schedule another meeting to discuss the additional item.

9

23. During a meeting, it becomes apparent that one or more key participants are *not* prepared for the meeting. What is the appropriate response?
    a. Stop the meeting for an appropriate time to allow the participants to ready the required material and prepare to continue.
    b. Stop the meeting and reschedule for another time.
    c. Continue with the meeting and encourage the unprepared participants to skim the material and get up to speed as quickly as possible.
    d. Request that the unprepared participants leave the meeting.
    e. Request an explanation as to why they are not prepared for the meeting.

24. Which of the following is *not* contained in a Communications Management Plan?
    a. Stakeholder communication requirements
    b. Frequency of communication
    c. User instructions from the project portal
    d. Person responsible for each communications item
    e. Communications methods

25. Which of the following is *not* a part of the Manage Communications process?
    a. Collecting information
    b. Analyzing information
    c. Distributing information
    d. Storing information
    e. Disposing of information

26. The Manage Communication process:
    a. Distributes project information to stakeholders.
    b. Ensures that the information being communicated is received and understood.
    c. Provides clarification and updates.
    d. All of the above.
    e. All except A.
    f. All except B.
    g. All except C.

27. Which of the following is the most effective method for project communications?
    a. Formal written documents
    b. Emails
    c. Project portals
    d. Meetings
    e. Presentations
    f. All of the above

28. Understanding the sender-receiver model is important for effective project communications because it:
    a. Defines the information requirements of the receiver.
    b. Documents the reading and comprehension level of the receiver.
    c. Incorporates feedback loops to improve comprehension and remove barriers to communication.
    d. Defines the frequency of communication.
    e. Defines how the communications should take place.

29. An effective strategy for managing project communications would include:
    a. Writing guides.
    b. Presentation styles.
    c. Facilitation techniques.
    d. Meeting guidelines.
    e. All of the above.
    f. None of the above.

30. Which of the following is an input to the Manage Communications process?
    a. Writing guides
    b. Work performance reports
    c. Portal policies
    d. Stakeholder analysis
    e. Budget performance

31. Performance reporting involves:
    a. Collecting and distributing performance information.
    b. Reporting of baseline versus actual results.
    c. Reporting on current forecasts.
    d. All of the above.
    e. None of the above.

32. The Control Communications process is focused on:
    a. Tracking status report submission from team members.
    b. Tracking timesheet compliance.
    c. Ensuring stakeholder information requirements are met.
    d. Conducting internal project status meetings.
    e. Conducting external project status meetings.

9

33. A Communications Management Plan should contain all the following except:
    a. A glossary of common terminology.
    b. The person responsible for creating reports.
    c. The person responsible for approving sensitive information.
    d. A communications timeline.
    e. The project budget.

34. Project managers spend the majority of their time doing _____ on a project.
    a. Schedule updates
    b. Communication
    c. Approval of project expenses
    d. Management of the work authorization system
    e. Work with the project scheduling software

35. The Issue Log is an effective tool for managing project stakeholders because:
    a. It ensures the stakeholders are notified when items are assigned to them.
    b. It tracks all open items of importance to the stakeholders and ensures that they are managed and closed.
    c. It allows the project manager to report progress on closing issues.
    d. It transfers responsibilities for issues from the project team to the project sponsor.
    e. It records items the project will not accomplish so that they can be added to the future project backlog report.

36. An Issue Log tracks:
    a. Issue name, description, status, and resolution actions.
    b. Issue name, responsible individual, cost, and impact.
    c. Issue name, date required, project impacts, and costs.
    d. Issue name, cost impact, and ramifications of not proceeding.
    e. Issue name, description, person causing the issue, and remediation required.

PROJECT RISK MANAGEMENT

1. There are _____ processes in Project Risk Management.
   a. 3
   b. 4
   c. 5
   d. 6
   e. 7

2. Project Risk Management is focused on:
   a. Overall project risk events.
   b. Specific activity risk events.
   c. Overall project opportunities.
   d. Specific activity opportunities.
   e. All of the above.
   f. None of the above.

3. A risk is the same as an opportunity from a risk management viewpoint.
   a. True
   b. False

4. Risk (or opportunities) can impact:
   a. Scope.
   b. Budget.
   c. Schedule.
   d. Quality.
   e. All of the above.
   f. None of the above.

5. Unknown risks that cannot be managed proactively should:
   a. Be ignored, since there are no direct actions that can be taken to minimize them.
   b. Be assigned a contingency reserve.
   c. Be documented to management so that the project is absolved of responsibility.
   d. Be assigned a management reserve.
   e. Be added as a WBS element so that resources can be assigned to it.

6. The Risk Management Plan is vital because:
   a. It identifies the project risks.
   b. It identifies the contingency required to deal with risks.
   c. It ensures that the risk approaches are appropriate for the risks and the project's appetite for risks.
   d. It defines how to deal with risks when they happen.
   e. It documents how to ensure that risks do not happen on a project.

7. Which of the following is considered when developing the risk impact matrix?
   a. Risk name
   b. Risk impact
   c. Risk date
   d. Risk resolution
   e. Risk trigger

8. The risk impact matrix is used to:
   a. Determine the contingency amounts for each risk.
   b. Plot risk impact and risk probability.
   c. Determine when risks are likely to occur.
   d. Validate requirements for contingency reserves versus management reserves.
   e. Record risk mitigation plans.

9. The project's risk tolerance is used to:
   a. Define when the project manager needs to use management reserves.
   b. Define when the project manager needs to use contingency reserves.
   c. Define when the project manager needs to ask for assistance.
   d. Define when the project must be stopped due to risk events.
   e. Define the willingness of the project team to accept or deal with risk.

10. A project that is willing to accept that some risks are inevitable, but that on average no more than 50 percent of the identified risks are likely to occur, would be classified as:
    a. Risk unconcerned.
    b. Risk seeking.
    c. Risk neutral.
    d. Risk concerned.
    e. Risk averse.

11. A project that is willing to accept that some risks are inevitable, and that by allowing risks to happen new opportunities for completing the project will be identified, would be classified as:
    a. Risk unconcerned.
    b. Risk seeking.
    c. Risk neutral.
    d. Risk concerned.
    e. Risk averse.

12. A project that is unwilling to accept that any impacts from risks are inevitable would be classified as:
    a. Risk unconcerned.
    b. Risk seeking.
    c. Risk neutral.
    d. Risk concerned.
    e. Risk averse.

13. Based on the following diagram, what would this project's risk profile be?

    a. Risk unconcerned
    b. Risk seeking
    c. Risk neutral
    d. Risk concerned
    e. Risk averse

10

14. Based on the following diagram, what would this project's risk profile be?

   a. Risk unconcerned
   b. Risk seeking
   c. Risk neutral
   d. Risk concerned
   e. Risk averse

15. Based on the following diagram, in which quadrant would a low probability/high impact risk be placed?

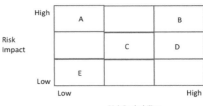

   a. A
   b. B
   c. C
   d. D
   e. E

16. Based on the following diagram, in which quadrant would a high probability/ medium impact risk be placed?

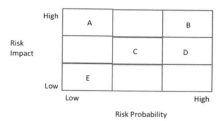

a. A
b. B
c. C
d. D
e. E

17. Based on the following diagram, in which quadrant would a low probability/low impact risk be placed?

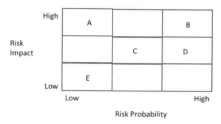

a. A
b. B
c. C
d. D
e. E

18. Who should be involved in project risk identification?
   a. Project management team only
   b. Project acceptor/sponsor
   c. Project management team and project acceptor/sponsor
   d. Project team
   e. All project stakeholders

10

19. Identification of risks is:
    a. A one-time activity completed as part of project planning.
    b. An activity completed at the beginning of each phase.
    c. A weekly activity discussed in the weekly status meeting.
    d. A monthly activity discussed in the monthly executive meeting.
    e. A continuous activity.

20. Which of the following would *not* be considered an input to risk identification?
    a. Activity duration estimates
    b. Scope Baseline
    c. Stakeholder register
    d. Change Management process
    e. Procurement documents

21. Which of the following would *not* be considered to be a technique for risk identification?
    a. Brainstorming
    b. Delphi technique
    c. Root cause analysis
    d. Schedule development
    e. Interviewing

22. Checklists can be effective for identification of risks.
    a. True
    b. False

23. It is *not* necessary to include assumptions in risk identification, as the assumptions clearly state the assumption and the expected result.
    a. True
    b. False

24. Which of the following is an appropriate technique for risk identification?
    a. Cause and effect diagrams
    b. System or process flowcharts
    c. Influence diagrams
    d. Strengths/weaknesses/opportunity/threat analysis
    e. All of the above
    f. None of the above

25. The Risk Register is used to:
    a. Record all risks.
    b. Record only critical risks.
    c. Record risks that have occurred.
    d. Record risks that have contingency assigned to them.
    e. Record risks that have been presented to senior management.

26. Qualitative Risk Analysis is focused on:
    a. Developing complex simulations to better understand risk.
    b. Tracking the results of risks to improve organizational risk processes.
    c. Reviewing risks during project delivery to determine whether they have happened.
    d. Prioritizing risks through Qualitative Risk Analysis.
    e. Controlling the project to minimize the occurrence of risks.

27. Qualitative Risk Analysis considers:
    a. The probability of a risk occurring.
    b. The impact of the risk if it happens.
    c. The timing of when the risk is likely to happen.
    d. The project's risk tolerance.
    e. All of the above.
    f. All except A.
    g. All except B.
    h. All except C.
    i. All except D.

28. Once Qualitative Risk Analysis is complete, the next step is to (select two answers):
    a. Develop risk contingency.
    b. Perform Quantitative Risk Analysis.
    c. Update the Risk Register.
    d. Plan risk responses.
    e. Implement risk mitigation plans.

29. Risk probability is determined by:
    a. Reviewing the characteristics of the risk against an established risk probability assessment guide.
    b. Comparing the characteristics of the risk against other similar risks.
    c. Interviewing subject-matter experts.
    d. Risk probability assessment meetings.
    e. All of the above.
    f. None of the above.

10

30. Risk impact is determined by:
    a. Reviewing the characteristics of the risk against an established risk impact assessment guide.
    b. Comparing the characteristics of the risk against other similar risks.
    c. Interviewing subject–matter experts.
    d. Risk impact assessment meetings.
    e. All of the above.
    f. None of the above.

31. Risk probability and impact are combined to determine the risk priority by:
    a. Multiplying the probability by the impact.
    b. Dividing the probability by the impact.
    c. Dividing the impact by the probability.
    d. Dividing each of the impact and the probability by the risk tolerance and summing the results.
    e. Plotting each on an impact matrix.

32. Risk data–quality assessment is used to:
    a. Determine the risk priority.
    b. Determine the risk impact.
    c. Determine both the risk priority and the risk impact.
    d. Assess the quality of the data used to determine the risk priority and impact.
    e. Scale the risk priority.

33. The timeframe when a risk is predicted to occur:
    a. Is used to increase the risk priority.
    b. Is used to factor into the probability determination.
    c. Is used to factor into the probability impact based on the future cost of money.
    d. Is used to determine when the project will monitor for the risk occurring.
    e. Has no value as risks are unpredictable.

34. During Qualitative Risk Analysis, the Risk Register:
    a. Is used to identify the risks that need to be analyzed.
    b. Is used to capture the results of the analysis.
    c. Is used to identify the risks that need to be analyzed and then capture the results of the analysis.
    d. Is sorted by priority to show the results of the analysis.
    e. Is sorted by impact and then probability to show the results of the analysis.

35. Quantitative Risk Analysis is focused on:
    a. Developing complex simulations to better understand risk.
    b. Tracking the results of risks to improve organizational risk processes.
    c. Reviewing risks during project delivery to determine whether they have occurred.
    d. Prioritizing risks through qualitative analysis.
    e. Controlling the project to minimize the occurrence of risks.

36. Quantitative Risk Analysis is:
    a. A one-time event completed during planning.
    b. An ongoing process repeated for each new risk identified.
    c. Always performed at the same time as Qualitative Risk Analysis.
    d. Performed after Qualitative Risk Analysis has identified a risk as having a high potential for impacting the project.
    e. Performed weekly in the project team meetings.

37. Quantitative Risk Analysis is:
    a. Only performed on risks where the data supports numerical analysis.
    b. Performed after Qualitative Risk Analysis.
    c. Performed after Qualitative Risk Analysis but only on the most critical risks.
    d. Performed after Qualitative Risk Analysis, but only on the risks where the data supports numerical analysis.
    e. Performed after Qualitative Risk Analysis, but only on the most critical risks where the data supports numerical analysis.

38. Which of the following is *not* a technique for performing Quantitative Risk Analysis?
    a. Interviewing
    b. Probability distributions
    c. Sensitivity analysis
    d. Expected Monetary Value analysis
    e. Modeling and simulation
    f. All of the above are Quantitative Risk Analysis methods

39. A probability distribution is used in Quantitative Risk Analysis because:
    a. It allows for graphing of the results.
    b. It is the easiest of the Quantitative Risk Analysis methods.
    c. It requires the least amount of data for Quantitative Risk Analysis.
    d. It represents the uncertainty of the risk values and therefore allows for better understanding of the risks.
    e. It doesn't require specialized analysis tools.

10

40. Sensitivity analysis is used in Quantitative Risk Analysis because:
    a. It allows for graphing of the results.
    b. It determines which risks have the most potential impact on the project.
    c. It requires the least amount of data for Quantitative Risk Analysis.
    d. It represents the uncertainty of the risk values and therefore allows for better understanding of the risks.
    e. It doesn't require specialized analysis tools.

41. A Tornado diagram is an example of:
    a. Three-point estimation.
    b. Probability distribution.
    c. Sensitivity analysis.
    d. Expected Monetary Value analysis.
    e. Modeling and simulation.

42. Expected Monetary Value analysis:
    a. Calculates the average outcome of a risk or an opportunity.
    b. Determines the total project cost considering the future cost of financing.
    c. Determines the resource costs by multiplying rate by hours.
    d. Discounts the project costs using an approved discount rate from finance.
    e. Determines when the project will exceed the risk contingency allocation.

43. Based on the following diagram, what is the Net Path Value for Result 1.1?

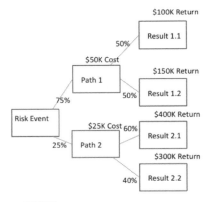

    a. $20K
    b. $25K
    c. $50K
    d. $100K
    e. $150K

44. Based on the following diagram, what is the decision EMV?

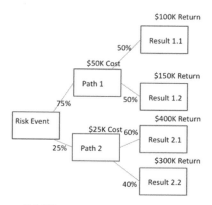

a. 56.25
b. 75
c. 83.75
d. 335
e. 500

45. If a project's risk has a 70 percent change of a $70K budget impact and a 30 percent change of a $100K budget impact, what is the Expected Monetary Value of the risk?
a. $30
b. $50
c. $79
d. $100
e. $170

46. A Monte Carlo simulation:
a. Uses cards drawn from a deck to randomly pick risk probabilities.
b. Uses a set of dice to randomly pick risk probabilities.
c. Uses a mathematical model run many times to simulate possible risk outcomes.
d. Used to use a die to pick probabilities, but now uses a computer random number generator.
e. Is a theoretical simulation example never used in real life.

10

47. During Quantitative Risk Analysis, the Risk Register:
    a. Is used to identify the risks that need to be analyzed.
    b. Is used to capture the results of the analysis.
    c. Is used to identify the risks that need to be analyzed and then captures the results of the analysis.
    d. Is sorted by priority to show the results of the analysis.
    e. Is sorted by impact and then probability to show the results of the analysis.

48. Which of the following is *not* a risk management strategy?
    a. Accept
    b. Avoid
    c. Manage
    d. Mitigate
    e. Transfer

49. When using the Avoid risk management strategy, what actions are taken?
    a. The project is cancelled to avoid the risk.
    b. The project delivery approach is changed to avoid the risk.
    c. The risk is deleted from the Risk Register to avoid any future reference to the risk.
    d. The team is instructed that the risk is to be avoided using whatever methods they feel are appropriate.
    e. The risk is reviewed with the project sponsor to ensure agreement that it can be avoided.

50. When using the Transfer risk management strategy, what actions are taken?
    a. The project manager finds another party willing and able to complete the risk portion of the project.
    b. The project team creates a document defining why the risk is not the responsibility of the project.
    c. A subcontractor is assigned the risk portion of the project.
    d. The team is instructed not to complete any of the activities associated with the risk.
    e. The risk is reviewed with the project sponsor to ensure agreement that it can be transferred outside the project scope.

51. When using the Mitigate risk management strategy, what actions are taken?
    a. The project manager assigns the task to someone up to the challenge.
    b. A subcontractor is assigned the risk portion of the project.
    c. The project delivery approach is adjusted to reduce either the probability or the impact of the risk.
    d. The team is instructed to consult with management prior to starting any of the work associated with the risk.
    e. The risk is reviewed with the project sponsor to ensure agreement that some project changes may need to be made if the risk occurs.

52. When using the Accept risk management strategy, what actions are taken?
    a. No actions are needed; the project team accepts the risk.
    b. A time and/or budget contingency is created.
    c. The project manager meets with the project acceptor and advises him or her that there are risks on the project.
    d. The team is advised to be on the lookout for the risk and immediately notify management.
    e. The project is immediately classified as "on watch" because the acceptance of a risk will make it late and over budget.

53. Which of the following risk management strategies requires time and/or budget contingencies (select two)?
    a. Avoid
    b. Accept
    c. Transfer
    d. Mitigate
    e. Eliminate

54. Purchasing insurance, buying products with extended warranties, and contracting with specialty firms are examples of which risk mitigation strategy?
    a. Avoid
    b. Accept
    c. Transfer
    d. Mitigate
    e. These are not risk mitigation approaches.

55. Adopting a less complex delivery approach, conducting early testing, and supplementing the team with experts are examples of which risk mitigation strategy?
    a. Avoid
    b. Accept
    c. Transfer
    d. Mitigate
    e. These are not risk mitigation approaches.

10

56. Developing a project schedule or a budget contingency is an example of which risk mitigation strategy?
    a. Avoid
    b. Accept
    c. Transfer
    d. Mitigate
    e. These are not risk mitigation approaches.

57. Which of the following defines a secondary risk?
    a. A secondary risk is a low-priority risk only managed when all high-priority risks are resolved.
    b. A secondary risk may result from implementing a Risk Response Plan.
    c. A secondary risk describes the risks deemed to be below the risk threshold for the project.
    d. A secondary risk is assigned to the business.
    e. A secondary risk is the residual risk from a mitigation strategy.

58. Which of the following is *not* an opportunity management strategy?
    a. Exploit
    b. Inspire
    c. Enhance
    d. Share
    e. Accept

59. Which of the following is *not* updated as part of risk response planning?
    a. Risk Register
    b. Project schedule
    c. Project budget
    d. Communications Management Plan
    e. Quality Management Plan

60. The Control Risk process does *not* consider which of the following?
    a. Implementing Risk Response Plans
    b. Notifying management of contingency plan consumption
    c. Tracking identified risks
    d. Identifying new risks
    e. Evaluating risk–management effectiveness

61. Implementing a Risk Response Plan may include:
    a. Consuming the risk contingency.
    b. Completing the actions in the Risk Response Plan.
    c. Identifying new or residual risks.
    d. Taking unplanned corrective actions.
    e. Updating the Risk Register.
    f. All of the above.
    g. None of the above.

62. The Control Risk process is:
    a. Driven by the Risk Register with a focus on all open identified risks.
    b. Driven by the Risk Register with a focus on open risks with a current trigger date.
    c. Focused on implementing risk plans.
    d. Focused on managing the project contingency.
    e. Focused on protecting the project contingency to ensure that the project is completed ahead of schedule and under budget.

63. Which of the following is *not* an input to the Control Risk process?
    a. Work performance data
    b. Risk Register
    c. Work performance reports
    d. Project Management Plan
    e. Project budget

64. A project risk is closed when:
    a. The project manager requests it.
    b. The project acceptor requests it.
    c. The risk owner confirms the risk event has passed.
    d. The risk contingency has been consumed.
    e. The risk target date has passed.

65. Risk audits are used to:
    a. Validate that the project is following the Risk Management Plan.
    b. Examine and document the effectiveness of the risk responses.
    c. Confirm the appropriate use of the risk contingencies.
    d. Review and close project risks.
    e. Confirm compliance with corporate risk-management policies.

10

66. A Project Change Request is a valid output of the Control Risk process.
    a. True
    b. False

11

PROJECT PROCUREMENT MANAGEMENT

1. There are _____ processes in Project Procurement Management.
    a. 3
    b. 4
    c. 5
    d. 6
    e. 7

2. Project Procurement Management is focused on:
    a. Ensuring that any projects being delivered under contact to a third party are managed to the terms of the contract.
    b. Selecting the components that the project requires from the corporate warehouse.
    c. Purchasing or acquiring the products, services, or results that the project needs from a third party.
    d. Negotiating with placement firms to hire the staff needed for the project.
    e. Communicating the list of components that the project requires to the purchasing department.

3. Procurement management applies only when the project is the deliverer of the third–party items.
    a. True
    b. False

11

4. The project procurement lifecycle:
   a. Follows the project lifecycle.
   b. Happens within a single phase of the project lifecycle.
   c. Is a unique lifecycle from the project lifecycle.
   d. Is a unique lifecycle for each item purchased.
   e. Is defined by the procurement department.

5. Procurement management is simply another term for a contract.
   a. True
   b. False

6. A contract can also be called a/an:
   a. Agreement.
   b. Understanding.
   c. Subcontract.
   d. Purchase order.
   e. All of the above.
   f. None of the above.

7. A complex project procurement requirement may result in:
   a. The seller developing a project plan, with the purchasing project manager becoming the acceptor.
   b. The seller developing a project plan, with the project acceptor also becoming the vendor's acceptor.
   c. The seller delivering the results based on the contract terms and conditions.
   d. The contract becoming the responsibility of the procurement department to allow the project manager to focus on other project components.
   e. The contract being separated from the project to simplify the project.

8. The Plan Procurement Management process is focused on:
   a. Creating the Procurement Management Plan.
   b. Identifying items the project must procure.
   c. Identifying how the project should procure required items.
   d. Identifying when the project should procure required items.
   e. All of the above.

9. Once a contract is signed for an item the project is procuring, the project manager should:
   a. Get out of the way and let the contracting firm deliver the items required.
   b. Integrate the seller's project plan into the main project plan and carefully manage all vendor activities.
   c. Manage the procurement to the terms and conditions of the contract.
   d. Develop acceptance criteria to be ready to receive and accept the purchased items.
   e. Demand weekly status reports from the seller's project manager.

10. The Risk Register may be used as part of procurement planning to:
   a. Identify opportunities to transfer risks.
   b. Capture risks associated with project procurement.
   c. Close risks once contracts have signed.
   d. All of the above.
   e. None of the above.

11. A fixed-price contract involves:
   a. A defined price per unit, with an undefined number of units to be purchased.
   b. A sliding rate per unit based on the number of units purchased.
   c. A defined price for delivering a defined amount of work.
   d. A fixed price per unit based on actual costs and an agreed profit margin per unit.
   e. An hourly rate per resource provided.

12. A time-and-materials contract involves:
   a. A defined price per unit, with an undefined number of units to be purchased.
   b. A sliding rate per unit based on the number of units purchased.
   c. A defined price for delivering a defined amount of work.
   d. A fixed price per unit based on actual costs and an agreed profit margin per unit.
   e. An hourly rate per resource provided.

13. A unit-price contract involves:
   a. A defined price per unit, with an undefined number of units to be purchased.
   b. A sliding rate per unit based on the number of units purchased.
   c. A defined price for delivering a defined amount of work.
   d. A fixed price per unit based on actual costs and an agreed profit margin per unit.
   e. An hourly rate per resource provider.

11

14. A cost-reimbursable contract involves:
    a. A defined price per unit, with an undefined number of units to be purchased.
    b. A sliding rate per unit based on the number of units purchased.
    c. A defined price for delivering a defined amount of work.
    d. A fixed price per unit based on actual costs and an agreed profit margin per unit.
    e. An hourly rate per resource provider.

15. Adding a subcontractor to augment the project team at a defined hourly rate is an example of what type of contract?
    a. Unit price
    b. Fixed price
    c. Cost plus
    d. Time and materials
    e. Risk sharing

16. Hiring a firm to complete a risky portion of the project for a prenegotiated price is an example of what type of contract?
    a. Unit price
    b. Fixed price
    c. Cost plus
    d. Time and materials
    e. Risk sharing

17. Negotiating a per-square-foot price for painting the interior of a new house is an example of what type of contract?
    a. Unit price
    b. Fixed price
    c. Cost plus
    d. Time and materials
    e. Risk sharing

18. A contract type such as fixed price with bonus for early delivery:
    a. Should never be considered in a project situation because it results in unpredictability in the schedule.
    b. Should only be considered if no other contract types can be agreed on.
    c. Should only be considered if an equivalent penalty clause is applied for late delivery.
    d. Is an acceptable contract type if it satisfies the project requirements.
    e. No contract deviations should be considered in a project environment.

19. A make-or-buy analysis is conducted during procurement planning:
    a. When a decision needs to be made about whether the component should be made by the team or contracted to a third party.
    b. For every activity in the WBS.
    c. When the team has the skills but lacks the capacity to complete a WBS activity.
    d. When the team does not have the skills to complete a WBS activity.
    e. When it is felt that a WBS activity can be completed more economically by a third party.

20. Which of the following is *not* contained in a Procurement Management Plan?
    a. Type of contracts to be used
    b. Penalty clauses for late delivery
    c. Standardized procurement documents
    d. Prequalified sellers
    e. Make-or-buy analysis process
    f. None of the above

21. Which type of contract represents the highest risk to the project?
    a. Fixed price
    b. Time and materials
    c. Cost plus
    d. Fixed price with an incentive for early delivery
    e. Fixed price with a penalty for late delivery

22. Which type of contract represents the least risk to a project?
    a. Fixed price
    b. Time and materials
    c. Cost plus fixed fee
    d. Cost plus cost-of-living increase
    e. Per diem

23. A procurement Statement of Work:
    a. Defines the process to be used during the procurement process.
    b. Defines the portion of the project scope to be delivered through a specific procurement.
    c. Defines the type of contract to be used for a specific procurement.
    d. Defines the terms and conditions of a specific procurement.
    e. Defines the acceptance process that will be applied to the finished product from a procurement.

11

24. A procurement Statement of Work should be:
    a. Loosely defined to ensure flexibility during contract negotiations.
    b. Loosely defined to allow the project to adjust the acceptance terms to ensure that the end result will meet the project's requirements.
    c. Clear, complete, and concise, to allow the vendors to accurately deliver the required results.
    d. An open-ended request that will be refined and closed down during contract negotiations.
    e. A direct extract from the Project Scope Statement to ensure that the results will fully integrate into the project.

25. A procurement Statement of Work is typically used as input to:
    a. The vendor's project plan.
    b. A contract.
    c. A RFP, RFQ, RFI, or similar procurement document.
    d. A bidder conference agenda.
    e. A purchase order.

26. A procurement document should be:
    a. Loosely defined requirements but highly defined expected results to give vendors flexibility in how to achieve the results.
    b. Loosely defined requirements and loosely defined expected results to allow the vendors to present their solution with the most flexibility.
    c. Highly defined requirements and highly defined expected results to ensure the solution performs exactly as specified.
    d. An open-ended request that will be refined and closed down during contract negotiations.
    e. A direct extract from the Project Scope Statement to ensure that the results will fully integrate into the project.

27. Source selection criteria should be defined:
    a. At the same time that the procurement documents are created.
    b. During the vendor response period.
    c. Once the vendor responses have been reviewed at a high level.
    d. Once the vendor responses have been reviewed in detail.
    e. Once the vendor responses have been ranked.

28. Which of the following would *not* be considered a source selection criterion?
    a. Overall cost
    b. Warranty
    c. Level of vendor participation on the pre-bidding process
    d. Business size and type
    e. Technical approach

29. The Plan Procurement process may result in updates to which of the following documents?
    a. Project Scope Document
    b. Project schedule
    c. Project budget
    d. Human resource plan
    e. Risk Register
    f. All of the above
    g. None of the above

30. Which of the following is *not* part of the Conduct Procurements process?
    a. Issue RFP.
    b. Obtain RFP responses.
    c. Select vendor.
    d. Award contract.
    e. All are part of the Conduct Procurements process.

31. Conduct Procurements is:
    a. A one-time process performed early in the project.
    b. A one-time process per procurement performed as the procurement is required.
    c. A process that is repeated as needed for each procurement and may be repeated for a single procurement.
    d. A weekly process performed as part of the weekly status process.
    e. A continuous process to ensure ongoing compliance in the procurement process.

32. Source selection criteria are used during the Conduct Procurement process to:
    a. Define the criteria against which the vendors will be evaluated.
    b. Evaluate vendor responses.
    c. Develop the procurement contract.
    d. Manage the procurement process.
    e. Document the results of the vendor evaluation.

11

33. Seller responses are:
    a. Reviewed by the evaluation team and voted on using a nominal group consensus process.
    b. Reviewed by the evaluation team and selected by a singular vote by team member.
    c. Evaluated against the source selection criteria using a weighted evaluation process to select the response with the highest score.
    d. Generally of limited value in the procurement process because a live demo should be used to select the successful vendor.
    e. Evaluated with separate technical and financial evaluation teams.

34. Bidder conferences are important because:
    a. They allow the organization to meet and get to know the vendor resources.
    b. They ensure that all vendors receive exactly the same information regarding clarifications and additional details related to the procurement.
    c. They let the vendors see who is competing to allow them to fine-tune their responses and provide the best possible price to the purchasing organization.
    d. They ensure a fair evaluation by having all participants together.
    e. They provide no value in ecommerce and should be eliminated.

35. During the Conduct Procurement process, the project management team can develop an independent estimate to:
    a. Give the vendors guidelines about how much the project is willing to spend.
    b. Develop a preliminary budget to ensure that the procurement can be funded by the project.
    c. Ensure that the make-or-buy decision is appropriate by ensuring that the project cannot make it cheaper than buying it.
    d. Provide a benchmark against which responses can be evaluated.
    e. Serve as a negotiation point to get a better price from the vendors.

36. Advertising is commonly used during the Conduct Procurement process to:
    a. Raise public awareness of the project to improve the company's image.
    b. Ensure that all potential vendors are aware of the procurement activities.
    c. Satisfy internal or governmental regulations.
    d. Raise the profile of the project to ensure that sufficient funds will be available to complete the procurements.
    e. Keep all parts of the organization aware of the procurement process.

37. Procurement negotiations should be:
    a. Performed by the project team exclusively to ensure the project requirements are met appropriately.
    b. Performed by legal counsel exclusively to ensure that the contract is binding and protects the project's legal rights.
    c. Performed by the project team and legal counsel as a team to address both project and legal requirements.
    d. Performed by the vendor's organization so that the project does not have to absorb any contract development costs.
    e. Performed by the project, legal counsel, and the vendor's organization to ensure a contract that supports all involved parties.

38. Which of the following is *not* included in a procurement agreement?
    a. Statement of Work
    b. Performance reporting
    c. Payment terms
    d. Acceptance criteria
    e. Source selection criteria

39. The Conduct Procurement process may result in updates to which of the following documents?
    a. Project Scope Document
    b. Project schedule
    c. Project budget
    d. Human resource plan
    e. Risk Register
    f. All of the above
    g. None of the above

40. The Control Procurements process is focused on:
    a. Ensuring contract compliance.
    b. Maximizing the value that the project can obtain from a contract.
    c. Searching for vendor contract violations so that penalty clauses can be enforced.
    d. Negotiating with the vendor to satisfy project requirements.
    e. Often not completed as part of the project, because the procurement department takes ownership of all contracts.

41. Which of the following is *not* a project management process that interfaces with the Control Procurements process?
    a. Control Quality
    b. Validate Scope
    c. Direct and Manage Project Work
    d. Control Risks
    e. Perform Integrated Change Control

42. Evaluating vendor performance and establishing corrective actions are part of which process?
    a. Control Scope
    b. Monitor and Control Project Work
    c. Control Quality
    d. Control Procurements
    e. Close Procurements

43. Once a procurement contract is signed:
    a. It cannot be changed; any required changes will require a new contract to be created.
    b. It can be changed as long as both parties agree that it is in the project's best interest.
    c. It can only be changed by the project; vendor changes are not allowed.
    d. It can be changed using an approved contract control process, which must be formally accepted by both organizations.
    e. It requires legal counsel to review and approve all changes.

44. Procurement performance reviews are used:
    a. Only when the vendor is not performing; they are used to identify remediation activities.
    b. As part of routine management to monitor performance against a project contract.
    c. To validate that a contract has satisfied all the stated obligations and that the contract can be closed.
    d. To make recommendations about whether the vendor should be considered for future work.
    e. Immediately prior to issuing payment to a vendor, to ensure that the payment terms have been met.

45. In the case of a contract dispute, which of the following would *not* considered a key input?
    a. Correspondence
    b. Work performance information
    c. Contract
    d. Contract change requests
    e. Vendor RFP

46. Which of the following is *not* required to authorize vendor payment?
    a. Contract payment terms and conditions
    b. Contract Performance Reviews
    c. Work Performance Data
    d. Contract Inspections and Audits
    e. Vendor invoice

47. The Close Procurement process is performed:
    a. Once at the close of the project.
    b. Once at the end of each phase of the project.
    c. As required based on the completion of each contract.
    d. As dictated by the project manager, as holdbacks and warranties may be required.
    e. By the procurement department as defined by corporate policies.

48. The Close Procurement process does *not* include which of the following?
    a. Enacting payment holdback and warranty clauses
    b. Evaluating vendor performance
    c. Completing vendor references
    d. Approving final vendor deliverable
    e. Approving final vendor payments

49. A vendor has completed the work as defined by the procurement Statement of Work. However, the project manager and project customer do not like the results. In this case, the contract is considered to be:
    a. Contested
    b. Incomplete
    c. Null and void
    d. Waived
    e. Completed

11

50. The project team is developing an RFP. What part of the procurement process does this occur in?
    a. Plan Procurement Management
    b. Conduct Procurements
    c. Develop Procurement Documents
    d. Control Procurements
    e. Close Procurements

51. The project management team has made a decision to procure a component that has a very poor definition of scope. What type of contract will provide the least financial risk to the project?
    a. Fixed price
    b. Time and materials
    c. Cost plus percentage of cost
    d. Cost plus fixed fee
    e. Fixed price with incentive for early delivery

12

PROJECT STAKEHOLDER MANAGEMENT

1. There are _____ processes in Project Stakeholder Management.
   a. 3
   b. 4
   c. 5
   d. 6
   e. 7

2. Project Stakeholder Management is focused on:
   a. Identifying the individuals interested in the project, analyzing their expectations, and then effectively managing the stakeholders.
   b. Ensuring that the project stakeholders complete their assigned WBS activities.
   c. Soliciting senior management as needed to resolve project issues.
   d. Defining the role that stakeholders will play in the project.
   e. Holding a project kickoff meeting to announce the project to the organization.

3. Stakeholder management is:
   a. Completed at the initial planning base only.
   b. Ongoing to address evolving stakeholder requirements.
   c. Only required when project communications are not effective.
   d. Only required when the project has to report to a senior stakeholder review board.
   e. Required to augment the project acceptor's role on the project.

12

4. Project stakeholders are:
   a. Senior management who have authority to make decisions on behalf of the project.
   b. Members of the business area the project is being completed for.
   c. Direct supervisors of the project manager, project acceptor, and project sponsor.
   d. Individuals who will be impacted by the project.
   e. Any individual or group, including external entities, that may affect or may be affected by the project.

5. A component of identifying project stakeholders is:
   a. Categorizing stakeholders by interest, influence, and involvement in the project.
   b. Developing individual communications plans for each stakeholder.
   c. Grouping stakeholders by department and management level.
   d. Eliminating stakeholders who do not have decision-making authority.
   e. Identifying key stakeholders.

6. Which of the following is *not* a stakeholder classification?
   a. Keep satisfied
   b. Manage closely
   c. Decision maker
   d. Monitor
   e. Keep informed

7. Which of the following is *not* a stakeholder classification model?
   a. Power/influence grid
   b. Power/interest grid
   c. Influence/impact grid
   d. Management level/impact grid
   e. Salience model

8. Project stakeholders are identified by:
   a. Organizational structure of involved departments.
   b. Project decision makers.
   c. Interviews with identified stakeholders.
   d. Open enrollment from the organization.
   e. All of the above.
   f. All except A.
   g. All except B.
   h. All except C.
   i. All except D.

9. You are classifying the project stakeholders based on the level of influence they have over the project, as well as the likelihood that this influence will be meaningful. What classification model are you using?
   a. Power/influence grid
   b. Power/interest grid
   c. Influence/impact grid
   d. Management level/impact grid
   e. Salience model

10. Which of the following is *not* captured in the stakeholder register?
    a. Name, position in organization, and contract details
    b. Reason for interest
    c. Stakeholder classification
    d. Assessment information, information requirements, and expectation and potential influence on the project
    e. All of the above are contained on the stakeholder register

11. The Plan Stakeholder Management process:
    a. Develops the plan for finding the appropriate project stakeholders.
    b. Develops the plan for communicating with the project stakeholders.
    c. Develops the plan for ensuring that the stakeholders complete their assigned project deliverables.
    d. Develops the management strategies for keeping the project stakeholders engaged.
    e. Develops the plan for tracking stakeholder satisfaction.

12. Stakeholder management is focused on:
    a. Effectively communicating project status to the project stakeholders.
    b. Keeping the stakeholders engaged for the duration of the project.
    c. Ensuring stakeholder satisfaction.
    d. Managing stakeholder participation in the project.
    e. Creating and maintaining effective relationships with the project stakeholders.

13. A stakeholder engagement assessment matrix is used to:
    a. Record the desired stakeholder engagement.
    b. Record the current stakeholder engagement.
    c. Record both the desired and the current stakeholder engagement.
    d. Plot desired versus current stakeholder engagement.
    e. Determine the stakeholder engagement for each stakeholder.

12

14. It is critical that all project stakeholders are fully engaged for the entire lifecycle of the project.
    a. True
    b. False

15. The Stakeholder Management Plan does *not* contain which of the following?
    a. Scope and impact of stakeholders
    b. Stakeholder communications requirements
    c. Action plans for maintaining stakeholder engagement
    d. Project status reports
    e. Timeframe and format of stakeholder communications

16. Effective stakeholder engagement can be achieved by:
    a. Meeting individually with each stakeholder on a weekly basis.
    b. Developing individual communications packaged and tailored to each stakeholder's needs.
    c. Managing stakeholder's expectations through negotiation and communication.
    d. Developing a common communication package for all stakeholders to ensure that all stakeholders receive the same information.
    e. Alerting senior management of all stakeholder engagement deficiencies.

17. Keeping stakeholders engaged will help ensure project success because:
    a. An informed stakeholder is a happy stakeholder.
    b. An informed stakeholder is better equipped to deal with project issues.
    c. An uninformed stakeholder will result in project delays.
    d. An uninformed stakeholder will stop the project and demand status.
    e. There is no relationship between stakeholders and project success.

18. The ability of a stakeholder to influence a project is typically:
    a. Constant throughout the project.
    b. Highest at the beginning of the project.
    c. Highest at the end of the project.
    d. Highest at the time deliverables are presented for approval.
    e. Only possible when the project manager requests assistance.

19. Which of the following techniques is *not* applicable for stakeholder management?
    a. Interpersonal skills
    b. Influence skills
    c. Communications methods
    d. Management skills
    e. All of the above are used

20. The Control Stakeholder Engagement process is focused on:
    a. Controlling the flow of information to stakeholders to manage the message.
    b. Controlling the work on the deliverables assigned to the stakeholders.
    c. Monitoring the overall stakeholder relationship and adjusting strategies for engaging stakeholders.
    d. Securing assistance from senior management for controlling stakeholders.
    e. Controlling access to the team to ensure that stakeholders don't get involved in day-to-day team work assignments.

21. What role does the Information Management System play in the Control Stakeholder Engagement process?
    a. It captures the feedback from the stakeholders.
    b. It allows for the consolidation of the information to be distributed to the stakeholders.
    c. It provides a portal used by stakeholders to get access to the desired information.
    d. It automates the creation of stakeholder status reports.
    e. It does not play a role in the Control Stakeholder Engagement process.

22. You are monitoring overall project stakeholder relationships and adjusting strategies and plans for engaging stakeholders. What is this process called?
    a. Identify Stakeholders
    b. Plan Stakeholder Management
    c. Manage Stakeholder Engagement
    d. Track Stakeholder Satisfaction
    e. Control Stakeholder Engagement

23. You are developing the strategies to engage stakeholders on the project. What is this process?
    a. Identify Stakeholders
    b. Plan Stakeholder Management
    c. Manage Stakeholder Engagement
    d. Track Stakeholder Satisfaction
    e. Control Stakeholder Engagement

12

13

POST-TEST

1. A lag of two days on a start-to-finish dependency results in:
   a. Nothing—there is no such thing as a lag.
   b. A delay of the start of the first activity by two days.
   c. An advance of the start of the first activity by two days.
   d. A delay of the start of the second activity by two days.
   e. An advance of the start of the second activity by two days.

2. Contingency reserves are depleted during the Control Costs process:
   a. When the schedule time for the risk event takes place.
   b. As needed to preserve on-budget performance.
   c. As mitigation plans are executed.
   d. As needed, but only to deal with a project risk.
   e. Contingency reserves should not be used until the end of the project to ensure that there is always a reserve.

3. The output of the Identify Stakeholder process is:
   a. The project organization chart.
   b. A RACI chart.
   c. A RAM matrix.
   d. The stakeholder register.
   e. A list of the most important project stakeholders.

4. Managing payments to a vendor is part of which process?
   a. Control Costs
   b. Monitor and Control Project Work
   c. Control Quality
   d. Control Procurements
   e. Perform Integrated Change Control

13

5. The acceptance criteria defined in the Project Scope Statement are:
   a. High level, typically specifying whether the deliverable requires acceptance.
   b. Detailed, identifying not only the acceptance criteria, but also any processes to be followed for defect remediation.
   c. A set of conditions that are required before the deliverable can be accepted.
   d. Optional.
   e. Both B and C.

6. Quality assurance:
   a. Tests the product.
   b. Ensures that quality processes are followed.
   c. Validates that the results satisfy the requirements.
   d. Audits the project and reports violations.
   e. Is typically not required on projects.

7. Extending the schedule, changing the strategy, and reducing the scope are examples of which risk mitigation strategy?
   a. Avoid
   b. Accept
   c. Transfer
   d. Mitigate
   e. These are not risk mitigation approaches.

8. Which of the following would *not* be considered the result of a project?
   a. A product
   b. Customer service
   c. A change in process
   d. An improvement in an existing product
   e. A result

9. Iterative or incremental lifecycles are preferred when:
   a. The organization wants predictable results.
   b. The project must be completed on a predefined date.
   c. The business needs to manage changing objectives and scope.
   d. The business would get value from early and partial delivery.
   e. All of the above.
   f. A and B.
   g. C and D.

10. Procurement management is involved with:
    a. Purchases that require formal legal contracts.
    b. Purchases that involve the procurement department.
    c. Purchases for standard off-the-shelf items.
    d. Purchases that are unique and haven't been made before in the company.
    e. All purchases.

11. A work authorization system is used to:
    a. Approve the project schedule.
    b. Approve the project budget.
    c. Manage who works on each project component.
    d. Manage the project schedule.
    e. Manage the project stakeholders.

12. A context diagram typically shows project scope using:
    a. Inputs.
    b. Outputs.
    c. Actors.
    d. Business processes.
    e. A, B, and C.
    f. A, C, and D.
    g. B, C, and D.
    h. All of the above.

13. You determine that the estimate for an activity is 50 hours based on a review of prior projects with similar activities. This is based on what estimating approach?
    a. Bottom-up
    b. Top-down
    c. Parametric
    d. Analogous
    e. Expert judgment

14. A Risk Breakdown Structure:
    a. Mirrors the Work Breakdown Structure and matches the risks to the activities.
    b. Groups risks into a set of predefined causes of the risks.
    c. Plots the risks on the project schedule.
    d. Matches mitigation plans to identified risks.
    e. Matches contingency reserves to identified risks.

13

15. Which of the following would be considered a project assumption?
    a. A business deadline defining the last possible date on which the project can be completed before the project benefits are no longer valid
    b. A concern that there will be a labor dispute at one of the project's vendors
    c. A milestone on the project schedule
    d. The assignment of a key project resource at 50 percent availability
    e. All of the above

16. The Project Management Information System provides:
    a. A work authorization system.
    b. A configuration management system.
    c. A communications management system.
    d. A project scheduling tool.
    e. All of the above.

17. There are _____ processes in Project Communications Management.
    a. 3
    b. 4
    c. 5
    d. 6
    e. 7

18. The Acquire Project Team process is focused on:
    a. Hiring the project team members that human resources can't supply with existing resources.
    b. Developing contracting relationships for the positions to be filled by external contractors.
    c. A one-time activity to obtain the team.
    d. An ongoing process to obtain the team.
    e. A project task delegated to the human resources department.

19. With respect to change, a portfolio:
    a. Defines processes, manages and controls changes.
    b. Expects change and is prepared to manage it.
    c. Monitors change in the broader internal and external environments.
    d. Manages change through an iterative development process.
    e. Does not support change.

20. Project stakeholders are:
    a. Internal to the organization.
    b. External to the organization.
    c. Supporters of the project.
    d. Distractors of the project.
    e. All of the above.
    f. A and B.
    g. A and C.
    h. A, B, and C.

21. The Estimate Costs process allows the Project Manager to:
    a. Define resource rates to be charged on the project.
    b. Obtain vendor quotes for items that must be purchased by the project.
    c. Identify the monetary resources needed to complete the project activities.
    d. Calculate overhead rates and allocations to bill the project for infrastructure needs.
    e. Multiply hours by rates to determine the project costs.

22. Selecting the appropriate media for communication is important because:
    a. Different stakeholders will prefer different media: written documentation versus email versus presentations.
    b. Social media and instant messaging must be included in an effective project communication strategy.
    c. Project communication should consider multimedia to ensure effective communications.
    d. Strategies for incorporating mobile communication must be included.
    e. Project portals form the backbone of effective project communication.

23. The Requirements Management Plan is:
    a. Produced at the same time as the Scope Management Plan.
    b. Produced once all of the requirements have been defined.
    c. Produced at the end of analysis.
    d. Required only on large or complex projects.
    e. Optional.

13

24. The Manage Stakeholder Engagement process:
   a. Develops and distributes the project communications package to the project stakeholders.
   b. Manages the completion of project deliverables by the stakeholders.
   c. Reports on stakeholder engagement.
   d. Conducts surveys to measure stakeholder engagement.
   e. Works with the project stakeholders to validate that the project is meeting their expectations and addressing any issues as they occur.

25. The project schedule should:
   a. Be created in its entirety during the initial plan.
   b. Be as complete as possible, given that it will be maintained weekly with project status updates.
   c. Support rolling-wave planning.
   d. Stop when the team feels that it is 75 percent complete, recognizing that no estimates are perfect.
   e. At a minimum, be fully complete for the next phase to advance, and then follow a rough order of magnitude for subsequent phases.

26. The relationship between organizational governance and a project is:
   a. Critical to project success, because the project should be aligned with organizational governance.
   b. Not important, because the project defines its own governance processes in the Project Management Plan.
   c. That project governance should always be a subset of the organizational governance.
   d. Important only when the project deliverables will be transferred to the operations department.
   e. Important only when senior management play an active role in the project.

27. The *Guide to the Project Management Body of Knowledge* (PMBOK) is:
   a. The international standard for project management.
   b. The North American standard for project management.
   c. A guidebook of project management best practices.
   d. The subset of the project management body of knowledge that is generally recognized as good practice.
   e. The master guide for project management.

28. Project organization charts can be documented as:
    a. Traditional organizational (tree-based) diagrams.
    b. Responsibility matrices.
    c. Role descriptions.
    d. All of the above.
    e. None of the above.

29. Procurement requirements are typically identified from:
    a. The Requirements Document.
    b. Matching the seller's catalog/service offerings to the Work Breakdown Structure activity list.
    c. Reviewing Request for Proposal responses.
    d. Reviewing Request for Information responses.
    e. Prior experience with vendors and their ability to help complete the project.

30. The project budget has been created. What Project Management Process Group are you in?
    a. Initiating
    b. Planning
    c. Executing
    d. Monitoring and controlling
    e. Closing

31. There are _____ processes in Project Human Resource Management.
    a. 3
    b. 4
    c. 5
    d. 6
    e. 7

32. Project Integration Management is focused on:
    a. Identifying, documenting, combining, and managing the Project Management Process Groups.
    b. Identifying, defining, combining, and managing the Project Management Process Groups.
    c. Identifying, documenting, combining, unifying, and managing the Project Management Process Groups.
    d. Identifying, defining, combining, unifying, and coordinating the Project Management Process Groups.
    e. Documenting, defining, combining, and coordinating the Project Management Process Groups.

13

33. Which of the following is *not* a step in negotiating?
    a. Analyze the situation.
    b. Differentiate between wants and needs.
    c. Ask high and offer low.
    d. Never make a concession.
    e. Listen attentively.

34. Budget reserve analysis:
    a. Combines known-unknowns and unknown-unknown contingencies together to determine reserve requirements.
    b. Validates contingencies against the project's risk profile to determine the risk reserve.
    c. Increases the calculated budget reserve to ensure adequate risk coverage.
    d. Decreases the calculated budget reserve to avoid over-risk aversion.
    e. Determines the budget reserve on the advice of the project manager and business owner.

35. An activity estimate is determined based on the number of units to be produced multiplied by an industry average. What type of estimate method was used?
    a. Bottom-up
    b. Top-down
    c. Analogous
    d. Parametric
    e. Expert

36. Which of the following statements defines the role of the project stakeholders?
    a. Act as decision makers on key project decisions
    b. Are interested parties but with limited project authority
    c. Help confirm project requirements and clarify assumptions
    d. Provide necessary resources for the project
    e. Confirm WBS activities

37. Who is responsible for project quality?
    a. Senior management
    b. Project manager
    c. Project acceptor
    d. Team
    e. All of the above

38. There are _____ processes in Project Scope Management.
    a. 4
    b. 5
    c. 6
    d. 7
    e. 8

39. During risk identification, the following elements should be recorded in the Risk Register:
    a. Risk name, description, effect of risk
    b. Risk name, description, effect of risk, impact and probability
    c. Risk name, description, effect of risk, impact and probability, analysis results
    d. Risk name, description, effect of risk, impact and probability, analysis results, mitigation plan
    e. Risk name, description, effect of risk, impact and probability, analysis results, mitigation plan, contingency

40. Project milestones are typically identified:
    a. After the schedule is fully developed.
    b. During initial WBS creation.
    c. Once the project sponsor reviews the schedule.
    d. By the project manager as the communications plan is developed.
    e. During the Define Activities process.

41. Lack of communications planning can result in:
    a. Inadequate communication.
    b. Delayed message delivery.
    c. Communication to the wrong audience.
    d. Misinterpretation of the message communicated.
    e. All of the above.

42. The Control Project Costs process involves:
    a. Tracking and approving project purchases.
    b. Verifying team members' timesheets to approve project charges.
    c. Approving vendor invoices.
    d. Managing costs against the project baseline.
    e. All of the above.

13

43. The make-or-buy analysis should consider:
    a. The total cost of the decision, including direct and indirect costs.
    b. Direct costs only if the project doesn't have to fund indirect costs.
    c. Costs should not be a factor. The decision should be made based on team capacity only.
    d. The organization's prior experience with a vendor.
    e. The project manager's prior experience with procurement.

44. Which of the following are used when determining a project's risk profile?
    a. Risk appetite, strategy, and threshold
    b. Risk strategy, tolerance, and threshold
    c. Risk appetite, strategy, and tolerance
    d. Risk appetite, tolerance, and threshold
    e. Risk appetite, strategy, tolerance, and threshold

45. A project can have:
    a. No critical paths.
    b. Only one critical path.
    c. Only one critical path, but multiple near-critical paths.
    d. Multiple critical paths.
    e. A maximum of three critical paths.

46. When developing the human resource plan, which of the following should *not* be considered?
    a. Skills required to complete the WBS activities
    b. Named individuals desired for the project
    c. Start and end times for project resources
    d. Reporting relationships for the project team
    e. Project training requirements

47. Monitor and Control Project Work is the focus of:
    a. The business sponsor.
    b. The business acceptor.
    c. The project team members.
    d. Executive management.
    e. The project managers.

48. During Project Scope Management:
    a. All project deliverables must be identified.
    b. All project deliverables must be fully decomposed.
    c. All project deliverables must be decomposed to at least two levels.
    d. Current phase deliverables must be fully decomposed.
    e. All of the above.
    f. All except A.
    g. A and C.
    h. A and D.
    i. B and D.

49. The process improvement plan is:
    a. Developed dynamically each time a process improvement is identified.
    b. Produced at the end of the project to capture all the process improvements for potential reuse in the organization.
    c. Produced by the organization's quality department and details the audit recommendations.
    d. Produced to obtain formal approval for implementing process improvements.
    e. Produced during planning and defines the steps to be used to analyze processes with the goal of enhancing their value.

50. The Identify Stakeholders process:
    a. Identifies all project stakeholders.
    b. Identifies all project stakeholders and their interest in the project.
    c. Is only required if the project must identify external stakeholders.
    d. Is only required if the project will have stakeholders from organizational units beyond the one for which the project is being delivered.
    e. Focuses on identifying those stakeholders who can make decisions on behalf of the project.

13

CHAPTER

14

EXAM DAY TIPS AND HINTS

Congratulations! I'm assuming if you're reading this chapter, you've completed all the questions in this book, including the post-test, and you have the confidence to schedule and take your PMP certification exam. Best of luck to you!

To help, I would like to offer a little advice for the days leading up to the exam, to help ensure that you will be successful when you sit down and start the 200 questions that make up the PMP exam.

First, schedule your actual exam day several weeks before you expect to be ready to take the exam. Most exam centers are very busy and are typically booking several weeks in advance. Don't leave it to the last day before the one-year expiration date on your eligibility letter, as you might be very disappointed. And don't just pick the first available time slot; ensure that it is a time slot that works for you. Are you most alert in the morning or the afternoon? Is a Monday or a Friday likely to be a better time, free from workplace or personal distractions? Make sure you select a time period that will allow you to be at your peak performance.

With the big date set, it's time to get yourself mentally prepared for the test. By now, you've done all the studying and preparation you need to know the material, so it's time to focus on being ready for the exam.

First and foremost, make sure you have the necessary documentation to present at the exam center. The exam center will require two pieces of ID, preferably government issued, with photos and signatures—the *PMP Credential Handbook* precisely defines what is and is not acceptable for ID.

A key consideration when selecting your IDs is the name on the ID. The name on the eligibility letter should exactly match the name on the ID. For example, my proper name is Stephen, but I typically go by Steve. While most exam centers will accept common nicknames, such as Steve for Stephen, it's always best to ensure that the name on your ID matches the name on your eligibility letter. Again, if you have any questions about whether the ID will be appropriate, review the *PMP Credential Handbook*.

14

Second, be prepared for the exam center, because the rules, regulations, and security will be very strict. Plan to arrive at least 30 minutes before your scheduled exam start time. You will be provided with a secure area to lock up virtually everything except for the clothing you are wearing. Cell phones, purses, wallets, snacks, reading materials, car keys, backpacks, and anything else you are carrying or have in your pockets must left outside the exam room in the provided secure area. The last time I took a PMI certification exam, the exam center used a handheld metal detector. I had to turn out my pockets and roll up my pants and sleeves to prove that I wasn't taking anything into the exam room. Bottom line: Be prepared for security as tight as in an airport (or at least it was in the center I used). And speaking of clothes, you're not even allowed to remove a sweater if you find the room too hot. (Well, you can, but first you have to get the attendant's attention, leave the exam room, remove the sweater, and then re-enter the room.) So again, be prepared with clothing you think will be adequate for a four-hour session in a traditional office.

A final comment about the exam center: Know in advance where it is located and how you're going to get there. In fact, I recommend making an advance dry run at approximately the time of your exam to allow you to properly estimate travel time and other logistics. Determining that it is a 25-minute commute on a Sunday isn't going to be very valuable on Monday, when you realize there is a significant issue from daily commuter traffic.

Plan to be early. I recommend arriving at least one hour before your scheduled exam time: That leaves you 30 minutes to deal with traffic and transportation issues, and 30 minutes to deal with check-in at the exam center. Arriving early and feeling relaxed will ensure a much better exam experience than stressing about whether you will get lost on the drive, where you will find parking, and/or whether you will get there on time.

Enough of the physical plan for arriving at the exam center; now let's focus on the mental preparation. By the time you have your exam scheduled, you shouldn't need to do any significant preparation. You need to have completed all the sample questions and have been successful with the post-test before you commit to an actual date. Use the time between booking and writing to do strategic reviews: Review Annex A-1, re-review Table A1-1, validate your memorization of the Earned Value Rules—EV always comes first; if it's Schedule, always use PV; if it's Budget, always use AC—and recheck your understanding of how to do forward and backward passes on the network diagram. I would even suggest creating a two- to five-page cram sheet you can use for one last review just before you enter the examination center.

Another important way to prepare is to keep reminding yourself of the exam format. There will be 200 questions, and you have four hours to complete the exam. This equates to completing a question every 1.2 minutes. (You'll complete some questions much faster than that, but some of them will likely take several minutes to complete.) Be prepared to do time checks versus number of questions completed every 30 minutes to ensure that you will complete the exam in the four hours allotted.

Be prepared for questions from every Knowledge Area and every Process Group. PMI even provides the Process Group distribution: Initiating 13%, Planning 24%, Executing 30%, Monitoring and Controlling 25%, and Closing 8%. Each question will have four possible answers, and you will select the *best* or *most appropriate* answer, recognizing there may be more than one right answer. A guideline for selecting the best or most appropriate answer is that it will typically be the one most closely aligned with the PMBOK and/or the one that is the most proactive to ensure future success rather than reactive to past issues.

There will be questions that validate your knowledge, questions that have you apply knowledge in a practical delivery situation, and even questions that will require you to make simple calculations. The exam center will provide note paper and calculators; in most instances, they will be integrated into the computer you're using for the test.

And now that much anticipated (dreaded?) time has arrived, and you are sitting in front of the exam computer. The four-hour clock has started, and you're presented with the first question.

Stop! Don't read the question until you are ready. If you need to make notes, write down the names of the Process Groups or Knowledge Areas or Earned Value formulas or anything else you have "memorized" and don't want to forget. Do it now, before you start. As mentioned a moment ago, you will be able to make notes—pencil and paper, erasable boards, and/or computer-based notepads will be provided. Make as many notes as you want before starting, but also remember that the four-hour clock has started, so do this as quickly as possible and then get going.

Now, read the complete question slowly and thoroughly. *Do not guess* what it is asking based on the first five words. Remember, these are well-written questions by professionals and they are field-tested—*read* them *carefully*. Then read each possible answer slowly and thoroughly. And then, select the *best answer*.

But what if, after reading the question and the possible answers, you don't have an answer? Skip it. You can always come back and review missed questions at the end. And don't let it bother you if you don't have an answer to the first question. Remember, the questions are distributed randomly. You are as likely to get as your first question the hardest question of the entire 200 as you are to get an easy, confidence-building question first. The key is to keep moving. If you have to skip the first five before you find the all-important first easy question, then go ahead and skip all five. Once you get several questions answered that you are confident are right, you will find that the exam jitters will go away, and you will be in the right mindset to continue the exam.

Don't go back; keep moving forward and do your first pass through the entire exam, completing as many of the "easy questions" as you can. Once you get your rhythm, all the months of preparation and sample questions from this book will pay off, and you will likely skip very few questions. If you find you are spending more than 1.2 minutes on a question and you aren't close to an answer, mark it for review on the next pass. Skipping one difficult question ensures that you won't run out of time to complete all the easy questions before the allotted four hours expires.

14

I will close this section with my top 10 tips for always getting the right answer:

1. Read each question and all possible answers slowly and carefully.

2. Eliminate the answers that are definitely *not* right.

3. Always select the *best* or *most appropriate* answer from the remaining possibilities.

4. Putting the question/answer into a real-life project situation will help you to select the best answer.

5. The best answer is always aligned with PMI principles and the PMBOK.

6. The best answer is always proactive, as opposed to reactive.

7. Always consider the PMI Code of Ethics and Professional Responsibility when selecting the best answer.

8. Most, if not all, questions are based on a project being delivered in the USA.

9. If you get a question that just doesn't make sense, assume it's an evaluation question, give it your best guess, and move on.

10. If you have less than 15 minutes left and you know you won't answer all remaining questions, *start guessing!* You are not penalized for wrong answers, so guessing is better than leaving a question unanswered. (But I am also confident you will never need to use this tip.)

GLOSSARY

acceptance criteria. Predefined criteria that must be satisfied for the project acceptor to accept a project deliverable.

activities. A defined unit of work that is directly linked to a project deliverable. An activity should be estimable, assignable, and trackable to ensure that the project schedule can be created and managed.

analogous estimating. An estimating technique based on using historical estimates from a previous project that was of similar scope.

assumption. A future condition that the project is assuming to be true. Clearly stating realistic project assumptions is key for successful projects because the project plans must be based on clearly stated conditions, some of which cannot be confirmed at the time of planning—in other words, assumptions.

baseline. An approved definition of work for a project. Typically, Schedule and Budget baselines are created when the project is formally approved. A baseline is not changed once it is created and is used for variance analysis against actual delivery results.

budget. The approved cost for the project. The budget is prepared during project planning and should contain the total costs of all work, materials, supplies, and other third-party costs required to complete the project.

Business Case. The Business Case is traditionally prepared by business unit management and defines both the preliminary scope for a project and the cost/benefit analysis for the project.

Change Control Board. A Change Control Board is composed of senior management representing all areas of the business. The Change Control Board reviews all Project Change Requests and considers the impact on both the project and the organization.

Change Management. A formal process to analyze, document, and approve all changes to a previously approved project condition. This is often referred to as *Integrated Change Management* because the analysis of changes must address the total impact on the project covering all 10 Knowledge Areas.

change request. A documented request to change a previously approved project condition.

Code of Ethics and Professional Conduct. A formal statement of how PMI members and PMI certified individuals are expected to behave. It covers responsibility, respect, fairness, and honesty.

G

Communications Management Plan. A formal document produced when developing the communications strategies for the project. The Communications Management Plan can either be a standalone document or be integrated into the Project Management Plan, depending on the project's specific needs and characteristics.

communications model. A model describing the communications process, which includes encoding, transmitting, decoding, acknowledging, and feedback.

conflict. Conflict can exist whenever two or more individuals work together for a common result. Conflict must be managed to ensure that it doesn't become destructive.

constraint. A future condition to which the project must adhere. Typically, constraints are timeframes that define a state the project must achieve for it to be considered successful.

context diagram. A diagram depicting the project scope. Context diagrams are typically drawn as a rectangle, where everything inside the rectangle is in the scope of the project and everything external is not. Key to a context diagram are the interfaces crossing the boundary of the rectangle, because these define the inputs to and outputs of the project.

contingency reserve. Typically, time and money reserved for use by the project to deal with the impacts of identified risks. Contingency reserves are identified in the Risk Response Plan and are managed by the project manager.

contract. A formal legal document defining the rights and obligations of two parties where one is the buyer and the other is the seller.

control account. A predefined management measurement where project specific costs are accumulated into a standardized control account. Control accounts are used to track and manage project performance on a standard basis across the organization.

Cost Baseline. The approved project budget. Typically, Budget Baselines are created when the project is formally approved. A baseline is not changed once it is created and is used for variance analysis against actual delivery results.

cost budget. The approved cost for the project. The budget is prepared during project planning and should contain the total costs of all work, materials, and supplies, as well as other third-party costs required to complete the project.

Cost Management Plan. A formal document produced when developing the cost management strategies for the project. The Cost Management Plan can either be a standalone document or be integrated into the Project Management Plan, depending on the project's specific needs and characteristics.

Cost of Quality. A method for tracking and measuring the costs and impacts of the project's quality system. Cost of Quality measures the cost of conformance (prevention costs) versus the cost of nonconformance (defect remediation) with the goal of increasing conformance costs to reduce nonconformance costs.

crashing. A technique to reduce the length of the project schedule by attempting to complete tasks faster, typically by adding resources or using a more efficient method of delivery.

critical path method. A schedule management technique that identifies the tasks that define the project's end date (the critical path tasks).

decomposition. A technique to break down the project WBS into smaller manageable pieces. For example, a project deliverable is decomposed into subdeliverables, which are decomposed into activities.

deliverable. A defined result delivered by a project. A deliverable can be a document, a physical product or a service. All project deliverables should directly contribute to satisfying the project's scope.

dependencies. Dependencies define a logical relationship that defines the order in which project activities can be completed. For example, building the walls of a house has a dependency that the floor must be complete before the walls can be started.

duration estimate. Duration estimates define the elapsed time (calendar time) required to complete a project activity.

Earned Value Management. A project evaluation technique that combines scope, budget, and work performance to evaluate overall project status and health.

effort estimate. Effort estimates define the amount of hands-on work time required to complete a project activity.

fast tracking. A technique to reduce the length of the project schedule by attempting to complete tasks in parallel to compress the overall project schedule.

float. Float defines the amount of time that the completion of a project task can be delayed without impacting the project end date (also called *slack*).

functional organization. An organizational structure where all staff report in a hierarchical structure to a functional manager. Functional organizations are grouped by a specialization, such as purchasing, manufacturing, or accounting.

governance. The alignment of project objectives within the larger organization.

Human Resources Management Plan. A formal document produced when developing the strategies for acquiring, developing, and managing the project team. The Human Resources Management Plan can either be a standalone document or be integrated into the Project Management Plan, depending on the project's specific needs and characteristics.

interpersonal skills. The "soft skills" required of a project manager to lead and motivate the project team. Interpersonal skills include coaching, leading, conflict resolution, motivation, training, and mentoring.

Issue Log. A log capturing the current status and next action date for all project issues.

lag. The amount of time that a successor must be delayed after the predecessor has been completed.

lead. The amount of time that a successor can start before the predecessor has completed.

G

make-or-buy analysis. A project decision about whether it is in the project's best interest for a specific activity to be completed by the project team (make) or purchased from an external supplier (buy).

management reserve. Typically, time and money reserved for use by senior management to deal with the unexpected impacts to a project's budget or schedule.

matrix organization. An organization structure where staff report to both a functional manager and a project manager. From a project management viewpoint, depending on which reporting relationship has the most power and authority, matrix organizations are referred to as *weak* (functional manager has the most power), *balanced*, or *strong* (project manager has the most power).

milestones. Specific points in the project that have significance to the team or management. A milestone is typically associated with the completion of a deliverable or project phase.

network diagram. A graphical representation of the project activities and the dependencies between the activities.

operations. The ongoing activities associated with the organization. Operations are repetitive activities that satisfy the functional objectives of the organization.

parametric estimating. An estimating technique based on using an established standard as the basis for estimating—for example, the amount of labor required to shingle one square foot of a residential roof.

PMBOK. The *Project Management Body of Knowledge* guide from the Project Management Institute. The PMBOK describes the sum of knowledge within the profession of project management.

PMI. The Project Management Institute. PMI is a not-for-profit professional organization for the project management profession with the purpose of advancing project management.

portfolios. A portfolio consists of projects, programs, sub-portfolios, and operations managed as a group to achieve strategic objectives.

Precedence Diagramming Method. A network diagramming technique where activities are shown on nodes and dependencies are shown on links between the nodes.

procurement document. A wide variety of documents created by a project to clearly define the procurement requirements. Examples of procurement documents include RFPs, RFIs, and RFQs.

Procurement Management Plan. A formal document produced when making the make-or-buy decision to formally document the items to be procured and the methods to be used during the procurement process. The Procurement Management Plan either can be a standalone document or can be integrated into the Project Management Plan, depending on the project's specific needs and characteristics.

program. A group of related projects managed together to achieve a common objective for the organization.

Program Evaluation and Review Technique (PERT). A technique for estimating activities that involves a pessimistic, most likely, and optimistic estimate. (Also called *three-point estimating.*)

progressive elaboration. An iterative method used to develop more detailed project plans because most information is obtained based on work completed to date. A common application of progressive elaboration is the development of a new project approach prior to the start of each new project lifecycle phase. (Also called *rolling-wave planning.*)

project. A temporary endeavor undertaken to create a unique product, service, or result.

project acceptor. A single individual with the power, authority, and knowledge to accept project deliverables and to make project decisions within the confines of the project scope.

project buffers. A project buffer is an allowance (typically of time) injected into the schedule to account for schedule uncertainty.

Project Charter. A Project Charter is a formal document, typically created by the business unit management, that formally introduces the project and provides the authority to begin the planning processes.

Project Communications Management. Project Communications Management identifies the processes to ensure effective project communication takes place, both inward within the project team and outward to the project stakeholders.

Project Cost Management. Project Cost Management identifies the processes to develop a complete and realistic project budget and the ongoing management activities required to manage and report on project performance against the Cost Baseline.

Project Human Resource Management. The processes to acquire, build, train, support, and maintain an effective project team.

Project Integration Management. Project Integration Management ensures that processes and activities encompassing the entire project delivery approach are delivered in an integrated fashion and that no project management actions are taken without consideration for the total project implications, including (but not limited to) scope, time, cost, and quality.

project lifecycle. The project lifecycle defines the approach or methodology to be used to execute the project.

Project Management Office. A central function in an organization focused on organizational project governance.

G

Project Management Plan. The Project Management Plan defines the overall management approach to be applied on a project. The Project Management Plan addresses the management approach from each of the 10 Knowledge Areas. Depending on the project's specific needs and characteristics, the individual management plans may be embedded directly into the Project Management Plan (typically as chapters) or as standalone documents referenced in the Project Management Plan.

Project Management Process Group. Project Management Process Groups represent the project management inputs, tools and techniques, and outputs for initiating, planning, executing, monitoring and controlling, and closing.

project manager. The single individual who has the power, authority, and responsibility to manage the assigned resources to achieve the results expected by the sponsoring business unit defined by the project scope.

Project Organization Chart. The Project Organization Chart defines the roles, responsibilities, and reporting relationships of the project team.

Project Procurement Management. Project Procurement Management defines the processes to be followed for selecting, purchasing, and managing the procurement process within a project.

Project Quality Management. Project Quality Management identifies the quality requirements for the project and then ensures that the results meet these requirements by applying the defined quality assurance and quality control processes.

Project Risk Management. Project Risk Management is focused on identifying the project's risk profile and then developing and delivering the appropriate risk management approaches to minimize the impact that risk events will have on the project's success based on the identified risk profile.

project scheduling tool. A project scheduling tool is used to automate the development of the project schedule. The WBS, estimates, and dependencies are input into the scheduling tool.

Project Scope Management. Project Scope Management is focused on defining the scope of the project and then managing the scope to ensure that the project is delivered within the defined scope. When scope changes are identified, the Change Management process is initiated to manage the changes.

project sponsor. Typically a senior business unit manager who has the power and authority to commit organizational resources to a project. The project sponsor often delegates day-to-day management to the project acceptor and gets involved only on an as-needed basis to deal with issues that cannot be addressed by the project acceptor.

Project Stakeholder Management. Project Stakeholder Management is focused on identifying all the individuals who have an interest in a project, and then manages the involvement of these individuals in the project as appropriate to maintain their commitment to the project.

Project Time Management. Project Time Management is focused on the activities associated with developing and managing the project schedule.

projectized organization. A projectized organization is focused on project delivery. In a projectized organization, staff are assigned to a project, typically on a full-time basis, and report directly and exclusively to a project manager.

Qualitative Risk Analysis. Qualitative risk management analyzes risks based on factors such as probability and impact to determine the potential impact or priority of each risk event analyzed. Risk probability/impact matrices are common qualitative risk management approaches.

Quality assurance. Quality assurance is focused on ensuring that the project follows the processes and procedures defined for it.

Quality audit. Quality audits are typically performed by an independent third party and focus on reviewing the adherence to the quality assurance and quality control processes, as well as evaluating the effectiveness of these defined processes.

quality control. Quality control is focused on ensuring that the results of the project activities will satisfy the project requirements.

Quality Management Plan. A formal document explaining the quality and grade requirements as well as the policies and procedures to be applied to ensure that these requirements are satisfied. The Quality Management Plan can either be a standalone document or be integrated into the Project Management Plan, depending on the project's specific needs and characteristics.

Quantitative Risk Analysis. Quantitative risk management analyzes risks based on established modeling and/or other numerical analysis methods and is used to determine the potential impact or priority of each risk event analyzed. Monte Carlo simulations are a common quantitative risk management approach.

RACI chart. A RACI (Responsible, Accountable, Consulted, and Informed) chart is used to assign roles and responsibilities to project components, typically activities and deliverables. The RACI chart clearly documents the involvement each team member has for the completion of the activities and deliverables.

Requirements Management Plan. A Requirements Management Plan documents the processes and procedures that will be used to document, trace, and manage the project's activities to satisfy all documented requirements.

Requirements Traceability Matrix. A Requirements Traceability Matrix (RTM) is used to trace how every requirement is documented, confirmed, clarified, delivered, and tested through the life of the project.

resource leveling. Resource leveling ensures that project team members are not allocated to work more hours than their allocation to the project defines.

G

resource smoothing. Resource smoothing balances the workload across project team members to ensure that all team members are used at their full allocation levels.

risk. An unknown future event that, if it occurs, would have a negative impact on the project.

Risk Management Plan. A formal document explaining how risks are to be identified, validated, and managed. The Risk Management Plan can either be a standalone document or be integrated into the Project Management Plan, depending on the project's specific needs and characteristics.

risk mitigation strategy. Once a risk has been fully analyzed (qualitative and/or quantitative) and remains a concern to the project, a risk mitigation strategy should be developed to identify what proactive actions the project can take to eliminate or minimize the potential impact the risk could have on the project. Risk mitigation strategies are eliminate, transfer, mitigate, or accept.

Risk Register. The Risk Register tracks all identified risks and records the results of the analysis and mitigation strategies as well as the current status and actions being taken.

risk tolerance. The "appetite" for risk on the project. Projects can be risk seeking, risk neutral, or risk averse.

rolling-wave planning. Rolling-wave planning is used to develop more detailed project plans because most information is obtained based on work completed to date. A common application of rolling-wave planning is the development of a new project approach prior to the start of each new project lifecycle phase. (Also called *progressive elaboration*.)

schedule. The schedule identifies the sequence and timeframe of when each WBS activity is to be completed.

Schedule Management Plan. A formal document explaining how the schedule is to be created and maintained. The Schedule Management Plan can either be a standalone document or be integrated into the Project Management Plan, depending on the project's specific needs and characteristics.

schedule model. A model/template schedule that can be used as a starting point for the development of a project schedule. The schedule contains all the key project components to help ensure that the resultant schedule is complete.

Scope Management Plan. A formal document explaining how the scope is to be identified, documented, validated, and managed. The Scope Management Plan can either be a standalone document or be integrated into the Project Management Plan, depending on the project's specific needs and characteristics.

Scope Statement. A clear and unambiguous statement of all the work (typically represented as deliverables) that the project has to produce to satisfy the business unit requirements.

secondary risk. A new risk created/identified as a risk mitigation plan is implemented.

slack. The amount of time that the completion of a project task can be delayed without impacting the project end date. (Also called *float*.)

staffing plan. Identifies the team member start and finish dates for a project.

stakeholder. Any individual (or group) who will be impacted in some way by a project.

stakeholder register. The stakeholder register identifies all project stakeholders as well as their interest, influence, and information requirements related to the project.

Statement of Work. A narrative describing the products, services, or results of a project. Statements of Work are often associated with procurement contracts to define what the project is procuring.

three-point estimating. A technique for estimating activities that involves a pessimistic, a most likely, and an optimistic estimate. [Also called *Program Evaluation and Review Technique (PERT)*.]

Tuckman model. A commonly applied team formulation model developed by Bruce Tuckman. It defines the team formulation as forming, storming, norming, performing, and adjourning.

virtual team. Virtual teams consist of team members who are not located at a single location. As a result of not being co-located, virtual teams need to use communication technology more extensively than co-located teams in order to function as a team.

WBS Dictionary. The WBS Dictionary contains detailed information about every component of the Work Breakdown Structure.

Work Breakdown Structure. A hierarchical decomposition of the project scope into deliverables, components, activity groups, and activities. The lowest level of the WBS, the activity, identifies a discrete unit of work to be performed by a team member.

work packages. A work package is the lowest level of the WBS for which cost and duration estimates are defined. (Also called *activities*.)

work performance data. The raw data of the performance measures related to team members completing WBS activities, such as timesheet hours worked and material consumption.

G

A

ANSWERS AND JUSTIFICATIONS

This appendix provides the answers and justifications for the questions in this book.

CHAPTER 1: PRE-TEST

Question	Chapter	Answer	Justification
1	5	B	The three-point estimating technique involves optimistic, pessimistic, and most likely estimates, which are then combined into a single estimate using the formula Estimate = (Optimistic + Most Likely + Pessimistic) / 3
2	2	A	A controlling PMO ensures compliance to established project management processes.
3	10	C	Planning risk responses takes place once Qualitative and Quantitative Risk Analysis are complete to ensure that strategies are documented for dealing with all high-priority risks on the project. This may involve changing the project approach to eliminate the possibility of a risk, introducing mitigation activities to minimize the probability or impact of a risk, and/or ensuring that time and budget contingency is planned in to deal with the risk, should it happen.
4	12	D	The five stakeholder engagement levels are: unaware, resistant, neutral, supportive, and leading.
5	8	F	Positive team environments are created by any number of factors that support both individual and team performance.

A

Question	Chapter	Answer	Justification
6	11	E	Contracts are required only for items where a formal definition of the procurement process is required. If the project will require periodic purchases of printer paper from a local office-supply store, a contract is not required, but the procurement process is still managed to ensure that there are funds available in the budget and that the purchases are managed by the project.
7	7	B	Cause-and-effect diagrams, such as the fishbone/Ishikawa diagrams, place the problem at the head of the diagram and then trace the problem back through all identifiable causes.
8	5	C	In a start-to-start dependency relationship, the first activity must be started before the second activity can start. For example, the house must be started before the inspections can begin.
9	3	D	While it is important to ensure that project management and other "overhead activities" are included in the WBS, they are included by identifying the required project management deliverables and including them in the deliverable list.
10	12	B	B is the best answer because it documents the complete stakeholder analysis process, which includes classifying the stakeholders and determining the power their positions may give them.
11	10	B	Project Risk Management is focused on taking proactive steps to ensure that positive events happen and that negative events don't happen. This could be as a result of changing the project approach to include/exclude the risk events altogether or by taking mitigation actions to increase/decrease the probability of the events occurring. When the project has no opportunity to influence the events, contingency is added to minimize the impact the events will have on successful completion of the project.
12	3	B	Product scope can be and often is broader than project scope—a product may contain several projects, which combine to address the larger product scope.
13	3	C	Develop Project Charter is focused on developing a document (the Project Charter) that formally authorizes the existence of a project. This also provides the project manager with the authority to apply organizational resources (time and money) to project activities.

Question	Chapter	Answer	Justification
14	6	E	Earned Value Management is a key principle defined in controlling project costs. It combines cost, schedule, and resource measurements to determine overall project performance.
15	9	E	The number of communications channels is calculated using the formula $n(n-1)/2$. In this case, it is $6 \star 5 / 2$.
16	8	D	A RACI chart, which is a form of matrix-based responsibility chart, is used to identify the resource that is Responsible (does the work), Accountable (accepts the work), Consulted (subject-matter expert), and Informed (interested bystander!). A RACI chart is an excellent tool for clearly identifying roles and responsibilities for a project where the activities are derived from the WBS and the RACI elements are based on the project organization.
17	2	B	When one item of the project triple constraints changes, at least one of the other constraints will change in the same direction. In the question, where scope has increased, either the schedule or the cost (or both) will have to increase to provide the capacity to deliver the increased scope.
18	6	E	The Cost Management Plan establishes the policies and procedures for planning, managing, expending, and controlling the project costs. Approval of the Cost Management Plan is done by management and not documented in the plan itself.
19	2	D	The PMI Code of Ethics and Professional Conduct defines the basic obligations of responsibility, respect, fairness, and honesty.
20	2	B	In a weak matrix organization, the primary reporting relationship remains with the functional manager. Project availability and reporting is secondary to the primary job responsibilities.
21	3	F	Inputs to the Scope Management Plan include the Project Management Plan, Project Charter, Enterprise Environmental Factors, and Organizational Process Assets.
22	10	B	Known risk at an activity level should have a contingency reserve assigned to it. The contingency reserve can be consumed if the risk event takes place.

A

Question	Chapter	Answer	Justification
23	5	C	Work packages is a higher-level definition of the WBS. Activities are children of work packages. Once the WBS is entered into the project scheduling tool, these terms typically are no longer used, and they are all simply WBS levels.
24	3	E	The Project Management Plan consolidates the management plans from all Knowledge Areas to ensure a comprehensive Project Management Plan exists. The Project Management Plan is one of the primary processes (Develop Project Management Plan) in the Integration Management Knowledge Area.
25	11	B	A fixed-price contract defines an agreed result for an agreed cost.
26	8	B	While C is also a correct answer, B is the better answer because the goal of the human resource plan is to define specific unique training requirements that must be provided prior to team members joining the project. While there may be specific resource training requirements needed due to skill gaps, these are typically addressed once the team members are identified and assigned, and not as part of the human resource plan.
27	2	D	According to the PMI Code of Ethics and Professional Conduct, respect is showing a high regard for ourselves, others, and the resources entrusted to us. Resources entrusted to us include people, money, reputation, the safety of others, and natural or environmental resources.
28	9	E	Project Communications Management is focused on all aspects of communication within a project: internal/external, formal/informal, and written/verbal. Project Communications Management ensures that the right information is provided to the right stakeholders in the right format at the right time.
29	6	B and D	Contingencies for known-unknowns should be allocated to the specific risk event. An additional project-wide contingency is required for unknown-unknowns.
30	2	A	Risk and uncertainty are typically highest at project startup, because there are so many unknowns. As the project progresses, risk and uncertainty typically decrease.

Question	Chapter	Answer	Justification
31	9	C	A message that is not understood because the receiver was not able to understand what the message meant suffers from decoding issues, whether it is the result of language, education, technical jargon, and so on.
32	10	C	During risk planning, it is important to identify any and all risks that could impact the project. Perform Quantitative and Perform Qualitative Risk Analysis will determine the appropriateness of the risks.
33	3	E	Perform Integrated Change Control is performed at any time in the project when a change to an approved project condition is detected. Perform Integrate Change Control ensures that all identified changes are documented and approved prior to introduction into the project.
34	7	E	E is the best answer because Project Quality Management is focused on ensuring that the project satisfies the business requirements from a completeness and accuracy standpoint. Defining quality assurance and quality control are the methods applied to satisfy the requirements. Project Quality Management will ensure that the processes applied are consistent with expectations. For example, the project can be determined a success with known defects, provided that is consistent with expectations—such as no more than 10 cosmetic defects (paint chips) in a new home.
35	2	E	Lessons learned are documented as part of the closing process. Lessons learned are part of the review processes conducted during the closing process.
36	2	A	In a functional organization, the project manager has little to no authority because the team members retain full reporting to their existing functional managers.
37	3	B	While both B and C are technically correct, the PMI exams are famous for their "best answer" approach. So technically, B is the better answer because the Requirements Traceability Matrix will be maintained throughout the project and therefore would be better supported with a spreadsheet versus paper for ongoing ease of maintenance.

A

Question	Chapter	Answer	Justification
38	5	D	While Develop Schedule is primarily a planning activity, it does occur throughout the project whenever a significant change to the schedule is required, either as a result of a Project Change Request or simply due to changes associated with project delivery. Develop Schedule is an iterative process, as the schedule will require refinement by changing resource allocations, refining estimates and dependencies, and so on to allow the project to change to correspond with overall project constraints. Develop Schedule requires input from all Project Time Management planning processes and will require constant interaction with these processes as the schedule refinements take place.
39	3	C	The WBS is an evolutionary document that originates in scope planning based on the deliverables identified in the Project Scope Statement. Having the WBS based on the deliverables helps ensure that all the work and only the work required to complete the project deliverables is identified. While the WBS will be decomposed into lower-level tasks during Project Time Management, it should initially be based on the deliverables.
40	12	B	Project stakeholders are any individuals who have a specific interest in the project. They are typically individuals who could impact or be impacted by the project.
41	8	E	Project Human Resource Management must be integrated across all Knowledge Areas, because any change to the project team could directly impact the schedule, budget, quality, risk, and so on. A new team member would have different skills, charge rates, and ability to complete assigned tasks, and therefore could impact many of the other components of the project.
42	11	E	Procurement management covers the complete spectrum of acquiring any items that the project requires from a third party. This begins with identifying the items that cannot be produced by the project team, determining the best way to acquire the needed items, developing the purchase terms (contracts), and finally managing the purchase of the items.
43	3	F	Requirements form the foundation for all project planning activities, and while they support the subsequent development for all Knowledge Areas, requirements are specifically prerequisites for WBS, budget, schedule, quality, and depending on the project, procurement.

Question	Chapter	Answer	Justification
44	2	D	Leadership involves focusing the team toward a common goal and enabling them to work as a team.
45	10	B	Qualitative Risk Analysis is typically the first analysis completed on new risks because it is a very rapid and cost-effective way of determining the priority of risks. That way, if the risk is determined to be of low priority, no additional time or attention needs to be paid to it.
46	3	D	Project deliverables can be printed documents, electronically delivered (video, computer-based training [CBT], audio), computer code, and so on. Deliverables are defined during project planning and address the specific requirements defined for the project.
47	5	B	Plan Schedule Management establishes the policies and procedures for planning, developing, managing, executing, and controlling the project schedule. It does not define how to use an automated scheduling tool.
48	5	E	While project scheduling software has complex algorithms for managing resource leveling, the project manager should be keenly aware of what is being done and the impact it has on the project schedule. This technique is typically used to level the load on specific resources to ensure that resources are not over-allocated. This typically extends the project schedule, as activities must be moved forward to reduce over-allocation of resources.
49	7	C	Quality assurance is focused on ensuring that the project does the right things (that is, follows the quality processes), and quality control is focused on ensuring that the project deliverables meet the requirements.
50	12	C	Stakeholder management will typically result in updates to the Issue Log because issues are opened, managed, and closed. It may require the issuance of a change request to change the project delivery approach and updates to the Communications Management Plan and stakeholder register because the stakeholder management process is continuously improved to ensure the highest possible level of stakeholder engagement.

A

Use the following table to validate your overall performance on this test as a whole and on a chapter-by-chapter basis. To complete this table, you will need to count the number of correct answers for the entire test as well as the number of right answers by chapter (column 2).

Test Section	Number of Questions Right	Total Questions Available	Score Calculation	Your Score
Total Test		50	Your Answer ★ 2	
Chapter 2		9	Your Answer ★ 11.11	
Chapter 3		4	Your Answer ★ 25	
Chapter 4		6	Your Answer ★ 16.67	
Chapter 5		6	Your Answer ★ 16.67	
Chapter 6		3	Your Answer ★ 33.33	
Chapter 7		3	Your Answer ★ 33.33	
Chapter 8		4	Your Answer ★ 25	
Chapter 9		3	Your Answer ★ 33.33	
Chapter 10		5	Your Answer ★ 20	
Chapter 11		3	Your Answer ★ 33.33	
Chapter 12		4	Your Answer ★ 25	

As mentioned in the Introduction, for several chapters the number of questions is relatively low, so your test results can move from 33 percent to 66 percent with as little as a single right/wrong answer. The distribution of questions is based on an expectation of how PMI will distribute the questions given the defined PMI distribution of questions based on the five Project Management Process Groups.

- Initiating: 13%
- Planning: 24%
- Executing: 30%
- Monitoring and Controlling: 25%
- Closing: 8%

Your actual distribution on your certification exam may vary from this. This distribution was designed to make exam preparation easier, as it aligns more closely with the PMBOK.

CHAPTER 2: PROJECT MANAGEMENT PROCESSES, ORGANIZATIONAL STRUCTURES, AND PROFESSIONALISM

Question	Answer	Justification
1	B	The PMI Code of Ethics and Professional Conduct guides practitioners of the profession and describes the expectations that practitioners should hold for themselves and others.
2	E	The PMBOK defines a project as a temporary endeavor to create a unique product, service, or result.
3	B	A project is temporary and focused on producing the unique result for which it was started. Operations refers to the ongoing operation of the company and typically involves producing a similar result on a recurring basis.
4	A	Portfolios refer to collections of projects, programs, sub-portfolios, or operations managed as a group to achieve strategic objectives. A program is composed of subprograms, projects, or other related work. A project achieves a defined and unique result.
5	C	The PMBOK defines the five project management processes as Initiating, Planning, Executing, Monitoring and Controlling, and Closing.
6	C	The PMBOK defines scope, quality, schedule, budget, resources, and risks as the main competing project constraints.
7	D	It is important for the project acceptor to define which of scope, time, or cost has the most flexibility to allow the project manager to define the optimal solution for managing project changes. For example, if the project acceptor defines cost as the most flexible, then the project manager will explore ways in which a change to scope or schedule can be controlled by increasing the cost of the project—for example, by adding another team member.
8	A	Progressive elaboration involves continuously evolving the project plan as more details become available, typically on a project-phase-by-project-phase basis.
9	B	Programs expect change from both inside and outside and are prepared to manage it.
10	C	Project success is measured by delivery of product and product quality, timeliness, budget compliance, and degree of customer satisfaction.
11	D	Program success is measured by the degree to which the program satisfies the needs and benefits for which it was undertaken.

A

Question	Answer	Justification
12	E	Portfolio success is measured in terms of the aggregate investment performance and benefit realization of the portfolio.
13	C	PMOs are typically classified as supportive, controlling, and directive.
14	D	A supportive PMO provides support to the project through the provision of templates, best practices, training, coaching, and other activities to help the project manager be more effective.
15	B	A directive PMO takes control and manages projects.
16	D	Operations management is responsible for overseeing, directing, and controlling business operations. Operations support the day-to-day operation of the business.
17	D	The main overlap between projects and operations occurs at the end of a phase and especially at the end of a project, when the project results are passed over to operations for ongoing use in the organization through knowledge transfer and ownership of the project deliverables. As well, projects may be undertaken to specifically develop a product or service to allow operations to be more efficient. In this case, the operations department becomes the business unit for which the project is being delivered.
18	B	Operations management should be included as part of stakeholder identification and included in the project at the appropriate level based on the project's characteristics.
19	C	A PBO conducts the majority of its work as projects and/or provides project services rather than functional approaches.
20	A	All projects should be aligned with organizational strategy to ensure that the project is consistent with the organization's direction. If the project is focused on breakthrough strategies, the project will not fit into an organization that is very conservative and focuses on cost reduction.
21	C	The PMBOK defines the following as the key competencies for a project manager: knowledge about project management, performance in the project management role, and personal interactions with the team and the stakeholders.
22	D	A project manager does not need requirements analysis skills, because requirements analysis is work completed by a team member, not a project manager. The PMBOK defines the skills needed by a project manager as leadership, team building, motivation, communication, influencing, decision making, political and cultural awareness, negotiating, trust building, conflict management, and coaching.

Question	Answer	Justification
23	C	All projects should be aligned with organizational culture to ensure that there is an understanding of values, priorities, and decision-making processes.
24	B	Functional, weak matrix, balanced matrix, strong matrix, and projectized are the recognized organizational structures.
25	D	In a strong matrix organization, the project manager has moderate to high authority because while the team members retain some reporting to their functional managers, the project manager has control over the team members and the ability to escalate issues to senior management.
26	C	In a balanced matrix organization, the project manager has the same level of authority over resource allocations as do the functional managers.
27	D	In a strong matrix organization, the project manager is fully responsible for the project budget.
28	B	In a functional organization, each member of the functional unit has a strong reporting relationship within the functional unit.
29	C	Functional organizations are typically structured by specialty—for example, engineering, production, or marketing.
30	E	In a balanced matrix organization, the project manager and functional manager work together to ensure that the staff support both functional and project requirements.
31	C	In a strong matrix organization, the project manager and functional manager work together to ensure that staff support both functional and project requirements, much like in a balanced matrix. However, in a strong matrix the project manager reports outside of the functional areas and has the ability to escalate issues to senior management when resource conflicts materialize.
32	A	In a weak matrix organization, the role of project manager is often not formally recognized and is often filled by a team member functioning more as a coordinator than as a project manager because he or she has limited to no power and authority over assigned staff.
33	D	In a balanced matrix organization, the role of project manager is filled by a member of the functional unit for which the project is being delivered. As a result, the project manager typically has moderate power and authority over staff from within the same functional area, but often has little more than a coordination role over staff from other functional areas.

A

Question	Answer	Justification
34	B	In a strong matrix organization, the role of project manager is filled from a separate functional area that focuses on project management (often a PMO). Because the project manager reports outside of the functional areas, he or she has the ability to escalate staffing issues outside the functional areas.
35	C	In a projectized organization, both the project manager and the team are assigned to a project. At the end of the assignment, both the project manager and the team are available for work on other projects.
36	D	The project sponsor is the individual, typically a senior manager, who has the power and authority to provide resources for the project and is able to make decisions to enable project success.
37	B	The project governance framework provides the project manager and the team with structure, processes, decision-making models, and tools for managing the project. It includes the processes for making decisions and defines roles, responsibilities, and accountability levels.
38	E	While E may sound like a weak answer; it is the best answer because the project lifecycle will vary depending on the type of project. For example, a software development project will have a different project lifecycle than a highway construction project.
39	B	Project lifecycles range from predictive and plan-driven, which define the entire project at the beginning, to adaptive and change-driven, which typically define the next phase of the project only.
40	B	A project lifecycle defines the activities that must be completed to satisfy the project objectives. The Project Management Process Groups define the project management activities that are repeated within each phase of the project lifecycle.
41	E	Cost of changes is typically highest at project completion because any change at that point will require a substantial retrofit. As the project progresses, cost of changes typically increases, most specifically after the design is completed.
42	B	A phase for a large project may take months or even years to complete. Therefore, the work may not be completed over a short timeframe.
43	A	A predictive lifecycle, which is also known as *plan-driven*, follows a defined set of phases where the scope, time, and schedule are planned early in the project lifecycle. Phases within a predictive lifecycle can be sequential or overlapped. Predictive lifecycles can also use a rolling-wave planning approach where more detailed plans are developed at the beginning of each phase.

Question	Answer	Justification
44	B	An iterative lifecycle, which is also known as *incremental*, intentionally repeats project phases to increase the understanding of the project and incrementally deliver the project. Phases within an iterative lifecycle can be sequential or overlapped.
45	E	An adaptive lifecycle, which is also known as *agile*, uses a series of very short iterations to incrementally deliver the project in very small increments.
46	C	An adaptive lifecycle is used when there is an expectation of very high levels of change. An adaptive lifecycle fixes the scope for each iteration (two to four weeks) and then allows for changes prior to developing the plan for the next iteration.
47	C	The Project Management Process Groups are initiating, planning, executing, monitoring and controlling, and closing.
48	D	Each phase or project should begin with the initiating processes, followed by planning and executing as repeating processes during delivery, with the closing processes terminating the phase or project. The monitoring and controlling processes should be performed throughout the entire phase.
49	A	The Project Charter is created as part of the initiating process. The Project Charter documents the results of the initiating process and is used to formally approve the project.
50	D	Ongoing risk management is completed as part of the monitoring and controlling process. Monitoring and controlling is focused on the project management activities required for successful project delivery.
51	C	Project deliverables are created during the executing process. The executing process is when the "project work" to achieve the project objectives is completed.
52	A	The Communications Management Plan, as with all management plans, is created as part of the initiating process. The planning process defines the approaches to be followed during the executing processes and forms the basis for the monitoring and controlling processes.
53	C	All project deliverables should be completed before the closing processes are started.
54	D	Obtaining acceptance of individual project deliverables is part of the Monitoring and Controlling Project Management Process Group. Obtaining final project acceptance, which encompasses all the individual deliverable acceptances, is part of the Closing Project Management Process Group.

A

Question	Answer	Justification
55	A	Work performance data are the raw facts gathered during project delivery based on measurements of work performed.
56	C	Work performance information results when work performance data are analyzed and compared to expected performance targets.
57	D	Work performance reports are the presentation of work performance information in the form of reports, presentations, or notes to stakeholders.
58	B	The main integration between the process groups is through inputs and outputs. For example, the output of the Initiating process group becomes the input to the Planning process group, and the output of the Executing process group is the input to the Closing process group.
59	E	Team building is the process of helping the team work together as a cohesive unit toward achieving the common project goals.
60	B	Team-building activities include such things as obtaining management support, encouraging team-member commitment, introducing appropriate rewards and recognition, creating a team identity, managing conflicts effectively, promoting trust, and encouraging open communication.
61	E	Team motivation is based on creating an environment that provides satisfaction to the team members. While a comfortable chair may make the workplace more enjoyable, it would not be a key motivator for high levels of team performance.
62	A	Effective communication within the project team and with the project stakeholders has been identified as the single biggest reason why projects succeed. Openness in communication ensures that all project participants have access to the information they need to help the project be a success. Openness in communication creates trust.
63	C	The four styles of decision making are command, consultation, consensus, and random (coin-flip).
64	E	The six steps of the decision-making model are problem definition, problem solution generation, ideas to action, solution action planning, solution evaluation planning, and evaluation of outcome and process.
65	D	The PMI Code of Ethics and Professional Conduct is based on responsibility, respect, fairness, and honesty.
66	C	The PMI Code of Ethics and Professional Conduct defines responsibility as taking ownership of the decisions we make or fail to make, the actions we take or fail to take, and the consequences of the result.

Question	Answer	Justification
67	C	The laws of each country are unique, and you should never assume that what may be considered a bribe in your own country is not a valid request in another. Therefore, you should validate the legality of the request.
68	B	The PMI Code of Ethics and Professional Conduct for responsibility states that you should only accept assignments that are consistent with your background, skills, and qualifications.
69	D	According to the PMI Code of Ethics and Professional Conduct, fairness is making decisions and acting impartially and objectively. Our conduct must be free from competing self-interest, prejudice, and favoritism.
70	D	As a PMI member, you are obligated to declare conflicts of interest, either personal or professional, and excuse yourself from the issue.
71	C	According to the PMI Code of Ethics and Professional Conduct, honesty is understanding the truth and acting in a truthful manner in our communications and in our conduct.
72	B	In a projectized organization, the project manager has the most power because he or she should be fully empowered to make project-based decisions.
73	C	In a functional environment, the functional manager has the most power because staff in the functional unit report to the functional manager.
74	D	The project schedule cannot be developed until the Work Breakdown Structure is completed, as the WBS defines all the activities that must be scheduled.
75	B	With the Project Charter approved, the project moves from initiating to planning. One of the first activities in planning is to define the project scope.
76	A	The optimal time to assign a project manager to a project is during initiation, because this ensures that all the project management activities in initiating are completed and ensures continuity when the project moves into planning.
77	C	The executing process typically requires the most time and resources, because this is the process where the project team is fully staffed and working on producing the required project deliverables.
78	D	A work authorization system ensures that the right resources work on the right WBS activities in the right order, because all work assignments must be made using the work authorization system, which is tightly connected to the project schedule.

A

Question	Answer	Justification
79	D	The Cost Baseline reflects the total amount of the project that is controlled by the project manager. Because the project manager does not control the management reserve, it is not included in the Cost Baseline.
80	D	The formal acceptance of the Project Charter signifies that senior management has approved the Project Charter, and therefore it is the official start of the project.
81	A	A constraint is a preexisting condition that must be met; otherwise, there will be some unwanted project consequences.
82	C	All projects, even cancelled projects, should have all closing processes completed to ensure that lessons learned are completed, staff performance evaluations are written, and reusable artifacts are collected. Many project managers feel there is more value in the closing processes for cancelled projects than for successful projects because there should be valuable lessons learned on why the project was cancelled.
83	C	The Requirements Traceability Matrix is used to trace all requirements from the original Scope Statement through all project development activities, including testing. The Requirements Traceability Matrix has nothing to do with project risks.
84	D	The PMI Code of Ethics and Professional Conduct requires full disclosure of any potential conflicts of interest.
85	A	The project Work Breakdown Structure identifies the work required to complete all the deliverables that satisfy the project's scope.
86	C	The Validate Scope process is focused on obtaining acceptance of each project deliverable as it is produced.
87	C	No matter the urgency or importance of any change, the Perform Integrate Change Control process must always be applied to ensure a full understanding of the change and its impacts before any work is initiated.
88	C	Because no one seemed to be offended by the story, publicly and immediately dealing with the storyteller would be an extreme measure, but the offense should definitely be dealt with in private to ensure that it does not happen again. If you notice that other team members begin to follow this example, it must be dealt with in a larger audience, but for a one-time, seemingly minor issue, a private discussion should be sufficient.

CHAPTER 3: PROJECT INTEGRATION MANAGEMENT

Question	Answer	Justification
1	C	Project Integration Management consists of the following processes: Develop Project Charter, Develop Project Management Plan, Direct and Manage Project Work, Monitor and Control Project Work, Perform Integrated Control, and Close Project or Phase.
2	B	Project Integration Management consists of the following processes: Develop Project Charter, Develop Project Management Plan, Direct and Manage Project Work, Monitor and Control Project Work, Perform Integrated Control, and Close Project or Phase. Manage and Control Project Team is not a valid process name.
3	B	Project Integration Management is necessary in situations where individual processes interact to ensure that the result has a full project view. Project Integration Management ensures that all related Knowledge Areas are applied for each project action—a risk mitigation plan may impact scope, time, cost, and human resources, for example.
4	B	The Develop Project Charter inputs are the Project Statement of Work, Business Case, Agreements, Enterprise Environmental Factors, and Organizational Process Assets.
5	C	A project manager is identified and assigned as early in the project as is feasible, preferably while the Project Charter is being developed and always prior to the start of planning.
6	E	The Sponsoring entity is responsible for the Project Charter. Because the Project Charter is primarily a business document, it is signed by the project sponsor—typically senior management, thus making it a formal document.
7	C	The SOW is a narrative description of products, services, or results to be delivered by the project. The SOW references the business need, project scope description, and strategic plan. The SOW defines what the business is requesting and why the request is important to them.
8	B	The Business Case is an input to the Develop Project Charter process.
9	C	The Project Charter would contain a summary milestone schedule. The detailed project schedule is developed during the planning phase of the project.
10	B	The Project Management Plan covers the complete project cycle.

A

Question	Answer	Justification
11	A	The Project Management Plan may require changes during any phase of the project. While the number of changes that would occur during closing is typically very limited, the possibility exists that a significant project event could occur during closing that would require an update to the Project Management Plan.
12	E	Any element of the Project Management Plan can be delivered as a subsidiary plan if it aids in overall usability of either the main or subsidiary plan.
13	A	Once the Project Management Plan is approved and signed off, all subsequent changes must be processed through a formal change request. Therefore, the only time when a change request is not required is during the initial creation, before the Project Management Plan is approved.
14	E	Direct and Manage Project Work is focused on leading and performing all the work defined in the Project Management Plan; therefore, it covers every Knowledge Area.
15	C	While Direct and Manage Project Work is focused on all activities associated with completing the project work, the main focus is the production of the project deliverables.
16	B	While your project may and will likely have status update meetings, status update meetings are not formally defined by PMI as part of the meeting technique. This is because the meeting technique is focused on obtaining the information needed to move forward with the work required to complete the project deliverables.
17	C	Meetings are most successful when the agenda is published in advance, participants are controlled, and the meetings are scheduled ahead of time to ensure that all participants are prepared.
18	B	Work performance data include any and all data that can be used to measure project performance. This can include schedule and budget information as well as defect details, quality measurements, and so on.
19	C	Change is inevitable on a project; changes will occur on a daily basis as the team works on producing a project deliverable. Change requests are required only when a change happens on a component of the project that has previously been accepted. Change requests can document budget changes or schedule changes, or simply record a change in a decision documented in a deliverable. Some changes are merely reactions to existing environments and could be already planned for or realized in the Risk Plan.
20	D	Monitor and Control Project Work is a process in the Project Integration Management Knowledge Area.

Question	Answer	Justification
21	C	Monitor and Control Project Work is focused on analysis and decision making based on the project performance data.
22	D	Anyone involved in the project can and should initiate a Project Change Request when a change is identified.
23	D	The Scope Management Plan should identify the individuals who can approve Project Change Requests.
24	C	All project documents impacted by an approved change, either current or previously approved, need to be updated to reflect the approved changes.
25	E	All changes to approved project conditions must be managed through a formal change process.
26	D	The Scope or Change Management Plan defines the processes to be followed for managing change on the project. The plan will identify the processes and procedures that the project must follow for processing changes.
27	D	A Project Change Log tracks all changes initiated for the project and is used to track and manage all changes as they move from initiated to approved/cancelled.
28	E	The closing activities should be completed at the end of each phase of a project to ensure that lessons learned are captured and that the work for the phase being completed is completed and made available to the organization.
29	D	Lessons learned are part of project closing to ensure that good practices are repeated and bad practices are improved.
30	B	The first step of any change, no matter the origin, is to evaluate the full impact that the change will have on the project.
31	D	If the project acceptor is unhappy, meeting with that person to understand his or her concerns should be one of the first things you do.
32	B	The Integrated Change Management process should be applied to all changes to ensure that the full impact of the change is considered for all Knowledge Areas.
33	D	A Change Control Board is composed of senior management representing all areas of the company who meet to review and approve all changes for all projects.
34	D	Close Project or Phase is applicable when a phase or project is being completed.

A

CHAPTER 4: PROJECT SCOPE MANAGEMENT

Question	Answer	Justification
1	C	Project Scope Management is about defining both what is in and what is not in scope for the project. Often defining what is *not* in scope does a better job of defining the scope of the project than providing an explicit definition of what *is* in scope. Project Scope Management is also concerned with controlling the scope of the project to ensure that the project delivers all of the scope and only the scope.
2	D	The Project Scope Baseline is initially set (and approved) during project planning. It is maintained for every approved change request to ensure that it continues to reflect the currently approved project scope.
3	B	The Project Scope Baseline is the foundation on which the project is controlled. While every effort should be made to make it accurate and complete during planning, change is inevitable, and therefore it becomes the basis for the Validate Scope and Control Scope processes.
4	B	The Scope Management Plan is a subsidiary of the Project Management Plan. The Project Management Plan defines how the project will be delivered and addresses all Knowledge Areas, while the Scope Management Plan addresses only scope.
5	J	The Scope Management Plan is mandatory on all projects. It can be produced as a standalone document or integrated into the Project Management Plan, depending on size, complexity, and overall project requirements.
6	C	Scope creep is inevitable, but with a well-defined Scope Management Plan, the project has predefined the processes for managing scope and processing Project Change Requests, and therefore positions the project to effectively control the project's scope.
7	C	The Scope Management Plan focuses on preparing the Project Scope Statement, creating the WBS, maintaining the WBS, accepting project deliverables, and processing changes to the project scope.
8	I	The Requirements Management Plan includes how requirements will be planned, tracked, and reported; configuration management processes; requirements prioritization processes; requirements metrics; and requirements traceability processes.

Question	Answer	Justification
9	A	While requirements are collected throughout the project, the high-level requirements *must* be captured during project planning to ensure that the project scope addresses all the project requirements—therefore, it is a planning activity. Subsequent requirements collection during execution should not identify new requirements (and if it does, a change request will be required), but rather should identify the details of the requirements identified during planning.
10	C	The requirements defined during planning must identify the needs and expectations of the business and form the basis for all subsequent planning activities. Requirements should be clearly documented and should include the "acceptance criteria," which will be used to confirm that the requirements have been met.
11	B	While project statements should be ignored, target dates and/or budget constraints are not project requirements. Target dates and budget constraints are important later in the planning process, when evaluating the feasibility of the project plan developed based on the identified requirements.
12	C	The PMBOK defines the following as appropriate techniques for collecting requirements: interviews, focus groups, facilitated workshops, group creativity techniques, group decision-making techniques, questionnaires and surveys, observations, prototypes, benchmarking, context diagrams, and document analysis. Requirements must be based on business needs. Web searches would be appropriate for identifying solutions for requirements.
13	F	Interviews can be both formal and informal. Interviews can follow a script, but they also can deviate to allow for spontaneous questions to further elicit a response.
14	D	Focus groups require a skilled moderator to ensure that they stay on track and that the goals are achieved. A well-moderated focus group will allow for the participants to explore new areas and achieve additional unexpected benefits.
15	C	With a skilled facilitator, facilitated workshops can be very effective for reconciling differences between stakeholders and/or business units.
16	B	Requirements review is typically an individual action where a document or presentation is reviewed for accuracy and completeness.
17	E	Group decision-making techniques include unanimity, majority, plurality, and dictatorship. Each method has advantages and disadvantages.

A

Question	Answer	Justification
18	E	Questionnaires and surveys are written sets of questions that can be distributed to a wide audience and require a limited response time. When designed appropriately, responses can be analyzed with numerical and statistical analysis methods.
19	B	One of the main disadvantages of the observations technique is that many people behave differently when they know they are being observed, and they complete their jobs as they think the job should be done, instead of how it's done every day.
20	A	Prototypes involve building a model to allow for direct observation of how the final product will look or act. They are often throw-away assets used just to identify and define requirements. Prototypes typically involve several iterations to refine the requirements to a complete state. It generally involves special skills from one or more project team members to actually develop the prototype.
21	G	Benchmarking will compare the actual results of the project against an established "norm." It is important to understand the area being benchmarked to ensure that relevant standards are being applied.
22	E	Document analysis involves reading existing documentation to determine requirements. As such, the value of this is directly related to the quality of the existing documents. Document analysis is often used as the first step in the requirements process to orient the project team to the overall business needs.
23	H	The initial Requirements Document identifies *all* of the business requirements, but at a high level only. Subsequent project activities will define the full details of each requirement during project delivery.
24	B	The Requirements Traceability Matrix is created at the same time as the requirements are identified and is then maintained through the complete project lifecycle.
25	C	The Define Scope process is done by the project team during planning and submitted to the key stakeholders for approval. Although it is an approved document, it must be maintained throughout the project to ensure that all approved change requests are reflected.
26	C	While all these are inputs to the Define Scope process, the Requirements Document is the key input, as it contains all the requirements that will become the project scope.
27	A	During scope definition, some requirements may be descoped from the project. Reasons for descoping can include difficulty, time to accomplish, cost to accomplish, better addresses outside the project, and so on. Requirements that are descoped must be documented and approved by key stakeholders.

Question	Answer	Justification
28	C	While the Requirements Document is a key input to the Define Scope process, it should also consider all other work completed to date, including any documentation from previous phases. Of particular interest are risks, issues, assumptions, and constraints identified during project initiation or in previous phases, as these may significantly impact the determination of what requirements should be in scope.
29	C	Define Scope is done initially during planning but also must be done as part of each Project Change Request. Although B might also be considered correct, C is a better answer because planning should be done as part of each phase plan automatically, and therefore does not need to be explicitly called out.
30	G	Expert judgment can come from any source. The project management team should seek out expert judgment to ensure that the project is maximizing its use of available resources.
31	J	The Project Scope Statement includes the project scope, acceptance criteria, deliverables, project exclusions, constraints, and assumptions. The project schedule is produced in Project Time Management.
32	B	The Project Scope Statement documents both the product and the project scope. This is important to ensure that readers of the Project Scope Statement clearly understand any differences between the product and the project scope. Listing exclusions is a common method of differentiating between product and project scope.
33	C	Because the project may produce many interim deliverables used by the project team, only the deliverables that will be presented to the project acceptor for formal acceptance are documented in the Project Scope Statement.
34	B	Clearly documenting the components that will not be delivered by the project can be critical for ensuring the stakeholders understand what the project will be delivering. It is often easier to say what the project *won't* do than what it *will* do. While D can also be considered a correct answer, it is not the best answer, because the Project Scope Statement is an outward-facing document rather than an inward-facing document.
35	C	Assumptions and constraints document the specific conditions on which the Project Scope Statement is based. They document factors that are outside the control of the project team and could impact the success of the project. Therefore, while B is also a correct answer, it is not the best answer, as the assumptions and constraints should be based on the most likely conditions under which the project will succeed.

A

Question	Answer	Justification
36	B	While the WBS will be decomposed into activities, this takes place during Project Time Management, not during Project Scope Management.
37	G	The WBS is based on the project deliverables and further defines the project scope. Therefore, completing the work in the WBS will satisfy the project's objectives. While the WBS will eventually identify the activities, this is done in Project Time Management, not Project Scope Management.
38	D	While the WBS must always be based on completing all identified project deliverables, the project team should consider all possible avenues for templates and skeletons to assist in developing a complete WBS.
39	E	Each branch (deliverable) in the WBS should be decomposed based on the level of detail required to clearly identify the work required to complete the deliverable. Large, complex deliverables may require many levels of decomposition, while small deliverables may require only one or two levels of decomposition.
40	F	The method of decomposition used will vary based on the project and may even vary based on the nature of a specific deliverable. While the fundamental expectation of WBS decomposition is to ensure that *all* project deliverables are produced, the WBS can be structured differently based on the team's preferences, availability of existing templates, or management disciplines to be applied.
41	B	The WBS has been decomposed initially by project delivery phase, and then by deliverable within the phase.
42	A	The WBS has been decomposed initially by deliverable, and then by the work packages to produce the deliverable.
43	C	The WBS has been decomposed initially by major project components, and then by deliverable within the component.
44	I	A WBS should identify all the work and only work required to complete the project deliverables. A WBS will typically be decomposed to different depths for each branch based on the size and complexity of the branch.
45	C	When enough is known about project deliverables, full decomposition should take place during initial planning, as this ensures the most accurate project plan (schedule and budget). However, because there is typically limited information known about the details for future deliverables, it is acceptable to do rolling-wave planning where only the deliverables for the next phase are fully decomposed.

Question	Answer	Justification
46	E	The Scope Baseline is the formally approved Scope Statement, which includes the WBS and WBS Dictionary.
47	D	A control account is assigned the lowest-level elements of each WBS branch (in other words, the elements that will be assigned to team members) as well as any additional management control points identified. For example, lowest-level elements are always considered to be management control points and are used to track cost, schedule, and resource information for each assigned work package.
48	A	A WBS Dictionary includes a control account identifier, a description of WBS elements, assumptions and constraints, a responsible organization, schedule details, resource requirements, costs, quality details, acceptance criteria, and other pertinent information. PMI is very explicit on the importance of the WBS Dictionary, and you should expect to see at least one question on the exam related to its use and importance.
49	E	Validate Scope is explicitly defined in the PMBOK as managing the formal acceptance of the project deliverables. It is focused on ensuring that the acceptance process defined for each deliverable is applied, and it therefore removes the objectivity from the acceptance process. Acceptance criteria defined in the "calm and quiet" of project planning are applied to the acceptance process to ensure that there are no surprises, and that "emotions" and "last-minute changes" do not impact the acceptance process.
50	B	Validate Scope is the process of ensuring that the acceptance criteria are applied to each deliverable. Control Quality is the process of ensuring that the deliverable meets the requirements for the deliverable.
51	E	Because Validate Scope is focused on ensuring that the predefined acceptance criteria are applied to each deliverable, the main outputs from this process are acceptance documents, defect reports, or Project Change Requests. If the deliverable is acceptable, an acceptance document is produced. If defects are identified, a defect report is produced. If the business requirements have changed, making the document no longer acceptable, a Project Change Request is produced. In all instances, work performance information is gathered to track information on deliverables accepted, defects raised, time to resolve defects, and so on.
52	B	Control Quality, which validates the "correctness" of the deliverable, is typically performed before Validate Scope, which obtains acceptance of the deliverable. It is possible, but not typical, for the two processes to be performed in parallel.

A

Question	Answer	Justification
53	D	Control Scope is focused on monitoring that the work on the project is consistent with the Scope Baseline. If deviations are identified, the Perform Integrate Change Control process is required to deal with the changes.
54	E	The focus of Control Scope is to monitor the status of the project against the Scope Baseline. If deviations are identified, either the work can be discontinued to return to the baseline or a change request can be processed to change the Scope Baseline.
55	E	The Control Scope process will often initiate the Perform Integrated Change Control process and should be fully integrated with the other control processes—Control Schedule, Control Costs, Control Quality, Control Communications, Control Risks, Control Procurements, and Control Stakeholders—to ensure that the impact of scope changes are fully integrated across all Knowledge Areas.
56	D	The Control Scope process uses the following project documents: Scope Baseline, Scope Management Plan, Change Management Plan, Configuration Management Plan, Requirements Management Plan, Requirements Document, Requirements Traceability Matrix, and Work Performance Data.
57	C	Variance analysis is used to examine any deviations between current project performance and the Scope Baseline.
58	C	The scope is based on the requirements. The other components are based on the project's scope.
59	B	Work packages are the lowest level that the WBS should be composed into. Work packages are estimable and assignable units of work—ideally with a 40- to 80-hour estimate that can be assigned to a single individual.
60	D	The Project Scope Baseline consists of the WBS, which identifies *all* the work required to complete the project (which therefore also contains the deliverables list as a high-level component of the WBS); the WBS Dictionary, which provides additional information about each element of the WBS; and the Scope Statement, which defines what is and is not in the project's scope.
61	B	Project acceptance documents are the output from the Validate Scope process.
62	C	Option C is the best answer because the primary purpose of the WBS is to decompose the scope of the project into deliverables, sub-deliverables, and activities. While the schedule is developed from the WBS, the prime purpose of the WBS is to define the scope of the project.

CHAPTER 5: PROJECT TIME MANAGEMENT

Question	Answer	Justification
1	D	Project Time Management consists of the following processes: Plan Schedule Management, Define Activities, Sequence Activities, Estimate Activity Resources, Estimate Activity Durations, Develop Schedule, and Control Schedule.
2	A	On smaller projects, these time management activities are typically done by an individual one WBS element at a time. The PMBOK presents these as separate activities because the tools and techniques are different, as opposed to a definitive statement in which each must be completed independently.
3	C	The project manager has developed this definition to clearly distinguish the application of the scheduling tool from the project processes and data defined by the Project Time Management processes.
4	B	The Schedule Management Plan must be produced for every project. It defines the processes the project will follow for defining and managing the project schedule. It can be a standalone document or integrated into the overall Project Management Plan.
5	B	While project scheduling tools automate some of the processes defined for Project Time Management, an automated tool is not mandatory (but is highly recommended for all but the simplest of projects) for a project to be effective with Project Time Management.
6	D	The usability of the project scheduling tools should not have a material impact on the project schedule. All other factors can significantly impact the overall project schedule.
7	F	The Schedule Management Plan defines the approach the project will take to create and manage the project schedule. This includes identifying the processes to be used to estimate activities, use the software, and adjust the schedule based on current project status.
8	D	The Schedule Management Plan contains scheduling methodology, level of accuracy, units of measure, schedule maintenance approach, control thresholds, performance measurement rules, and reporting formats. Assignment of resources is completed during Project Time Management, but it is not part of the Schedule Management Plan.
9	C	In the Create WBS process, the WBS identifies all project deliverables and the work packages that are necessary to produce the deliverables. In the Define Activities process, the WBS is further decomposed into activities, which can be estimated and assigned to resources.

A

Question	Answer	Justification
10	C	The Define Activities process decomposes the WBS work packages into activities. An activity is defined as a WBS element that can be accurately estimated, assigned to a single resource, and effectively tracked and managed to completion. An activity ideally has an estimate in the 40- to 80-hour range. Individual team members can further break activities into tasks to help them manage their daily (or even hourly) work, but this level of decomposition is not considered in the PMBOK.
11	F	Activity decomposition should be completed to ensure that a WBS is estimable and assignable. While it is possible that some low-end/free tools may have some WBS restrictions, most commercial project scheduling tools will support the WBS developed to PMI standards.
12	D	Activities should be decomposed until the lowest level can be estimated with a 40- to 80-hour estimate and the activities can be assigned to and completed by a single resource.
13	C	The WBS Dictionary must be maintained throughout the WBS decomposition process, both for WBS and for activity elements.
14	E	Where feasible, the team members should participate in the decomposition process to ensure that they understand and buy into the activities.
15	E	The WBS is decomposed until the bottom level (activity) is estimable and can be resourced. For some deliverables, this could be two levels—project and deliverable (where the deliverable can be produced by a single resource with 60 hours of effort)—and for other deliverables on the same project, it could be 10 levels, with project/deliverable/major section/subsection/activity group/activity subgroup.
16	A	The information contained in the activity list and activity attributes is the same as that maintained in the WBS Dictionary. Each project can decide whether these activity components are best documented separately or as part of the overall WBS Dictionary.
17	B	Because the activity will typically be referred to as a standalone work assignment and will appear on project status reports and timesheets without the full context of the project schedule/WBS structure, each activity should have a self-sufficient name so that it can easily be put into the overall schedule context.
18	A	Milestones are points in time when the project records a significant event. Therefore, milestones are activities that have no duration.

Question	Answer	Justification
19	E	Sequence Activities is not optional, as it identifies the order in which the project activities must be completed to ensure that predecessor/successor relationships are satisfied and that the activities are completed in the correct order.
20	B	Current best practices for effective schedule development suggest that all activities in the project should be part of the dependency network to ensure that the activities are executed in the desired order, as opposed to how the tool schedules it or what the team feels like working on that particular day. Finish-to-start dependencies are the main dependency type that should be used.
21	C	The activity attributes (or WBS Dictionary) should clearly identify the order in which activities are to be completed—that is, predecessor and successors. A subject-matter expert may be required to define these activity attributes, but this work should be done at the time the activity is defined.
22	B	Milestones should be sequenced in the same way as any other project activity.
23	D	The four dependency types defined by the Precedence Diagramming Method (PDM) are finish-to-start (FS), finish-to-finish (FF), start-to-start (SS), and start-to-finish (SF).
24	A	In a finish-to-start dependency relationship, the first activity must be finished before the second activity can start. For example, when building a house, the foundation must be in place before the first floor can be built.
25	B	In a finish-to-finish dependency relationship, the first activity must be finished before the second activity can finish. For example, the house must be completed before the inspections can be stopped.
26	E	In a start-to-finish dependency relationship, the first activity cannot finish before the second activity starts. For example, your preparation for your PMP exam does not finish until the exam starts (so keep studying until the moment you walk into the exam).
27	A	Most activities in a project are completed in a serial fashion. For example, for a house the foundation must be in place before the first floor can be built, the first floor must be built before the walls can be constructed, the walls must be constructed before the roof can be put on, and so on.
28	D	While some examples can be found where an activity should continue until the successor starts, in most projects, this dependency type is rarely used.

A

Question	Answer	Justification
29	A	The diagram shows the first activity completing, and then the dependency allows the second activity to start.
30	C	The diagram shows the first activity starting, and then the dependency allows the second activity to start.
31	B	The diagram shows the first activity finishing, and then the dependency allows the second activity to finish.
32	D	The diagram shows the first activity finishing, and then the second activity starts.
33	G	The PDM, while rarely manually drawn by a project manager, is the method used by most project management software packages, as activity on nodes with relationships on the nodes is the main method used by automated tools.
34	B	The four dependency types are mandatory, discretionary, internal, and external.
35	A	Mandatory dependencies represent the true dependencies that must be honored for the project activities to be completed successfully. The floor must be built before the walls can be constructed. All mandatory dependencies should be defined for the project.
36	C	Discretionary dependencies should be used with caution, because discretionary dependencies may constrain the project and result in less than optimal resource allocations, as the schedule must wait for the discretionary dependencies to be completed.
37	D	External dependencies link project and nonproject activities. These should be used when the external dependency is absolutely critical to project success. Care should be taken with using external dependencies, as they must be maintained manually and could result in project delays if not updated in a timely fashion.
38	B	Only one dependency type can exist between two activities. The dependency can be modified by adding lead or lag, which defines a time period that adjusts the dependency. For example a finish-to-start with a lead of two days allows the second activity to start two days before the successor finishes. Similarly, a finish-to-start with a lag of two days delays the start of the second activity to two days after the first activity completes.
39	E	A lead impacts the second half of a dependency relationship. A lead allows the second activity to start early. In this case, it allows the second activity to start two days before the first activity finishes.

Question	Answer	Justification
40	D	A lag impacts the second half of a dependency relationship. A lag delays the end of the second activity. In this case it delays the finish of the second activity by two days—for example, allowing the final inspection to be completed two days after the house is constructed.
41	B	The project schedule network diagram is a graphical representation of the logical relationships between the project schedule activities.
42	C	Based on the assumption that project scheduling software will be used on the project, most commercial packages will produce a network diagram based on the activity list and the dependency network.
43	E	Estimate Activity Resources determines the requirements for all resources required to complete an activity. While human resources (team) is typically the main resource assignment, this process also identifies the requirements for materials, equipment, or supplies required by the activity. With the quantity of resources identified, the budget is calculated based on usage times cost.
44	B	When estimating activity resources, it is important to know the resource availability to ensure that resources are available as needed by the project. Equipment is typically scheduled the same as human resources and therefore is also supported by resource calendars. Material is assumed to have an unlimited availability, as more can always be purchased (with a budget impact). If material is of limited availability, it is also typically supported by resource calendars.
45	B	While cost for resources should not be a major consideration when determining which resources should be assigned to an activity, the cost should always be a secondary consideration to select the least expensive but still qualified resource.
46	E	Estimating activity resources is focused on selecting the appropriate resources to complete each project activity. Therefore, expert judgment is a key factor in selecting the correct resource, but careful consideration should be given to evaluating alternative resource options to select the best combination of resources to complete each activity. Existing data, either internal or external, can often be used to establish standards for resource assignment. For example, a house can typically be wired most effectively by a certified electrician, two trainees, and one general laborer. Bottom-up estimating can be used individually to determine the resource requirements at the activity level.

A

Question	Answer	Justification
47	B	Although estimating activity resources is not an exact science, you must ensure that the resources assigned are as accurate and appropriate as possible. Therefore, if an activity cannot be accurately resourced, the activity can be temporarily further decomposed to a point where you are more confident, and then the resources can be aggregated back to the activity level.
48	K	The outputs from the Estimate Activity Resources process are activity resource requirements, the Resource Breakdown Structure, and updated project documents.
49	C	The activity duration estimate can only be determined after the activity resources are identified. The number and skills of the assigned resources are key inputs to the duration estimating process.
50	E	To develop realistic activity duration estimates, it is important that you have an accurate understanding of the activity and the skills and availability of the resources to complete the activity.
51	G	The three estimating techniques identified by the PMBOK are analogous, parametric, and three-point.
52	A	The parametric estimating method involves using a standardized measure, such as the industry standard that a roofer can lay 100 square feet of roofing in an hour. Based on this standard measure, the project estimate can be determined by the number of units the project requires. For example, we have 1,500 square feet of roof; therefore, the activity will take 15 hours for a single roofer.
53	C	Analogous estimating involves finding a similar project or activity and then basing the estimate on this historical fact. For example, the last time we conducted business area interviews, it took 65 hours. For this project, we will be conducting similar interviews but to a smaller group of users; therefore, it should take 50 hours for this project.
54	E	The three-point estimating technique supports two formulas: triangulation, which is (Optimistic + Most Likely + Pessimistic) / 3, and beta, which is (Optimistic + 4 ★ Most Likely + Pessimistic) / 6.
55	A	The three-point estimating technique supports two formulas: triangulation, which is (Optimistic + Most Likely + Pessimistic) / 3, and beta, which is (Optimistic + 4 ★ Most Likely + Pessimistic) / 6.
56	B	Triangular and beta distribution are the two most used formulas for PERT. PERT is a technique that uses most likely, optimistic, and pessimistic estimates to derive a more accurate activity estimate.

Question	Answer	Justification
57	A	Bottom–up estimating is based on individual estimates for a detailed list of items. The individual estimates are then added to determine the activity estimate.
58	C	Because all activity duration estimates have some degree of inaccuracy, each estimate should also consider the accuracy of the estimate and include an additional estimate for a contingency reserve.
59	C	Beta distribution is (Pessimistic + 4 ★ Most Likely + Optimistic) / 6. In this case, it is (20 + 4 ★ 12 + 10) / 6.
60	D	Triangular distribution is (Pessimistic + Most Likely + Optimistic) / 3. In this case, it is (20 + 12 + 10) / 3.
61	A	A milestone is a marker to indicate a significant event in a project. A milestone has no duration.
62	C	While not all activities will require a contingency reserve, any activities that are considered to have risk, or activities where the duration estimates are considered to be inaccurate, should have a contingency reserve determined to address these uncertainties. Contingency reserves should be developed as a separate component of the activity duration estimate to provide maximum management control.
63	B and D	Contingency reserves are also referred to as *time reserves* and *buffers* by the PMBOK. It is important to understand that these three terms are the same, and they may be used interchangeably in the PMP exam.
64	B	Risk reserves at the activity level are associated with identified risk events and risk mitigations plans. Therefore, they are known-unknown. For example, the project may identify that there is a risk that weather will delay project construction during the winter season. This is a known event (inclement weather during winter) but unknown impact to the project (will storms delay the project by no, one, five, or ten days?).
65	D	Risk reserves at the deliverable or project level are based on the general or high-level riskiness of the project. For example, the project may be attempting to develop a customer service solution that has not been done before. Therefore, there is a high level of risk associated with the project, but the team really has no insight into the source or the types of risks that will occur. These are unknown-unknown impacts, as the team simply feels that there will be delays from a wide variety of sources.
66	A	Because the term *unknown-unknown contingency reserves* is long and doesn't inspire confidence, these contingency reserves are often referred to *management reserves*.

A

Question	Answer	Justification
67	C	In an ideal situation, activity duration estimates should always be presented as a single number. However, in some circumstances, the estimating team doesn't have the confidence to develop a single number due to uncertainties in the basis for estimation. In these circumstances, the estimate should be presented with the range of possible results to provide the project management team with the best information known. Estimating accuracy ranges is totally independent of contingency reserves, which are focused on delivery risks.
68	B	The Develop Schedule process is the last process in the Project Time Management Planning activities. It requires the input from all the prior Project Time Management processes, specifically Define Activities, Sequence Activities, Estimate Activity Resources, and Estimate Activity Durations. Costs are not required to develop the project schedule.
69	C	While A, B, and D can be considered to be correct answers, the best answer is C because the primary reason for a project schedule Baseline is to measure project progress against and to identify any corrective actions needed to keep the project on schedule.
70	B and C	Development of the project schedule is typically done using project scheduling software, as it is a very labor-intensive process to perform manually. Even with the use of specialized software, it is an iterative process and may require several iterations before an optimal schedule is developed.
71	E	Whether the schedule is developed manually or using software, critical path, critical chain, what-if analysis, and resource optimization techniques are used to develop the project schedule.
72	C	The critical path method remains the preferred approach for both manual and automated project scheduling.
73	E	The critical path method first calculates the early start for each activity, then the early finish for each activity. This is known as a *forward pass*. Once all early starts and early finishes are calculated, you would perform a *backward pass* through the network diagram to calculate the late finish and the late start for each activity.
74	B	A project with multiple critical paths is hard to manage because the project manager must carefully manage all activities on all critical paths, therefore increasing the number of items that must be monitored closely.

Question	Answer	Justification
75	D	Minimum project duration is calculated on the forward pass as the last with the earliest early finish date. Scheduling flexibility is determined from the backward pass comparing the early start and late start (or early finish and late finish) dates for each task. With the scheduling flexibility, the maximum project duration can be calculated.
76	A	The critical path is calculated by the critical path method and identifies the project's end date by defining the sequence of tasks that define the shortest possible timeframe over which the project can be completed.
77	B	The project end date is the day on which the final project activity completes. In this case it is Day 16.
78	B	The project critical path consists of the activities that have no slack. In this case it is B–C–D.
79	B	The project slack is calculated as the difference between early start and late start (or early finish and late finish). In this example, Task A is the only activity with a difference, which is 2: 0 (or 7: 5). This results in a slack of 2.
80	B	The critical path method focuses exclusively on activity duration estimates and sequences.
81	A	Task C is on the critical path (slack is zero); therefore, any movement on any of start/finish or duration will impact the project end date.
82	C	Task A has a slack of two days; therefore, any combination of movement on any start/finish or duration up to a maximum of two days will not impact the project end date.
83	B	Negative slack is what happens when an unrealistic constraint is placed on a project. For example, if the project's critical path indicates that it will take 16 days to complete the project, and the project sponsor insists the project be completed in 14 days, all tasks on the original critical path will get a negative slack of 2 days (–2).
84	F	All schedules will have at least one critical path, even if it is the *only* path. The project's critical path will likely change throughout the project, and at any time there could be a single critical path, multiple critical paths, or—what is often the case—a single critical path with several near-critical paths where a single change in an activity could make a new critical path. It is important for a project manager to manage not only the critical path, but also the almost-critical paths.

A

Question	Answer	Justification
85	B and C	The critical chain method builds from the critical path method and allows for the introduction of buffers to adjust the schedule to accommodate limited resources or other project contingencies.
86	B	The critical chain method adds buffer activities at appropriate places in the project schedule to account for limited resources or other project uncertainties. From a critical path/critical chain viewpoint, the buffer activities are treated the same way as any project activity. But the buffer activities are not added to the WBS or activity lists, as they are used purely for adjusting the project schedule.
87	C	While some project managers still introduce buffers into the project schedule to allow them to control the total schedule, with automated scheduling software buffers are not required for resource management, because the software has very sophisticated algorithms for managing resource leveling.
88	A and C	Resource smoothing moves activity dates only within the available slack in an effort to remove resource over-allocations. Because resource smoothing is constrained by available slack, the result may still have some resource over-allocations.
89	C	The term *crashing* applies to the technique of shortening a project schedule by adding resources and/or finding a different way to achieve the activity's required result. Crashing should only be applied to critical path tasks, because crashing non-critical path tasks will not impact the project end date.
90	D	The term *fast tracking* applies to the technique of shortening a project schedule by removing or changing dependencies to allow more activities to be completed in parallel. Fast tracking should be applied only to critical path tasks because fast tracking non-critical path tasks will not change the end date.
91	D	Crashing involves adding resources to complete a project activity. Resources may be human resources, tools, equipment, or supplies. Crashing also can be done by changing the approach to completing the task.
92	B	Any project activity where the early start/late start or early finish/late finish dates are different has slack and therefore is not on the critical path.
93	C	The best alternative is to explore fast tracking and crashing options and present the results of this analysis to the project sponsor.
94	D	Fast tracking involves changing the dependencies between activities to allow for more work to be completed in parallel.

Question	Answer	Justification
95	A	The Schedule Baseline, which is produced at the end of Project Time Management planning, is a formal document that is presented for approval and then subject to change management processes. Because the Schedule Baseline is used to track project progress and analyze delivery variances, it is important that this is a controlled project deliverable.
96	D	Although typically, the project schedule is presented using the output from the project scheduling software, the most common outputs used are bar charts (often referred to as Gantt charts), milestone charts, and schedule network diagrams. Depending on who you are communicating the schedule to, you can use any of the various types.
97	A	While technically a Gantt is a very specific bar chart associated with the work of Henry Gantt, the term has been adopted to generally refer to the type of bar charts typically developed as a result of project schedule development.
98	C	The Control Schedule process is focused on obtaining the current status of the project schedule and then comparing the current status to the Schedule Baseline to determine whether any corrective actions are needed.
99	B	Work performance data must be provided by the team members based on the Schedule Management Plan. The data are then used to update the current project schedule.
100	C	The Control Schedule, Monitor and Control Project Work, and Perform Integrated Change Control processes are all closely integrated and combine to ensure that the project schedule is properly controlled and that any resulting updates to the baseline schedule are properly reviewed and approved.
101	E	The Control Schedule process is focused on understanding the current schedule status and then reacting to any changes to ensure that the project remains on schedule.
102	C	Timesheets is not a technique to be used for the Control Schedule process. Timesheets are typically inputs to work performance data. It is simply raw data that would need further analysis. Any trend, critical path, critical chain, or Earned Value Management analysis would be appropriate for identifying and validating deviations from the Schedule Baseline.

A

Question	Answer	Justification
103	B	Trend analysis is a very useful technique for controlling the schedule because it allows for the analysis of variations over time. On projects, it is not uncommon to have a particularly bad (or good) week as a result of excessive distraction from the project by other company activities or a rapidly spreading cold/flu. Taken in isolation, the project is in a terrible state, and immediate and drastic remediation is required. But when considered over a several-week trend, it may be seen as a minor bump in the schedule. Compare this to a very small schedule "overrun" that is barely recognized on a weekly basis, such as 0.05 percent. This is not significant enough to warrant remediation, but when examined over several weeks, this is an ongoing trend that will soon result in a true schedule deviation if not corrected.
104	E	Critical path analysis is not just a technique for schedule development. It is also an important technique for controlling the schedule, because it allows identification of any changes to the critical path and/or emergence of new critical paths. Understanding the project's critical path is important for effective schedule control because these are the activities that must be managed most carefully.
105	C	During schedule development, buffers are added to the project to accommodate resource constraints or other delivery concerns. During schedule control examining, the changes in the project buffers allow for the determination of where corrective actions are needed.
106	C	Earned Value Management is a powerful tool for schedule control because the schedule variance (SV) and schedule performance index (SPI) allow the project manager to quickly identify whether there are any schedule performance issues that require further investigation.
107	A and B	Formal outputs from the Control Schedule process are limited to updated schedule forecasts and Project Change Requests. Outputs such as remediation actions are the output of the Monitor and Control Project Work process, and senior management updates are output from the Manage Communications process.
108	C	Parametric estimating uses a standard measure (in this case, 5 hours per interview) times the number of occurrences (in this case, 12) to determine the total estimate.
109	A	A mandatory dependency dictates that the predecessor task (the floor) must be completed before the successor (the walls) can be built.

CHAPTER 6: PROJECT COST MANAGEMENT

Question	Answer	Justification
1	A	Project Cost Management consists of the following processes: Plan Cost Management, Estimate Costs, Determine Budget, and Control Costs.
2	B	PMI states that no Knowledge Area is more important than another. For a project to be successful, all Knowledge Areas must be applied.
3	A	On small projects, which generally implies a short duration, cost estimating and cost budgeting are typically tightly linked and performed by a single person. While the tools and techniques are different, the shortened timeframe of a small project makes the combination feasible.
4	A	Because Project Cost Management typically has to integrate with the corporate financial systems and comply with corporate financial policies, it should be closely integrated with the corporate finance department.
5	E	Project Cost Management must consider all monetary aspects of the project. Depending on corporate policies and project size, there may be very significant financial requirements for the project to ensure that it accurately predicts and manages the total financial environment in which the project must operate.
6	C	The Cost Management Plan can be delivered as a separate plan or as part of the Project Management Plan. The project can determine which method will provide the most clarity and ease of use.
7	D	The Cost Management Plan defines the total environment under which the project's finances will be managed. This includes units of measure, level of precision, level of accuracy, organizational procedure links, control thresholds, rules of performance measurement, reporting formats, and process descriptions. Identification of funding sources is not typically documented in the Cost Management Plan.
8	B and D	The project costs should be based directly on the cost of completing each activity in the WBS. The WBS contains *all* the activities to complete the project; therefore, if the project costs for each activity in the WBS are properly calculated, the total cost for the project should be known. However, because risks and contingencies are excluded from the WBS, additional consideration must be given to ensure that additional costs are included for all identified risks and contingencies.

A

Question	Answer	Justification
9	E	Cost estimates must include all costs to complete each WBS activity. This will typically include resource, material, equipment, and supply costs, but it could include other specific costs unique to each WBS activity.
10	B	While cost estimates are typically expressed in the operating currency ($) of the project, there may be instances where costs can be expressed in other terms, such as staff hours. This is especially relevant when the project will be delivered by full-time salaried staff.
11	E	While E may sound like a copout answer, cost estimates should be as accurate as possible. But as with all estimating/planning processes, especially for large projects, it is impossible to develop firm cost estimates at the beginning of the project. Therefore, accurate estimates should be developed for the next phase, and then rolling-wave cost estimating can be applied for the remainder of the project. Degree of accuracy in cost estimates should always be clearly stated when supplying an estimate.
12	D	The Human Resources Management Plan identifies the project staffing attributes, personnel rates, training costs, and any other costs associated with having staff assigned to a project.
13	G	While you will never see a question on your PMP exam with an answer like "it depends!", there will be answers that suggest the right answer will vary based on specific project and organizational politics. There is no absolute right answer to this question, because each organization and even sometimes each project within an organization will have different policies for what costs are attributable to a project. In some instances, projects bear the full burden of overhead and even corporate overhead allocations, and in others the project will bear direct costs only.
14	B	Multiplying hours times rate is definitely the right first step for determining human resource costs. But you also need to consider how the resources are assigned to the project. If a resource is assigned to the project full time but only scheduled for project activities an average of 20 hours per week, the project will likely be charged for a full week because the resource has no other project assignments. Therefore, you must consider the assignment level versus the level of scheduled activities.
15	E	Cost estimating uses the same estimating tools as defined for activity estimating. Each method has advantages and disadvantages and should be considered for appropriateness for each activity on the project. The key to successful cost estimating is to not get lulled into a sense that hours times resource rate equals cost estimate.

Question	Answer	Justification
16	C	While the project scheduling tool will typically provide a significant amount of the input to the cost estimate, cost estimates are typically developed outside the project scheduling tool using a spreadsheet for the cost estimates. In addition to the costs produced from the scheduling tool, costs for contingency, material and supply costs, corporate allocations and other costs are determined from additional modeling and simulation software tools. The spreadsheet would be used to consolidate the multiple budget components.
17	E	The project budget determines the Cost Baseline against which project performance is measured and controlled.
18	C	The human resource plan is not required when determining the project budget, because the resource costs by time were already determined during activity cost estimating.
19	F	Determining the project budget can be a considerable amount of work, especially on large projects. Determining the project budget is much more than just adding the costs for the work packages. Proper project budgets typically require several levels of summary, and for all but very short projects should be allocated over time to allow for the allocation of financial principles for present/future value calculations.
20	A	Contingency reserves are set aside for known-unknowns. Management reserves are set aside for unknown-unknowns.
21	B	Management reserves are typically not included in the Cost Baseline. The project manager is responsible for and has approval authority for the Cost Baseline. By the very name, management reserves are in addition to the Cost Baseline, but they require management approval before they can be spent to cover project risks (unknown-unknowns).
22	A	Management reserves are included in the project budget to ensure that money is available to cover the risks the management reserves are to cover (unknown-unknowns). By the very name, management reserves require management approval before they can be spent.
23	E	While the preferred route for obtaining project costs is from corporate accounting systems, often the time delays and availability of data necessitates alternatives for obtaining project costs. Depending on the accuracy of these alternative sources, a reconciliation may be required on a regular basis. The processes for obtaining project actual costs should be defined in the Cost Management Plan.

A

Question	Answer	Justification
24	C	While some project cost overruns may be accepted and result in an over-budget situation, in most instances where an uncontrollable cost overrun occurs (material costs increase, for example), the project manager should alert project stakeholders to the changes and secure approval to adjust the project baseline through a Project Change Request.
25	B	While project costs are often considered to be a single measurement factor for projects, in reality cost status in isolation is meaningless. At Month 2, saying that the project is $10,000 over budget is a meaningless fact. Is the project also ahead of schedule, which would indicate the extra expenditure is probably acceptable? Or, if the project is over budget and also behind schedule, that is doubly bad.
26	E	Effective project cost control involves ensuring that project costs do not exceed approved funding by time period, WBS component, or activity. If costs are managed at this level, it will also ensure that the total approved Cost Baseline is not exceeded.
27	C	The valid EVM terms are PV (planned value), AC (actual cost), CPI (cost performance index), and BAC (budget at completion).
28	E	Earned Value Management applies to all types and sizes of projects.
29	E	For EVM to work, scope, cost, and schedule must be baselines, as they form the basis for EVM. Actual results are then applied against these baselines to determine the earned value for the project.
30	A	Planned value is the original baseline developed for the project.
31	B	Earned value is the amount of actual work completed for a given time period.
32	C	Actual cost is the actual costs charged to the project.
33	C	The planned value consists of the accumulation of all planned costs up to a specified period in the project.
34	B	Earned value is the measurement of the work actually completed. Earned value can be considered the work efficiency, because it measures the amount of actual work completed versus the level of effort required to complete it. For example, if an activity with a 10-hour estimate was completed in 12 hours, the efficiency would be .83, meaning for every hour of work put into the activity, only .83 hours of expected work was completed.
35	A	Actual costs are the actual charges allocated to the project.

Question	Answer	Justification
36	A	SV = EV – PV.
37	C	CV = EV – AC.
38	B	SPI = EV / PV.
39	D	CPI = EV / AC.
40	B	Schedule variance measures the amount that the project is ahead of or behind schedule at a given point in time. It is the difference between the earned value and the planned value. Schedule variance is not expressed in calendar days; rather, it is expressed as the "relative deviation from schedule" where zero is on schedule, positive numbers are ahead (where a larger positive number is farther ahead than a small positive number), and negative numbers are behind (where again, the larger [smaller?] the negative number, the farther behind the project is).
41	B	Cost variance measures the amount that the budget is over or under plan at a given point in time. It is the difference between the earned value and the actual cost. Cost variance is not expressed in financial terms ($); rather, it is expressed as the "relative deviation from budget" where zero is on budget, positive numbers are under (where a larger positive number is farther under than a small positive number), and negative numbers are over (where again, the larger [smaller?] the negative number, the farther over budget the project is).
42	B	SV = EV – PV; therefore, –20 = 980: 1000.
43	E	CV = EV – AC; therefore, –270 = 980: 1250.
44	D	CPI = EV / AC; therefore, .78 = 980 / 1250.
45	A	SPI = EV / PV; therefore, .98 = 980 / 1000.
46	C	With both SV and CV reporting negative numbers (and SPI and CPI both less than 1), the project is experiencing both budget and schedule issues.
47	B	With a positive CV, the budget is okay, but an SPI less than 1.0 indicates that there are schedule issues.
48	D	With a positive SV, the schedule is okay. With a CPI greater than 1, the budget performance is also in good condition.
49	D	EAC is an EVM term that stands for *estimate at completion*.

A

Question	Answer	Justification
50	E	Calculation of EAC, unlike all the other EVM formulas, depends on assumptions. The most accurate formula for EAC is Option A, and it doesn't involve EVM, as it uses actual cost to date plus a comprehensive reforecast of all remaining ETC. However, this method typically takes a significant amount of effort to reforecast the remaining ETC. Therefore, other formulas are often used based on assumptions of the future. If you assume future work will progress at the budget rate, the formula is Option B. If you assume future work will be performed at the present CPI (that is, current performance), the formula is Option C. If you assume both SPI and CPI will determine EAC, the formula is Option D. Because these multiple options are "too difficult to present in a PMP question," you should be okay for your exam if you assume Statement C is the formula to be used for EAC.
51	C	EAC = BAC / SPI; therefore, 51,020 = 50,000 / .98.
52	A	EAC = BAC / SPI; therefore, 48,076 = 50,000 / 1.04.
53	A	The TCPI is a measure of the cost performance that is required to be achieved with the remaining resources in order to meet a specified management goal.
54	B	There are actually two TCPI formulas. Based on BAC, it is (BAC: EV) / (BAC: AC). Based on EAC, it is (BAC: EV) / (EAC: AC).
55	A, C and E	Schedule variance (SV) = EV: PV, cost variance (CV) = EV: AC, variance at completion = BAC: EAC.
56	A	During the Determine Budget process, the risk profile was applied to the individual contingency amounts to determine how much should be allocated to the contingency reserve. Therefore, on all but the most risk-averse project, the contingency reserve will be less than the sum on the contingency amounts. Therefore, it is expected that some risk events will not transpire, and it is appropriate to keep the contingency reserve as large as possible for future risks that are not fully funded.

CHAPTER 7: PROJECT QUALITY MANAGEMENT

Question	Answer	Justification
1	A	Project Quality Management consists of the following processes: Plan Quality Management, Perform Quality Assurance, and Control Quality.
2	D	Planning project quality is key to ensuring that the quality expectations are well understood and that the project processes are designed to support them.
3	C	The project's quality management processes must be designed to satisfy business expectations. When this is not possible within existing corporate policies, the deviations should be documented and resolved.
4	A	The project quality statement should include provisions for implementing continuous process improvement as identified during project execution.
5	D	Quality assurance is important to ensure that processes are followed that will ensure the completeness and appropriateness of each deliverable. Quality control will ensure that the results are appropriate. Therefore, both are required. For example, if a housing inspector is only concerned that the house contains an electrical system, it might pass an inspection (QA—the electrical system is installed properly and safely). However, the house may be unlivable because the electrical system is undersized and cannot support more than two electrical devices being used at a time (QC—the electrical system is not usable).
6	E	A project does not need to deliver high quality and grade for it to be acceptable; it simply has to meet stated requirements. For example, a house can be accepted based on a predefined number of defects (quality is not high) and may even have missing requirements (no outside deck; grade is not high).
7	A	From a quality perspective, grade refers to the usability of the project. Using a housing example, the usability of a house might be based on the number of rooms, bathrooms, and so on, and not involve the "cost" of components. A bedroom is usable if it is properly painted and has acceptable floor covering, as opposed to requiring gold-embossed figurines in each corner and the finest Italian marble tile on the floor. Grade measures usability, not the elaborateness of the result.
8	C	From a quality perspective, quality measures whether the project meets the defined requirements.

A

Question	Answer	Justification
9	A	Because grade measures the usability of the solution, a low-grade solution, such as a starter home, could be acceptable.
10	B	While it is possible that a low-quality project could be accepted, it is not recommended because the quality measures whether the project satisfies the requirements. Therefore, a project with low quality either simply doesn't satisfy the requirements or does it with a high level of defects.
11	F	The International Standards Organization recognizes the importance of customer satisfaction, prevention over inspection, continuous improvement, management responsibility, and Cost of Quality.
12	B	Effective quality management is focused on doing the right things the first time (plan and design), as opposed to relying on inspection and defect resolution.
13	A	Plan-Do-Act-Check as defined by Shewhart and modified by Denning is one of the principles of effective project quality and defines the process for continuous improvement.
14	E	PMI considers all the principles defined in this question to be acceptable continuous improvement techniques.
15	C	Cost of Quality is a specific quality measurement process that measures the cost of inspections (conformance work) and the cost of resolving defects (nonconformance work). The goal of Cost of Quality is to increase spending on conformance work to reduce spending on nonconformance work, with the understanding that conformance work delivers higher value to the project than nonconformance work.
16	A	All projects require a Quality Management Plan. The Quality Management Plan identifies the quality requirements for the project and defines how the project will satisfy these requirements.
17	E	Quality planning should be integrated with all other planning activities to ensure that quality standards accurately reflect the total project. Specifically, it is important to ensure that the schedule and cost reflect the time and effort to ensure that the quality activities are executed.
18	B	The human resource plan is not required to develop the Project Quality Plan. While the project team will be responsible for executing the Project Quality Plan, the team details are not required to develop the plan.

Question	Answer	Justification
19	F	The Quality Management Plan should consider not just internal requirements, but also external requirements from the government, industry standards, operating conditions, and even cultural and social considerations.
20	D	While the Quality Management Plan for each project will be unique based on the specific quality requirements for the project, it should consider all available support material, including organizational quality policies, procedures, and guidelines; historical databases; and lessons learned from other phases or projects.
21	D	Because planning quality is based on identifying the project approaches that will maximize quality at the lowest possible cost, cost-benefit analysis, Cost of Quality, benchmarking, and statistical sampling are all valid techniques to be used in planning quality.
22	C	Cost of Quality focuses on cost of conformance measurements, which consist of prevention costs and appraisal costs, and cost of nonconformance, which consists of internal failure costs and external failure costs. Contract negotiation costs are related to Project Procurement Management.
23	B	Cost of conformance costs are associated with ensuring that the work is done right the first time; therefore, prevention costs are valid cost of conformance costs.
24	D	Cost of nonconformance costs are associated with fixing work done incorrectly the first time; therefore, rework costs are a valid cost of nonconformance cost.
25	C	The 7QC tools are cause-and-effect diagrams, flowcharts, checksheets, Pareto diagrams, histograms, control charts, and scatter diagrams.
26	E	Histograms, control charts, and scatter diagrams provide different ways to take typically large amounts of quality measurements and group (central tendency, dispersion, tolerances, and correlation) and present them for further analysis.
27	B	Checksheets, also called *tally sheets*, are used to gather data by organizing the facts in a manner that facilitates the collection of data about a particular problem area.
28	B	Pareto diagrams are a special form of bar chart used to identify the main sources of a problem. The Pareto diagram allows you to identify and focus on the key areas that are causing a specific project issue.
29	C	A Pareto diagram is a special form of vertical bar chart used to identify the sources of a problem.

A

Question	Answer	Justification
30	B	A control chart is used to determine whether a process is stable and whether the performance is within acceptable boundaries. The upper and lower control limits help notify the team if sampling shows a process that is out of control. This then requires analysis of an assignable cause.
31	D	Benchmarking compares actual project performance against comparable projects, either internal or external, to determine whether the project is performing "on standard" and identify areas for improvement where the project performance falls below the benchmark.
32	D	Design of experiments is a process used to manage the various factors involved in an outcome with the goal of being able to measure the impact of change one factor at a time.
33	A	A quality checklist defines the specific steps in the form of an actual checklist required to complete a defined process or procedure. The checklist is designed to be "checked off" each time the process is applied.
34	D	Quality assurance is the process of auditing the project to ensure that the appropriate quality standards and processes are being followed.
35	B	Quality assurance is focused on doing the right things; one of the items it is focused on is ensuring that all deliverables follow the standards defined during planning.
36	B	Quality assurance validates that the deliverables meet defined standards. Therefore, if a deliverable is missing a section, QA is likely to detect this, because the missing section would have been defined as required by the standard.
37	D	Because quality assurance is focused on ensuring compliance to standards, project-specific knowledge is not mandatory to be able to perform QA activities. Therefore, it is often common for an external QA department to be assigned to this work on a project.
38	B	Quality assurance is a conformance cost within the appraisal category.
39	D	While quality assurance's main objective is to ensure that the project's standards are being applied, it is also likely that continuous improvement opportunities will be identified to improve standards and processes.
40	A	The 7QC tools are all commonly used when performing QA activities.
41	C	An affinity diagram is used to generate ideas that can be linked to form organized patterns of thought about a problem.

Question	Answer	Justification
42	C	A Process Decision Program Chart is used to relate the steps required to obtain a goal. PDPCs are often used for contingency planning because they help clarify the steps that could impact reaching the goal.
43	C	Interrelationship digraphs are typically used when other methods, such as affinity diagrams, tree diagrams, or fishbone diagrams, are inadequate. However, interrelationship digraphs also have practical limitations and are usable for only up to 50 relevant items.
44	A	Tree diagrams, also known as *systematic diagrams* or *decision trees*, start from a single point and then branch to accommodate parent/child or decision paths.
45	E	Tree diagrams are useful for any situation where there is a "root" or parent and then decomposition of the parent to children. This applies to all of the examples in the question.
46	B	Prioritization matrices allow for issues to be prioritized based on evaluation criteria and assigned weights. This allows the most important issues to be identified and acted on.
47	B	Prioritization matrices are preloaded with evaluation criteria and relative weights. As issues are identified, the evaluation criteria are applied and the issue is prioritized based on the mathematical score. This allows the issued to be ranked in order of priorities based on this scope.
48	D	Matrix diagrams seek to show the strength of relationships between factors, causes, and objectives that exist between the rows and columns that form the matrix. Matrix diagrams are very useful in quality assurance activities because they provide a method of analyzing large amounts of data related to quality measurement.
49	A	Project audits are conducted to validate whether projects are applying the processes defined on the quality plans.
50	B	Quality audits should be conducted regularly on the project to validate that the quality processes are being followed as well as to identify process improvement opportunities that might not be obvious while directly executing the processes. Quality audits should be seen as opportunities to improve the project's likelihood of successful delivery rather than as a "policing action to catch offenders."
51	F	A quality audit should be designed to identity what is working well and what needs to be improved from a quality assurance perspective.

A

Question	Answer	Justification
52	E	The Perform Quality Assurance process is focused on validating that processes are being followed and that the processes are effective. If deficiencies are identified, change requests are used to make the necessary changes to allow process improvements to be implemented.
53	C	Quality control is focused on ensuring that the project deliverables satisfy the stated requirements so that when they are presented for formal acceptance, there should be few to no errors detected.
54	E	Quality control is focused on ensuring that the deliverables meet the requirements specified for the project deliverables—essentially, that it does what the customer expects.
55	E	Quality control involves reviewing each deliverable to validate that it meets requirements. Depending on the type of deliverable, peer reviews, inspections, walkthroughs, testing, and other appropriate validation methods will be used.
56	D	Quality control is an internal project process that validates the deliverable's readiness for delivery to the business. This may result in validation that the document is ready to be delivered or identification of defects that must be resolved and revalidated. Acceptance documents are provided by the business once the quality control processes are completed and the validated document is presented for formal approval.
57	B	All changes to the project must go through formal change control processes. While the team may be right that this change is needed, it shouldn't be done simply because the team believes it is a good idea.

CHAPTER 8: PROJECT HUMAN RESOURCE MANAGEMENT

Question	Answer	Justification
1	C	Project Human Resource Management is focused on organizing, managing, and leading the project team, where the project team consists of all resources who will do work on the project, full-time or part-time.
2	D	While it would be ideal if the project team was fixed and assigned to the project as needed, in real life this is rarely possible because the project needs will change over time, resources will resign and be replaced with new hires, and/or resources will be adjusted to accommodate other organizational requirements.

Question	Answer	Justification
3	C	Resource changes are inevitable, except on very short projects. Therefore, the project manager should be prepared to accept these changes, but also should clearly document in a Project Change Request the impact the resource change will have on the project, and then have the change request approved.
4	B	While a team kickoff party could be a very good idea to facilitate the "forming stage," planning the kickoff party is not defined as one of the activities for Plan Human Resource Management.
5	B	The staffing plan should clearly identify resource requirements by skill set, the date the resource(s) must start, the level of effort required (full-time, part-time), and the date the resource can be released from the project.
6	A	The human resource plan clearly defines the reporting relationship for the project. This is required during the planning stage to ensure that the project is staffed with the appropriate resources needed to support the management of the overall team.
7	B	While the project should consider how it can support individual career plans, this takes place once the resource is assigned to the project. The human resource plan is developed before individual team members are identified and assigned to the project.
8	C	The Human Resources Management Plan must always be produced, but whether it is integrated with the Project Management Plan or produced as a standalone document will be determined by unique project requirements.
9	D	The project budget is developed once the resources are assigned to the project, because the costs for the assigned resources must be known for the budget to be developed.
10	C	Understanding the project lifecycle and the processes that will be used on the project is important for the Human Resources Management Plan because the lifecycle will define when staff typically join and leave the team, and the processes to be used will help define the skills required.
11	D	The WBS defines all the work that must be completed for the project. Therefore, the human resource requirements can be determined from the WBS, because the team will be responsible for completing all the work identified in the WBS.
12	E	Project organization charts serve many important roles on a project. The main objectives are to ensure that each work package has an unambiguous owner and that all team members have a clear understanding of their roles and responsibilities.

A

Question	Answer	Justification
13	D	Typically, a tree-based chart is used to represent the overall project structure and reporting relationships, while a text-based format is better suited for documenting detailed responsibilities.
14	C	The Organizational Breakdown Structure is arranged according to the organization's existing structure. An OBS is useful to the project team to help them understand which organizational resource they can contact to better understand requirements.
15	C	The Resource Breakdown Structure is another name for a tree-based project organization chart. The RBS is useful because it can be used to facilitate planning and controlling of project work.
16	D	RACI charts can be developed from any level of the WBS. For large projects, multiple levels of RACI charts are often developed, with deliverable or major activity RACI charts used for management reporting and detailed RACI charts used for detailed work management.
17	A	For a RACI chart to have maximum value, a single resource should be designated as responsible for each line. The goal is to have each activity assigned to a single individual to clearly define ownership.
18	D	While a single resource should be accountable to identify a single point of acceptance, it is acceptable to have a number of resources consulted or informed.
19	E	The staffing plan should identify staff requirements, resource calendars to identify availability, release dates, training needs, recognition and rewards, compliance, and safety.
20	D	While in an ideal world, human resources would be able to deliver the desired team exactly as planned, this is often not the case because human resources have to work within organizational constraints. Therefore, it is important to work with the human resources department to determine the optimal staffing plan based on known constraints. Once the project is staffed, a change request should be created to identify any changes in schedule, budget, or any other project component that results from the revised staffing plan.
21	A	While it would be ideal if the Acquire Project Team process simply followed the human resource plan, there are often changes in staff availability between when the plan was written and when the project is staffed. Therefore, there is often one more round of negotiations to ensure that the best possible team is available.

Question	Answer	Justification
22	E	While A through D can all be considered correct answers, they do not follow the spirit of the PMBOK, which explicitly defines pre-assignment as a requirement of a competitive process or due to specific domain knowledge.
23	D	In an ideal world, the human resources department will provide the exact team requested in the human resource plan. However, because this is often not the case, it is in the project management team's best interest to be prepared to negotiate with functional managers or other project managers to obtain access to resources with the skills but not necessarily the availability to work on the project. When this fails, the project management team should be prepared to look to external organizations to hire or subcontract the needed resources.
24	B	Virtual teams may well provide an optimal team as specialized resources, better business area coverage/access, and more working hours per day are possible with the virtual team. However, virtual teams should be considered as just one of the resourcing options available to the project management team because PMI still favors a physically co-located team.
25	C	While it is always nice to know team members personally, selecting team members based on prior work experience rather than true project needs may result in a suboptimal team because others with better credentials could be passed over in order to select a friendly face.
26	E	While a multi-criteria decision matrix allows for the ranking of potential team members on factors such as availability, cost, experience, ability, knowledge, skills, attitude, and other factors, it should be just one of the factors used for selecting team members.
27	A	The Develop Project Team process is focused on improving the competencies of team members and developing the best possible environment to facilitate effective team interactions.
28	D	While the project managers may involve outside specialists, such as the human resources department, to ensure effective team performance, they are directly responsible for ensuring that the project develops and fosters a healthy team environment.
29	B	For a project team to perform effectively, it is important that the team have a common goal/vision. However, in a multicultural team, care and attention must be paid to individual cultures to ensure that all team members are respected.
30	D	The recommended techniques for Develop Project Team are interpersonal skills, training, team-building activities, ground rules, co-location, recognition and rewards, and personal assessment tools.

A

Question	Answer	Justification
31	D	Interpersonal skills are critical for a project manager to be able to deal with any and all "human issues" that come up during daily project delivery.
32	D	Project-specific training should be identified in the human resource plan and should be delivered as planned to ensure that all team members have the appropriate project-specific training required. Additional training may be identified during the Acquire Project Team process and may or may not be a project responsibility, but should be delivered to ensure that the assigned resources have the skills necessary to complete project assignments.
33	B	The Tuckman model defines the team-building model as forming, storming, norming, performing, and adjourning.
34	B	Adding even a single new team member to an existing performing team can be very disruptive and will require the entire model to be exercised, although likely in an abbreviated timeframe.
35	A	While it might take a shorter amount of time through each stage, you will still begin with the forming stage whenever new members are added to the team.
36	E	Removing even a single new team member from an existing performing team should follow the adjourning process to ensure that adequate knowledge transfer takes place for the departing team member(s).
37	C	Ground rules are important to ensure a common understanding of code of conduct, communications, meeting etiquette, and general team norms.
38	D	The team should develop the project ground rules. This ensures that the rules are acceptable and will be applied.
39	D	The team should share responsibility for enforcing the project ground rules.
40	A	Project-level rewards and recognition should be planned into the Human Resources Management Plan and applied throughout the project to recognize and reward desirable behavior at project, team, and/or individual levels.
41	E	Finding an effective reward and recognition system can be very challenging because different team members will find different rewards appropriate.
42	C	Integration of project performance into the annual employee review process needs to be well defined and known by all team members.

Question	Answer	Justification
43	A	All team members will have strengths that should be leveraged and weaknesses that should be improved. Effectively identifying both during project delivery will increase the project's likelihood of successful completion.
44	D	The Manage Project Team process is focused on tracking team-member performance, providing feedback, resolving issues, and managing changes to the team.
45	B	Managing the project team is heavily focused on the soft skills to help the team become a high-performance team. This requires effective communication, conflict resolution, motivation, and other general team-building skills.
46	B	Conflicts are unavoidable when humans interact with each other. While conflicts resolved quickly can actually be beneficial and can lead to better understanding between the parties and/or creative solutions, conflicts that don't get resolved quickly can soon become worse and may impact the entire project. When this happens, the project manager needs to get involved and help find a solution.
47	D	A key technique for managing the project team is simply listening and learning—being present and available to the project team to stay in touch with their problems, issues, successes, and career aspirations.
48	A	Integrating team-member performance appraisals into the overall team management approach ensures that known strengths and weaknesses are understood prior to the project start and are leveraged/addressed by project assignments. Similarly, integrating mid-project performance appraisals may allow for adjustments in assignments to better support both project and career goals.
49	C	Conflict is inevitable in a project situation. The act of bringing together individuals and forming a team will result in conflicts. Therefore, the project management team should monitor and ensure that conflict never escalates to a dangerous level.
50	E	Project conflict can be caused by project and human dynamics. Project conflicts can come from a wide variety of sources.
51	E	Having ground rules and group norms in place will significantly lessen the human personality conflicts because these rules establish how the team members should interact with one other. Having good project management and an achievable plan in place will reduce stress-generated conflicts.

A

Question	Answer	Justification
52	A	While excessive amounts of conflict are never beneficial for a project, some conflict can be good because it will allow the team members to better understand each other and establish acceptable ways of working together. Similarly, conflict over how best to satisfy project requirements will often result in a solution that uses the best of all options.
53	E	Collaboration is the result of working together to form an optimal solution.
54	A	The team member is withdrawing from the conflict using the reason that he or she is too busy to bother. More likely, the person simply is avoiding the conflict and is using lack of time as an excuse.
55	D	The RACI chart identifies the Responsible, Accountable, Consulted, and Informed resources for each activity in the WBS.
56	C	Because this is a weak matrix organization, the project manager has little power over the team members; therefore, expert power may be most effective to show them how following the techniques successfully used on other projects can help.
57	B	The five general techniques for resolving conflict are withdrawal/avoid, smooth/accommodate, compromise/reconcile, force/direct, and collaborate/problem solve.
58	G	There is no one preferred conflict-resolution approach. While compromise and collaborate often produce good results, there will be instances where withdrawal or force may be the optimal solution. Each conflict needs to be examined to determine the best option. It is also important to recognize that the optimal solution may need to change if the conflict escalates.
59	E	This is another of the "best answers." While immediately and only when requested are not appropriate factors for project management intervention, it may be appropriate for intervention when the conflict worsens or escalates. However, the best answer is for the project management team to intervene only when resolution appears to be impossible, because it is still highly likely that a worsening or escalating conflict can be satisfactorily resolved without intervention.
60	B	Interpersonal skills most often used by project managers include leadership, influencing, and decision making. There is no single best management approach for project management. Each project manager will bring his or her own unique combination of interpersonal skills to the job.
61	C	The Resource histogram graphs the workload per time unit for each resource.

Question	Answer	Justification
62	A and B	Identification of staff release dates is important to both human resources and the team members to allow them to plan for their next assignments proactively.
63	D	Factors that the team cannot control should not be factors in a recognition and reward system.
64	D	While team building can be a formal process with external consultants and specialized environments, it can also be a simple five-minute agenda as part of a regular team meeting.
65	C	While project managers may be experts in their field of project management, this does not necessarily give them expert power on a project, because they may have limited knowledge of the subject matter area the project is addressing. Additionally, while they may be expert project managers, they must earn "expert power" by demonstrating their abilities to the team.
66	C	All changes to the accepted project "facts" should be documented on a change request and presented for approval.

CHAPTER 9: PROJECT COMMUNICATIONS MANAGEMENT

Question	Answer	Justification
1	B	Project Communications Management ensures the timely and appropriate planning, collection, creation, and distribution of project information to all project stakeholders.
2	A	The Plan Communications Management process is critical on all projects to ensure that an effective and efficient communications strategy is defined to satisfy all stakeholders' information needs and requirements.
3	E	Planning effective project communications begins at the source, ensuring that effective processes are in place to collect information from team members, to store this raw data in a way that it can be effectively extracted, to process the raw data into the required information needed, and finally to distribute the information to the project stakeholders.
4	C	The stakeholder register is an input to the communications planning process because it identifies the stakeholders and their information needs.
5	C	The formula for calculating the total number of potential communications channels is $n(n - 1) / 2$.

A

Question	Answer	Justification
6	B	Creating independent sub-teams will limit the communication to just the members of each sub-team, with an additional communications channel between the leaders of each sub-team.
7	D	The language is typically not considered when determining a communication approach because any effective communication approach should be able to transmit information in any language.
8	A	A message that is not properly encoded will never be understood because the message doesn't contain the correct information. Encoding is preparing the message for transmission.
9	D	Acknowledgement from the receiver that the message was received and understood is an important step in effective communication.
10	B	A message that cannot be understood because of issues with sending the message (noise in the room) suffers from issues in the transmit step in the communications model.
11	D	The Communications Management Plan should identify how acknowledgement of all project communications should be delivered. For example, absence of feedback from a stakeholder within five days of a scheduled delivery can be recorded as acknowledgement of the deliverable. (In other words, they have five days to either notify the project manager that the communication was not received or identify any issues they may have with the deliverable.)
12	A and E	The sender is responsible for encoding the message in the best possible way to ensure that it is understood and for participating in the feedback process to ensure full understanding of the message.
13	C	While it could be said that the issue was with the encoding step—where the document should not contain buzzwords and industry-specific terms, with the assumption that the document was meant for an appropriately educated audience—the issue in this case is assumed to be in the decoding step because the reader was from a different department.
14	C	Communications distribution tools include a wide range of tools that allow for the distribution of information to the project stakeholders. A database of project data is not a communications distribution tool because it is simply a repository of project data.
15	D	The project status report should always be a formal written document because it must be preserved as evidence of project performance at a point in time.
16	A	In this case, interactive communication is the appropriate communication method because a conversation is likely required to review and understand the options.

Question	Answer	Justification
17	B	Push communication is the appropriate first step to send the monthly status report to the identified stakeholders. Follow-up interactive communication may be required if there are questions, but the appropriate initial approach is push.
18	C	In this case, pull communications would be appropriate. The project manager would load all the project status reports into a project portal and then make the portal available to the stakeholders to retrieve old reports whenever needed.
19	D	When retrieving project updates from the team, the project manager would most likely use all possible communications options. Push technology could be used to send the request for updates to the team, pull technology could be used to retrieve timesheet information from a centralized database, and interactive communication could be used for follow-ups and clarifications.
20	C	Meetings are inevitable for projects because they are an effective way to gather information and reach consensus for a group of people. However, meetings should be carefully managed with a defined agenda, identified participants only, strict time management, and published minutes.
21	C	While the invitees to a meeting should be well thought out and validated, there is always a possibility that a participant may be missed. Therefore, it would be appropriate to understand why this individual wishes to attend.
22	E	While Answers B or C might be considered to be correct, Answer E is the best answer because it ensures that the appropriate participants are present to discuss the new item (as it may require a different audience than this meeting) and that the participants have time to prepare for the discussion.
23	B	If the key participant(s) are not prepared for the meeting, the meeting should be rescheduled to allow the participants to prepare and to respect the time of those who are prepared, ensuring that the meeting doesn't take any more of their valuable time.
24	C	A project portal, although commonly used for effective project communications, is not a mandatory communications tool. Even if a project portal is used as part of the project's communications strategy, the user instructions would not be contained in the Communications Management Plan.
25	B	The Manage Communications process is focused on the creation, collection, distribution, storage, retrieval, and destruction of project information. Analyzing the information is not done as part of this process.

A

Question	Answer	Justification
26	D	The Manage Communications process goes beyond the distribution of the relevant information and ensures that the information is appropriate and that it has been received and understood.
27	F	Effective project communication requires all forms of communication. The key is the determination of the most effective method for each unique communication requirement.
28	C	The sender-receiver model defines the encode-transmit-decode-acknowledge-feedback process to ensure that the messages the project intends to send are being received and understood properly.
29	E	The Manage Communications process should clearly document the approaches to be used for effective project communication. This should include defining the appropriate writing styles (formal/informal, active/passive voice, sentence structures, and so on), meeting guidelines, presentation techniques, facilitation techniques, and active listening guidelines.
30	B	Work performance reports provide the raw data that is reported by the project. The Manage Communications process uses the work performance reports to facilitate discussion and create communications.
31	D	Performance reporting is the collection and reporting of current status, actual versus baseline, and forecasts of future project performance.
32	C	The Control Communications process monitors and controls project communication throughout the entire project with the goal of ensuring that the information needs of the stakeholders are met.
33	E	The project budget is not contained in the Communications Management Plan. While the performance of the project versus budget is definitely one of the items that will be communicated, the budget itself is not included in the Communications Management Plan.
34	B	Communicating takes more time than any other single item that a project manager must do on a successful project.
35	B	The Issue Log is vital for communication management because it tracks all open discussion items with the stakeholders and allows for everyone to review the current status of the issue as it moves toward closure.
36	A	An Issue Log will typically track issue number, issue name and description, date added, raised by, assigned to, due date, status, date resolved, and resolution.

CHAPTER 10: PROJECT RISK MANAGEMENT

Question	Answer	Justification
1	D	Project Risk Management consists of the following processes: Plan Risk Management, Identify Risks, Perform Qualitative Risk Analysis, Perform Quantitative Risk Analysis, Plan Risk Responses, and Control Risks.
2	E	Project Risk Management is focused on any risk or opportunity that could impact either the overall project or an individual task within the project.
3	B	While risk management is focused on both risks and opportunities, the treatment is very different. Project Risk Management is focused on making opportunities happen and making risks not happen.
4	E	Risk (or opportunities) can impact any aspect of the project, but most notably can impact the scope, budget, schedule, or quality of the project.
5	D	Unknown risk should have a management reserve assigned to it. The management reserve can be consumed if the risk event takes place.
6	C	The Risk Management Plan identifies the project's risk profile and, based on the profile documents, the strategies for dealing with project risks. A project with a risk-averse profile will have a very different strategy for dealing with risks than a risk-neutral project, for example.
7	B	The risk impact matrix plots risk impact versus risk probability to help determine which risks should receive attention. For example, a high-probability, high-impact risk will require more attention than a low-probability, low-impact risk.
8	B	The risk impact matrix plots risk impact versus risk probability to help determine which risks should receive attention. For example, a high-probability, high-impact risk will require more attention than a low-probability, low-impact risk.

A

Question	Answer	Justification
9	E	The project's risk tolerance defines the appetite of the project for risk. For example, a research and development project could have a very high risk tolerance, while a project to replace a critical internal system could have a very low risk tolerance. On a high risk tolerant project, there would be very few contingency plans worked into the project, and instead the project would simply accept the consequences of failure. (Thomas Edison has been credited with saying, "I know now 101 ways to not make a light bulb!) Contrary to that is a risk-averse project, which would have a considerable amount of contingency to ensure that no matter what risk event takes place, the replacement of the critical internal system will still be able to be completed by taking advantage of the contingency to deal with the risks.
10	C	A project that expects no more than 50 percent of the identified risks to occur would be classified as risk neutral and therefore would typically allocate about 50 percent of the total contingency amounts (budget and schedule).
11	A	Very few projects are ever classified as risk unconcerned, as the approach of exploring new opportunities is contrary to the principles of defining scope, schedule, and budget. A risk-unconcerned project would by its very definition have no scope and would simply run until time or budget runs out.
12	E	A project that is fully risk averse would define sufficient contingency to cover all identified risks plus an additional management contingency for a significant number of unidentified risks.
13	D	With only low probability/low impact and low probability/medium impact risks on the "ignore list," this project would be very risk concerned and would allocate a significant amount of time and budget to contingency.
14	C	With four quadrants in the manage category and four quadrants in the ignore category, this project would be classified as risk neutral. Risk-neutral projects often allocate approximately 50 percent of the schedule and budget contingency to ensure that some contingency is available, but also expect that not all risks will likely occur.
15	A	Quadrant A represents all risks where the probability is low and the impact is high.
16	D	Quadrant D represents all risks where the probability is high and the impact is medium.
17	E	Quadrant E represents all risks where the probability is low and the impact is low.

Question	Answer	Justification
18	E	All project participants should be encouraged to participate in identification of risks because different individuals with different roles and responsibilities will have a very different perspective on what the risks are for a project.
19	E	While there is always a focused period of identifying risks as part of a project or phase planning process, identification of risks should be a continuous activity at any time during the project.
20	D	The Change Management process should have no impact on the identification of risks. The Change Management process defines the steps to be followed to document and approve all project changes.
21	D	The schedule development defines the process for developing the project schedule and does not directly introduce risk into the project.
22	B	Risk checklists can be developed based on prior project experience to document known project risks. Reviewing risk checklists can be a very effective way of identifying risks.
23	B	The assumptions and constraints are an important source of risks. While the assumption does clearly state the assumption and expected result, the assumption does not assign mitigation plans or contingency, should the assumption prove to be invalid. Therefore, any assumptions where there is a possibility that the assumption will not prove to be true should be included as potential project risks.
24	E	Risk identification should use any technique that allows for a systematic exploration and identification of project risks.
25	A	The Risk Register is a living document that is started with risk identification. All risks identified should be recorded in the Risk Register. This ensures that the risk is logged and that it is considered during Quantitative and Qualitative Risk Analysis.
26	D	Qualitative Risk Analysis reviews each possible risk and does further analysis on the probability and impact to assess the likelihood and magnitude of the risk.
27	E	Although Qualitative Risk Analysis is primarily focused on probability and impact, it also considers the timing of when a risk might occur and the project's risk tolerance to develop the treatment each identified risk should receive.
28	B and D	Depending on the nature of the risk, once Qualitative Risk Analysis is complete, the next step will be either to perform Quantitative Risk Analysis or to directly develop the risk responses.

A

Question	Answer	Justification
29	E	Determining a risk's probability by using an established risk priority guide is the main method typically used. However, often the project team members may not have enough insight into the risk, and therefore expert judgment, interviews, and risk-ranking meetings may also be required.
30	E	Determining a risk's impact by using an established risk impact guide is the main method typically used. However, often the project team members may not have enough insight into the risk, and therefore expert judgment, interviews, and risk-ranking meetings may also be required.
31	E	The Risk Management Plan should define an impact matrix, which will be used to determine the priority of risks. Impact would be placed on one axis and probability on the other. Each risk is then positioned on the matrix.
32	D	Risk data-quality assessment is used to validate the accuracy of the raw data used to determine the risk priority and impact. If it is determined that the quality of the data is low, then the priority and impact values are suspect and would be of limited use to the project.
33	D	The timeframe when a risk will occur doesn't impact the risk priority. A high-priority risk will always be a high-priority risk, whether it is predicted to occur in the next three months or not for over a year when the project enters the testing phase. However, it does impact the timeframe for monitoring the risk because there is no value in tracking the testing risk until the project enters that timeframe (in this case, phase).
34	B	The Risk Register is a living document that is updated throughout the project. Once Qualitative Risk Analysis is completed on a risk, the Risk Register is updated with the results.
35	A	Quantitative Risk Analysis is the process of numerically analyzing the identified risk for a project.
36	D	Because Quantitative Risk Analysis typically involves considerable effort, it is typically only done after Qualitative Risk Analysis has identified the high-probability/high-impact risks.
37	E	Because Quantitative Risk Analysis typically involves considerable effort, it is typically done only after Qualitative Risk Analysis has identified the high-probability/high-impact risks.

Question	Answer	Justification
38	F	All of the items in the list are valid techniques for performing Quantitative Risk Analysis. Interviewing is likely to be the one item most questioned, but interviewing is a vital technique because interviews are often required to obtain the necessary data for the numerical analysis. For example, interviewing can be used to obtain pessimistic, optimistic, and most likely risk results, which can then be used to complete a three-point estimate.
39	D	While E can be considered a correct answer because probability distributions can be done with spreadsheet software, D is a better answer because it represents the value that probability distributions bring to Quantitative Risk Analysis.
40	B	Sensitivity analysis graphs the variations between the project's objectives and the project's risks to allow for identification of the risks that have the highest potential impact.
41	C	A Tornado diagram is a special type of bar chart used in sensitivity analysis to highlight where possible benefits are greater than the identified impacts.
42	A	Expected Monetary Value is a statistical analysis approach that explores all possible outcomes of a risk, considering costs and probabilities to develop an average cost of the risk.
43	C	Expected Monetary Value is $100K Return – $50K Cost.
44	C	All paths must be calculated. Result 1.1 = $50K, Result 1.2 = $100K, Result 2.1 = $375K, and Result 2.2 = $275K. Then EMV for the two paths is calculated: Path 1 50% ($50K) + 50% ($100K) = $75K. Path 2 60% ($375K) + 40% ($275K) = $335. Next, the percentages of each path must be factored in, where Path 1 75% (75) versus Path 2 25% (335) results in Path 1 = 56.25 and Path 2 = 83.75. Therefore, the answer is 83.75, since the largest value is selected.
45	C	EMV = 70% ($70) + 30% ($100) = $79
46	C	A Monte Carlo simulation translates the risk uncertainties into potential impacts by running many mathematical-model simulations of the various parameters that could impact the risk and the outcome.
47	B	The Risk Register is a living document that is updated throughout the project. Once Qualitative Risk Analysis is completed on a risk, the Risk Register is updated with the results.
48	C	The four risk management strategies are Avoid, Transfer, Mitigate, and Accept.

A

Question	Answer	Justification
49	B	When the Avoid strategy is applied to a project, the project is changed to eliminate the risk. For example, if there is a risk that the learning curve for a new tool could be higher than expected, the risk can be avoided by not using the new tool.
50	A	A is the best answer because it involves finding a qualified third party willing and able to deal with the risk, unlike C, where the risk is simply assigned to someone else who may be even less prepared for the risk. A Transfer strategy must be accepted by both parties. An example would be when an extremely complex portion of the project is contracted to a specialty firm that has advanced knowledge, skills, or tools.
51	C	Risk mitigation involved making some changes to reduce the probability or impact of a risk occurring. Risk mitigation often is done when risk avoidance is not possible; therefore, the next best alternative is to reduce the impact of the risk. An example would be if there is a risk that the learning curve for a new tool could be higher than expected, then the risk can be mitigated by ensuring that both introductory and advanced training are provided to the team, or possibly that an experienced consultant is on standby to assist the team through the learning-curve period.
52	B	When the project manager and team accept that there are no workable risk management strategies besides acceptance, funds and schedule contingency should be created to allow the project team to deal with the risk if it occurs. For example, the project manager accepts that there will be weather delays for a major construction project on the Florida waterfront during hurricane season and adds time and budget to deal with the delays.
53	B and D	Only Mitigate and Accept strategies require contingency. With Avoid and Transfer strategies, the risk is eliminated and therefore does not require contingency. With the Mitigate strategy, the contingency is required for only the residual risk that the mitigation action was not able to eliminate.
54	C	The approaches in the question assign a project risk to a third party, which is a Transfer risk mitigation strategy.
55	D	The approaches in the question attempt to reduce the risk, which is a risk mitigation strategy.
56	B	The approaches in the question create project contingencies, which is an Accept risk mitigation strategy.

Question	Answer	Justification
57	B	Implementing a Risk Response Plan should address the primary risk that the response was developed for. However, as a result, new risks may be created. These new risks are called *secondary risks*, because they are the unexpected result of a Risk Response Plan. Secondary risks should be managed carefully, because they could be high impact and high probability.
58	B	The four opportunity management strategies are Exploit, Enhance, Share, and Accept.
59	D	Risk responses would typically not require an update to the Communications Management Plan. The Risk Register would be updated to reflect the results of each Risk Response Plan, and depending on the risk management strategy chosen, the schedule, budget, and quality approaches to the project may be changed. For example, contingency would increase both the schedule and the budget, and a mitigation strategy to do early testing would change the quality approach.
60	B	Notifying management of contingency plan consumption would be done as part of communications management.
61	F	Implementing a Risk Response Plan typically begins with executing the actions predefined for dealing with an identified risk. This may or may not involve use of the risk contingency. Once the plan has been executed, a risk identification process should be completed to determine whether there are residual risks that may require future action and/or new risks for identification. In a worst-case situation, when the planned actions either are no longer appropriate or are ineffective, additional unplanned actions may be required to deal with the risk (which may or may not require contingency).
62	B	The Risk Register is the main input to the Control Risk process. However, as there will be high-priority risk on the register that cannot be influenced at this time, the Control Risk process should focus on the current risks only.
63	E	The project budget is not an input to the Control Risk process. While the Control Risk process may consume the project budget, it does so through the allocated risk contingency or through a Project Change Request if adequate contingency does not exist.
64	C	A risk should be closed only when the risk owner confirms that the risk event has passed. This may mean that the risk has occurred and has been dealt with by the project or that the events that could cause the risk have been eliminated, thereby eliminating the risk.
65	B	Risk audits are used to examine and document how effectively the identified risk response is dealing with the project's risks.

A

Question	Answer	Justification
66	A	A Project Change Request may be required as a result of implementing a Risk Response Plan. The Project Change Request would obtain approval for any corrective and/or preventative actions identified as the project risks are managed.

Chapter 11: Project Procurement Management

Question	Answer	Justification
1	B	Project Procurement Management consists of the following processes: Plan Procurement Management, Conduct Procurements, Control Procurements, and Close Procurements.
2	C	Project Procurement Management defines the processes necessary to purchase the products, services, or results from outside the project team.
3	B	Procurement management applies whether the project is the buyer or the seller of the third-party items.
4	D	Each item purchased by the project will have its own unique lifecycle. Some procurements may be complete in a single phase of the project—for example, a contract with an SME to develop the Project Scope Statement during the planning phase—while other procurements may cover the entire lifecycle of the project—for example, a contract to provide temporary office space for the project team.
5	B	Procurement management is much more encompassing than a contract. While procurement management may involve creating a contract to specify the terms and conditions for purchasing something for a project, procurement management also involves identifying what needs to be purchased, how it should be purchased, and the actual management of the purchase (which is the component covered by the contract).
6	E	While the term "contract" typically brings to mind a formal legal document crafted by teams of lawyers from both organizations, in reality a contract can be a very simple document that is a binding agreement binding the seller to provide something of value and the buyer to provide compensation ($) to the seller. Depending on the purchase requirements of a project, a contract can be very simple or very complex.

Question	Answer	Justification
7	A	From a seller's viewpoint, large and complex procurements often become projects where the purchasing project manager becomes the acceptor. It is critical that the purchasing project manager becomes the acceptor because the delivery of the expected results is a component of the overall project the purchasing project manager is responsible for. The purchasing project manager may choose to involve the project acceptor and/or purchasing department, but must always retain full ownership of the procurement process.
8	E	The Plan Procurement Management process is focused on identifying what, how, and when the project will purchase required items. The output from the procurement planning process is the Procurement Management Plan. Plan Procurement Management is the process of documenting the project procurement decisions, specifying the approach, and identifying potential sellers.
9	C	Different procurements/contracts will require different management approaches. A fixed-price contract will typically be managed in a very hands-off fashion because the project has limited capacity to influence the results after the contract has been signed, while a per-diem staff augmentation contract should be managed with the same care and attention as any other project activity.
10	D	Procurement may allow for closing of risks, because risks can be transferred to qualified third parties, or new risks could be identified based on the results of procurement planning.
11	C	A fixed-price contract has a defined price to be paid for a defined scope of work. A fixed-price contract reduces the project's financial and delivery risks due the fixed nature of the contract, but also reduces the project's flexibility to change because the terms and delivery are fixed and cannot be changed (without penalty).
12	E	A time-and-materials (T&M) contract can also be called a per-diem contract. It defines a rate per resource. The project has the ability to use as few or as many hours from this resource as it requires. A per-diem contract increases the project's financial and delivery risks because the project is "paying by the hour," but it also increases the project's flexibility to change as the project defines how many hours are required and what work should be completed.
13	A	A unit-price contract has a defined price to be paid for delivered unit (for example, $/square foot of roofing material). A unit-price contract allows the project to predict the cost if (and only if) it can predict the number of units required.

A

Question	Answer	Justification
14	D	A cost-reimbursable contract involves the vendor providing evidence of the actual cost to produce a unit of result (product of service). The seller and purchasing companies then agree to an acceptable markup (profit) over cost.
15	D	A time-and-materials contract is typically used to provide skilled resources to augment the project team with additional resources.
16	B	A fixed-price contract defines an agreed result for an agreed cost. The fact that this transfers a project risk to the seller doesn't change the nature of the contract type.
17	A	A unit-price contract defines the cost for a unit of result for a project. This can be a unit price for a material, such as $/ream of paper, or a defined fee for a measurable amount of work, such as $/square foot of wall painted.
18	D	D is the best answer because it is based on ensuring that the best contract type is in place for the project's requirements. Generally, if a contract is going to be customized, such as offering a bonus for early delivery, a similar and opposite penalty should also be considered. But, as already stated, this may not be required in all situations, and therefore the best answer is whatever best satisfies the project's requirements.
19	B	A make-or-buy analysis is done for every element of the WBS. In a lot of instances, the result of the make-or-buy analysis is an automatic make, and the activity is assigned to a team member, but the analysis is always completed on an activity-by-activity basis. A more formal or complete make-or-buy analysis is completed when the team lacks the capacity or skills to complete an activity.
20	B	While you might find guidelines on creating them, penalty clauses for late delivery would be defined in individual contracts and would be consistent with the type of contract.
21	B′	Time-and-materials contracts represent the highest risk to a project because the project assumes the risk that the work can be completed as planned. It is also considered the higher risk for the buyer (project).
22	A	A fixed-price contract reduces the risk to the project because the project cost will always be a predetermined amount—the project has no risk associated with completing the work as planned.
23	B	A procurement Statement of Work defines the exact nature of the work that is to be delivered to the project through a specific procurement. The procurement Statement of Work should be developed from the Project Scope Baseline and defines only the portion of the project scope that is to be included in the specific procurement.

Question	Answer	Justification
24	C	A procurement Statement of Work should be written with the same care and attention that was given to the original Project Scope Statement. It needs to be clear, complete, and concise to allow the vendors to validate whether they can deliver as requested and to allow the definition of equally clear and complete acceptance criteria.
25	C	While it is possible that a procurement Statement of Work could be the input to a purchase order, generally purchase orders are made for material purchases directly from the make-or-buy results, while more complex procurements require Statements of Work, which are then used to prepare a Request for Proposal, Request for Information, or other similar documents to solicit information or quotes from prospective vendors.
26	C	Defining the high-level requirements with well-defined expected results ensures that the result of the procurement will meet project expectations while allowing the vendors maximum flexibility in how to achieve the result.
27	A	The source selection criteria should be developed at the same time as the procurement documents to ensure that the selection criteria match the procurement documents, and prior to any contact with the vendors to ensure no contamination of the selection criteria. Many procurement documents are issued with the selection criteria included to allow the vendors to better understand how the responses will be evaluated.
28	C	Acceptable source selection criteria include the following: meets requirements, costs, technical capacity, management approach, solution approach, warranty, size of vendor, production capacity, business size and type, and references.
29	F	As a result of the make-or-buy analysis, decision changes may be required to many of the existing project documents. For example, the decision to purchase a project component may increase the project scope because the purchased component (assuming it's a package solution) will deliver additional functionality, increase the project cost, decrease the project schedule, and change the team member composition. Risks can be added or removed as a result of procurement decisions because risks transferred to vendors through procurement or procurement activities can add new risks to the project.
30	A	Issue RFP is part of the Plan Procurement process.

A

Question	Answer	Justification
31	C	Conduct Procurements is a process that, as a minimum, is repeated once for each procurement because it is the process where vendors are evaluated and selected (including the development of a contract). For large, complex procurements, the Conduct Procurement process may be repeated more than once as the list of vendors is narrowed through short lists and other evaluation processes.
32	B	The source selection criteria contain the evaluation criteria that are to be used to evaluate vendor response. Each vendor response is evaluated against the evaluation criteria and scored using a weighted scoring system to select vendors that best satisfy the stated requirements.
33	C	Vendor responses should be evaluated on a point-by-point basis using the source selection criteria. Each evaluation point receives a score that is accumulated into a total score using a predefined weight per evaluation point.
34	B	Bidder conferences ensure that all bidders have the opportunity to receive the same information at the same time, ensuring there is no preferential treatment.
35	D	Having an evaluation benchmark allows the evaluators to confirm that the vendor responses are appropriate based on the project's requirements. For example, if the benchmark is substantially higher than most vendor's responses, it could be an indicator that the procurement Statement of Work does not adequately define the project's requirements.
36	B	Advertising through general circulation or trade-specific publications ensures a wider audience for the procurement process, which could result in more and potentially better responses to the procurement Statement of Work.
37	E	The best contracts are those that provide a win-win for all involved parties. The best contracts are those that are developed in partnership between the project and the vendor to ensure that the project's requirements are met in a way that allows the vendor to successfully deliver. Legal counsel should also be involved in procurement negotiations to ensure that the organization's rights are protected.
38	E	Source selection criteria are used to evaluate vendor responses and select the successful vendor. Source selection criteria are not included in contract documents.

Question	Answer	Justification
39	F	As a result of the Conduct Procurement process, changes may be required to many of the existing project documents. For example, the contract negotiations may result in a decision to purchase a project component, which may increase the project scope, because the purchased component (assuming it's a package solution) will deliver additional functionality, increase the project cost, decrease the project schedule, and change the team-member composition. Risks can be added or removed as a result of procurement decisions because risks can be transferred to vendors through procurement, or procurement activities can add new risks to the project.
40	A	The Control Procurements process is focused on both seller and purchasing organizations ensuring overall contract compliance and making the appropriate changes to the contracts as needed. Control procurements provides the best results when both selling and purchasing organizations work together to maximize joint value, as opposed to focusing on only their own organization.
41	B	The Control Procurements process is focused on both seller and purchasing organizations ensuring overall contract compliance and making the appropriate changes to the contracts as needed. Control procurements provides the best results when both selling and purchasing organizations work together to maximize joint value, as opposed to focusing on only their own organization.
42	D	Monitoring vendor performance and identifying corrective actions are part of the Control Procurements process. This information can be used to complete a vendor performance review, which could be used to determine the viability of future work with a vendor.
43	D	Contract change control processes should be defined and documented as part of the original contract, and define the processes that must be followed for all changes to a signed contract.
44	B	Procurement performance reviews are structured reviews of the vendor's progress to deliver the scope and quality defined in the contract. The objective of the review is to measure the vendor's performance.
45	E	Once a contract is in place, the terms and conditions in the contract override statements made in the RFP.

A

Question	Answer	Justification
46	B	While a Contract Performance Review may indicate completion of a contract payment milestone or conversely indicate that a contract payment milestone may be missed, the Contract Performance Review is not a formal document used to review and validate that the vendor's performance has satisfied approval for payment. Work performance data and Contract Inspections and Audits, however, report specific performance and should be considered when validating approval for payments.
47	C	Individual contracts can be closed at any time during a project. Once a vendor has satisfied all the terms and conditions in a contract, the contract should be closed.
48	C	Typically, a project manager or lead is not obligated to provide vendor references. If the vendor's performance was positive and it is acceptable by organizational policy, vendor references can be provided, but it is not a defined component of the Close Procurement process.
49	E	If the vendor has clearly satisfied all the requirements defined in the procurement Statement of Work, the contract is considered to be complete. The fact that the project manager is unhappy with the results doesn't negate the fact that the vendor has satisfied the contract requirements.
50	A	Development of procurement documents is part of the Plan Procurement Management process.
51	D	With limited scope definition, vendors either will be unwilling to enter into a fixed-price contact or will make the fixed price excessively large to cover their scope risk. Either cost plus percentage of cost or time and materials provides the project with high financial risk because the cost could increase due to the lack of scope. Cost plus fixed fee could still increase from a cost factor, but at least the fixed-fee portion would remain constant, making it the best alternative for reducing financial risk.

CHAPTER 12: PROJECT STAKEHOLDER MANAGEMENT

Question	Answer	Justification
1	B	The processes in Project Stakeholder Management are Identify Stakeholders, Plan Stakeholder Management, Manage Stakeholder Engagement, and Control Stakeholder Engagement.
2	A	Project Stakeholder Management includes the processes to identify the individuals (or groups) who could impact or be impacted by the project, analyze their expectations, and develop the strategies for effectively engaging the stakeholders in project decisions and execution.
3	B	Stakeholder management is a vital component of effective project management because it ensures active engagement of the project stakeholders for the life of the project. As stakeholder information requirements may change, effective stakeholder management must change to ensuring ongoing satisfaction of all stakeholders' requirements.
4	E	While all responses are correct, E is the best answer because stakeholders consist of anyone who has an interest in the project.
5	A	Because project managers have limited time, it is important to categorize stakeholders by interest, influence, and involvement in the project to allow for the development of communications strategies focused on each category of stakeholder.
6	C	A common classification method used in a power/interest grid is: keep satisfied, manage closely, monitor, and keep informed.
7	D	The four common stakeholder classification models are: power/interest, power/influence, influence/impact, and salience model.
8	I	The first step to identifying project stakeholders is to identify members of the organization who have a direct involvement in the project. Next, the managers of the identified members would be included. Finally, meeting with these identified stakeholders would identify any remaining stakeholder who may have an interest or impact on the project.
9	C	An influence/impact classification grid tracks each stakeholder's influence and the level of impact he or she has on the project.
10	B	While the reason a stakeholder is interested in the project may be a factor in the stakeholder classification and assessment information, the stakeholder register does not explicitly capture the reason a stakeholder is interested in a project.

A

Question	Answer	Justification
11	D	The Plan Stakeholder Management process develops the management strategies to keep the project stakeholders engaged throughout the project.
12	E	Project Stakeholder Management is more than just providing effective communication to the project stakeholders. It is about the creation and maintenance of effective relationships with the aim of satisfying the needs of the stakeholders within the project boundaries.
13	C	A stakeholder engagement assessment matrix is a matrix with the stakeholder engagement classification as columns and with a row for each stakeholder. Using a legend such as C for Current and D for Desired, the current and desired levels of engagement for each stakeholder can be recorded. Action plans can then be created to deal with any deficiencies in stakeholder engagement.
14	B	Level of stakeholder engagement will vary by stakeholder group/classification at different phases of the project. For example, during planning and approval, senior stakeholders will be very engaged to ensure that the project is properly positioned for success, and then they may reduce their involvement until such time as the project again requires senior management attention to deal with issues. During planning and approval, business unit stakeholders will likely not be involved, but they will become very active once the project enters the delivery phases.
15	D	The Stakeholder Management Plan identifies engagement levels of stakeholders, scope and impact of stakeholders, interrelationships between stakeholders, stakeholder communications requirements, information requirements of stakeholders, timeframe and format of stakeholder communications, and methods for maintaining the Stakeholder Management Plan.
16	C	Effective stakeholder engagement can be achieved by engaging stakeholders as appropriate for their interest in the current project phase, managing stakeholder's expectations through negotiation and communication, addressing concerns before they become issues, and clarifying and resolving all identified issues.
17	B	Keeping stakeholders engaged ensures that they are aware of current project status and therefore are informed and ready to deal with any project issues that are appropriate for their level of power and authority.
18	B	A stakeholder's ability to influence a project is highest during the planning phases because that is when the scope, budget, and timeline are defined for the project.

Question	Answer	Justification
19	B	Effective stakeholder management is based on strong interpersonal, communications, and management skills. Influence skills would not be appropriate for stakeholder management, as it is the project team's responsibility to satisfy the stakeholders' expectations.
20	C	Control Stakeholder Engagement is the process of monitoring stakeholder relationships and adjusting the strategies for ensuring that the stakeholders are engaged.
21	B	The Information Management System provides a standard tool for the project manager to capture, store, and distribute information to stakeholders about the project cost, schedule progress, and performance.
22	E	Control Stakeholder Engagement is the process for monitoring overall project stakeholder relationships and adjusting strategies and plans for engaging stakeholders.
23	B	Plan Stakeholder Management is the process for developing the strategies to engage stakeholders on the project.

CHAPTER 13: POST-TEST

Question	Chapter	Answer	Justification
1	5	D	A lag impacts the second half of a dependency relationship. A lag delays the start of the second activity. In this case it delays the start of the second activity by two days after the first activity finishes.
2	6	C	Contingency reserves should only be used when identified mitigation plans for which the contingency reserve was developed are executed.
3	12	D	The stakeholder register documents all project stakeholders and documents: name and contact details, stakeholder classification, and information requirements.
4	11	D	The approval of payments to vendors is completed as part of the Control Procurements process. Vendor payments are often closely tied to vendor performance, which is also part of the Control Procurements process.

A

Question	Chapter	Answer	Justification
5	3	E	The acceptance criteria clearly outline the conditions (tests) that must be satisfied before a deliverable can be accepted. Remediation actions, such as turnaround time-frames, re-acceptance criteria, and approval to proceed, must also be defined clearly to prevent never-ending acceptance processes.
6	7	B	Quality assurance is focused on ensuring that the project does the right things (that is, follows the quality processes), and quality control is focused on ensuring that the project does things right (in other words, satisfies the business requirements).
7	10	A	The approaches in the question change the project delivery approach, which is an Avoid risk mitigation strategy.
8	2	B	Customer service would be an example of the result of operations.
9	2	G	An iterative or incremental lifecycle allows for the management of changing objectives and scope, as the overall project direction can be adjusted during the planning process for each iteration. As well, with an iterative lifecycle, it should be possible to implement the results of early iterations to provide early but partial benefits to the business.
10	11	E	Procurement management is involved in all purchases required by a project, no matter the size or type. If the project must purchase something, whether it's an off-the-shelf purchase of a box of printer paper from a local office-supply store or a complex purchase requiring legal counsel to create a formal contract, project procurement management defines what must be purchased and how it should be purchased, and ensures that the purchase process is well managed.
11	3	C	A work authorization system ensures that no team member begins work on a project component until authorized to do so. This ensures that the right team members work on the correct tasks in the appropriate order.
12	3	H	A context diagram identifies the inputs, actors using the inputs, processes applied, outputs, and actors using the outputs.
13	5	D	Analogous estimating is based on similar experiences from other projects.

Question	Chapter	Answer	Justification
14	10	B	A Risk Breakdown Structure is used by the project team to look at the various sources of risks on the project. The RBS could be based on categorization frameworks previously used in the organization and can be used to categorize risks into common groups for further analysis using beta or triangular distribution methods.
15	2	B	An assumption is a statement about a future event that you believe will be true but don't have the facts to back up.
16	3	E	The Project Management Information System consists of all the tools that can aid in successful project delivery.
17	9	A	Project Communications Management consists of the following processes: Plan Communications Management, Manage Communications, and Control Communications.
18	8	D	Acquire Project Team is an ongoing process because team members will be added to and removed from the project throughout its life. Some team changes will be planned in the human resource plan, and some will be unplanned due to organizational demands and/or staff resignations.
19	2	C	Portfolios continuously monitor changes in the broader internal and external environments.
20	2	E	Project stakeholders can be internal or external, positive or negative. A project stakeholder is anyone who has interest in the project. Positive stakeholders can be leveraged to help ensure project success, and negative stakeholders need to be managed to ensure that they don't overtly or covertly damage the possibility of project success.
21	6	C	C is the best answer because it ensures that all costs required to complete project activities are calculated. This includes resource costs, material costs, infrastructure costs, and so on.
22	9	A	Different stakeholders will prefer different communications media. Where possible, the project should use the best communications media for each type of communication.

A

Question	Chapter	Answer	Justification
23	3	A	The Requirements Management Plan is produced during project planning and is a companion document to the Scope Management Plan. While the Scope Management Plan defines the processes to be followed for defining and controlling the overall project scope, the Requirements Management Plan focuses on defining the processes to be followed for defining and controlling the individual requirements that the project must address. In effect, the sum of the project's requirements becomes the project's scope.
24	12	E	Manage Stakeholder Engagement is the process of communicating and working with the project stakeholders to meet expectations and address any issues where expectations are not being met.
25	5	E	While E and C are very similar answers, E is a better answer because the project plan does not need to support rolling-wave planning. Smaller projects should be scheduled in their entirety to more accurately forecast total project duration.
26	2	A	All projects should be aligned with organizational governance to ensure that the project will integrate with the organization on completion. If the project is loosely governed or produces a result that has limited governance, the project will not fit into an organization that has stringent governance—for example, a project with limited governance would be inappropriate for a health care organization due to the level of reporting required.
27	2	D	The PMBOK is defined as the subset of all knowledge of project management that is generally recognized as good practices for successful project management.
28	8	D	The format used to document the project organization can vary based on individual project requirements. The key is that the project organization is clearly documented so that all project stakeholders understand who is on the project and what the appropriate reporting/escalation point is.
29	11	A	Procurement requirements should always be based on the project requirement documentation. All procurement requirements should be driven from project requirements that cannot be completed internally by the project team.
30	2	B	The project budget is created as part of the Planning Project Management Process Group.

Question	Chapter	Answer	Justification
31	8	B	Project Human Resource Management consists of the following processes: Plan Human Resource Management, Acquire Project Team, Develop Project Team, and Manage Project Team.
32	3	D	Project Integration Management includes the processes and activities to identify, define, unify, and coordinate the various processes and project management activities within the Project Management Process Groups.
33	2	D	The steps in negotiating are to analyze the situation, differentiate between wants and needs, focus on interests and issues, ask high and offer low, when making concessions ensure value in the concession, focus on win-win, and listen attentively.
34	6	B	The budget reserve will adjust the individual risk contingencies based on the project's risk profile to ensure an appropriate budget reserve is calculated. For example, if the project has a total of five risk contingencies for a total of $50,000, but a risk profile of "risk neutral" (or 50 percent risk-taking/risk-fearing), then the budget reserve should be calculated at only $25,000, as it assumes only 50 percent of the risks will occur based on the risk profile. Or, to phrase it differently, the project assumes that 50 percent of the identified risks should be able to be absorbed by the project without impacting the approved budget.
35	5	D	Parametric estimating is based on a standard calculation times the number of units—for example, three hours per electrical outlet times the number of electrical outlets in a house.
36	2	C	Project stakeholders serve many roles on a project, ranging from fully engaged business-unit stakeholders who have approval authority on the project to relatively non-engaged stakeholders who have little more than a passing interest in the project and no authority. However, all stakeholders should have a sufficient level of engagement to be able to confirm requirements and clarify assumptions.
37	7	A	A is considered the best answer due to the fact that senior management must remain ultimately responsible for project quality, principally by ensuring that suitable resources at adequate capacities are made available to the team. If senior management does not satisfy this requirement, then the team is unlikely to be able to satisfy the quality expectations for the project.

A

Question	Chapter	Answer	Justification
38	3	C	Project Scope Management consists of the following processes: Plan Scope Management, Collect Requirements, Define Scope, Create WBS, Validate Scope, and Control Scope.
39	10	A	During risk identification, only the risk name, description, and effect of the risk are captured. The remaining components of the Risk Register are added as the risks progress through the risk management processes.
40	5	E	A milestone is a significant point or event in the project. Milestones are typically identified during WBS decomposition as part of the Define Activities process, as the schedule details are known at that time.
41	9	E	Communications planning is critical to ensure effective communication on a project. Effective communication is a deliberate process that requires planning to ensure that the right information is communicated to the right people at the right time and in the right format.
42	6	D	Controlling project costs is focused on managing the project costs against the project baseline.
43	11	A	The make-or-buy analysis should consider all costs associated with the procurement. This should include the effort to develop the procurement documents and conduct the procurement, as well as the direct costs for the procurement itself.
44	10	D	A project's risk profile is based on appetite (the amount of uncertainty the project is willing to take on), tolerance (the amount of uncertainty that can be accepted), and threshold (an absolute measure of the amount of risk that can be tolerated).
45	5	D	A project can have multiple critical paths. The critical path defines the longest duration for project completion. Project dependency networks with many paths can have multiple paths with identical completion durations.
46	8	B	While there may be instances when a named individual absolutely must be assigned to a project to provide very unique knowledge, most project human resource plans should be developed with a focus on the skills required to provide the maximum staffing flexibility.

Question	Chapter	Answer	Justification
47	3	E	While all team members are involved in Monitor and Control Project Work, this process is focused on the work completed by the project management team to manage the work being completed on the project.
48	3	H	All deliverables must be identified during Project Scope Management. If sufficient information is available, they should also be fully decomposed, but often there isn't enough information to fully decompose future deliverables. Therefore, it is acceptable for only the next-phase deliverables to be fully decomposed, with the future deliverables addressed by rolling-wave planning.
49	7	E	The process improvement plan is often a component of the Quality or Project Management Plans and details the steps for analyzing project management and product development processes to identify ways in which their value can be enhanced.
50	12	B	The Identify Stakeholders process is focused on identifying all project stakeholders and the reason why the stakeholder has an interest in the project. Stakeholders may be at any authority level in the organization and may or may not be directly involved in the project. Key stakeholders to be identified are any project adversaries, as management processes must be put in place to neutralize them.

A

Use the following table to validate your overall performance on this test as a whole and on a chapter-by-chapter basis. To complete this table, you will need to count the number of correct answers for the entire test as well as the number of right answers by chapter (column 2).

Test Section	Number of Questions Right	Total Questions Available	Score Calculation	Your Score
Total Test		50	Your Answer ★ 2	
Chapter 2		9	Your Answer ★ 11.11	
Chapter 3		4	Your Answer ★ 25	
Chapter 4		6	Your Answer ★ 16.67	
Chapter 5		6	Your Answer ★ 16.67	
Chapter 6		3	Your Answer ★ 33.33	
Chapter 7		3	Your Answer ★ 33.33	
Chapter 8		4	Your Answer ★ 25	
Chapter 9		3	Your Answer ★ 33.33	
Chapter 10		5	Your Answer ★ 20	
Chapter 11		3	Your Answer ★ 33.33	
Chapter 12		4	Your Answer ★ 25	

As mentioned in the Introduction, for several chapters the number of questions is relatively low, so your test results can move from 33 percent to 66 percent with as little as a single right/wrong answer. The distribution of questions is based on an expectation of how PMI will distribute the questions given the defined PMI distribution of questions based on the five Project Management Process Groups.

- Initiating: 13%
- Planning: 24%
- Executing: 30%
- Monitoring and Controlling: 25%
- Closing: 8%

Your actual distribution on your certification exam may vary from this. This distribution was designed to make exam preparation easier, as it aligns more closely with the PMBOK.

INDEX

Like the Book?

Let us know on Facebook or Twitter!

facebook.com/cengagelearningptr

www.twitter.com/cengageptr